LADS

LADS

A MEMOIR OF MANHOOD

Dave Itzkoff

VILLARD   NEW YORK

Lads is a work of nonfiction. Some names
and identifying details have been changed.

Grateful acknowledgment is made to Sony/ ATV Music Publishing and Universal Music
Publishing Group to reprint an excerpt from "Everybody Knows" by Leonard Cohen and
Sharon Teresa Robinson. Copyright © 1988 by Sony / ATV Songs LLC, MCA Music, Inc.,
and Robinhill Music. Copyright © 1988 by Universal-Geffen Music on behalf of itself and
Robinhill Music. All rights for Sony / ATV Songs LLC administered by Sony / ATV Music
Publishing, 8 Music Square West, Nashville, TN 37203. All rights reserved. Used by
permission of Sony / ATV Music Publishing and Universal Music Publishing Group.

Library of Congress Cataloging-in-Publication Data

Itzkoff, Dave.
Lads : a memoir of manhood / Dave Itzkoff.
p.   cm.
ISBN 1-4000-6113-X
1. Itzkoff, Dave. 2. Periodical editors—United States—Biography.
3. Maxim (New York, N.Y.) I. Title.
PN4874.I88A3 2004
070.5'1'092—dc22
[B]
2004041945

Villard Books website address: www.villard.com

Printed in the United States of America

2 4 6 8 9 7 5 3 1

FIRST EDITION

Book design by Barbara M. Bachman

for my father—
who else?

I have looked upon the world for four times seven years,

and since I could distinguish betwixt a benefit and an injury,

I never found man that knew how to love himself.

—IAGO, *Othello*

LADS

1.

ALL GOOD THINGS

WHAT I WANTED AFTER COLLEGE WAS A JOB AND MY own apartment, but what I needed was a good comeuppance, and that's what I got. A liberal arts education had provided me with many valuable lessons: Do not attempt to take the determinant of a nonsymmetrical matrix. Do not carry a balance on your credit card. Do not enroll in two consecutive semesters of any course taught by Joyce Carol Oates. Do not mistake two hundred and fifty years of consistency for proud tradition. And do not, under any circumstances, tell a girl that you're attracted to her unless you're absolutely certain that she reciprocates those feelings, and even then, do not do so unless she's already confessed as much to you first. But only some of these lessons would prove useful outside the classroom, and I desperately needed to find out which.

The days leading up to graduation had been a flurry of activity, of neglecting to say good-bye to the people I hoped to stay in touch with, of constantly crossing paths with the people I prayed never to see again, and of trying to cram all my possessions into four equal-size cardboard boxes. And then it was over. Hours before the ceremony, I had been listening to varsity rowers–turned–investment bankers and mechanical engineers–turned–management consultants discuss how they were going to divide up the known universe. Now, in the time it took me to drive the length of the New Jersey

Turnpike, I had completed my transformation into another shut-in who lived with his parents. All I had to show for the experience was a piece of paper written entirely in Latin, mounted on a plaque with my alma mater's name at the bottom. Still, it wasn't a total wash. "Don't you get it?" a former roommate had explained to me. "Your résumé is going to say 'Princeton' on it. You *automatically win.*"

The meager amount of defiance I could muster at the time had been channeled into my entry in the senior class yearbook, the same stock picture of a yawning tiger that stood in for every student who didn't bother to submit a photograph, accompanied by my insightful parting words for the class of 1998: a lyric from a Bob Dylan song that ended with the line "I'm goin' back to New York City, I do believe I've had enough." To the extent that rock music can ever mean anything, it was a perfect encapsulation of my feelings in that final semester—my overwhelming urge to get as far away from institutional insularity as possible and return to Manhattan. It was more than just the city of my birth—it was the town where my fellow Jews had turned up their ample noses at my arriving ancestors and sentenced them to a life of sharecropping in the South, where previous generations of Princetonians had come to seek themselves in alcoholic binges and the arms of dubious women with names like Zelda, where no one cared if you succeeded and everyone hoped that you'd fail. I thought I had a score to settle, but the quotation was more of a boast than a battle plan. Instead of going back to New York City, I found myself driving parallel to it, and then past it, to resume my life in exile, in a suburb so sleepy and unremarkable that not even Billy Joel would have bothered to commemorate it in verse.

As a sort of graduation gift, my parents had offered me their assistance in transporting some of my belongings home, and when I pulled into the family garage they were waiting for me, shuffling things around, preparing to turn the space into a permanent shrine to the four years I spent apart from them.

"It's the college boy," my father bellowed. "Mama, come see

the college boy!" This wasn't his normal speaking voice, but a special tone he adopted when one of his children was within earshot.

"Aaaaay," my mother called back, clapping her hands. She was every bit as wiry and willowy as he was big and burly. I was the first member of the family to have earned a college degree, and they were the last generation who hoped to see their children grow up to be smarter than they were.

"So, college boy, what did they teach you? Say something clever."

"Do you think it would be all right if I just unpacked in peace?" I was carrying one of the four heavy boxes, and I was angry. It was too early to be feeling so weary—too early in the day, too early in the summer, too early in my life.

It had been seven years since my parents had moved the family to a town called New City, a community every bit as generic as the name suggested, and one they had never even heard of until they traveled there to buy their first SUV. After a combined ninety-seven years of living in New York, they had thrown in the towel. My father had a good year in business—his first ever, as far as any of us could recall—and decided it was his turn to acquire property, just as he had seen his friends do during the previous decade. "What is this rent?" went his carefully reasoned rationale. "Why should I be flushing my money down the toilet when I could be putting it into something I can own?" His irrational exuberance did not quite explain why he was taking out a thirty-year mortgage at the age of fifty-one.

For my sister, starting a new high school posed no problem and she adjusted marvelously, but for me, it was an adolescent nightmare more scarring than acne. My parents bought me whatever they could afford to help me adapt—new clothes, new car, new nose—but I made no enduring friendships, put down no roots. As badly as I wanted to get out of college, I had once wanted to get *in* just as intensely. And as sure as I was that I had no desire to return to suburbia, I was starting to feel with equal certainty that I would never escape it. "You know, that bedroom will always be yours," my father would remind me during the occasional phone conversations we shared while I was away. "You can come back to it any time you want." I know, Dad, *and that's what I'm afraid of*!

Aside from the odor of cat urine that now permeated the air, that ammonia aroma that people who have lived in houses smelling of cat urine for several years never seem to notice, everything about my parents' home was just the way I had left it, just the way I'd remembered it. Entering my own bedroom was like wiping away the last four years of my existence—the walls remained covered with posters and newspaper clippings from an era when my affections for Walt Disney movies and professional hockey could still be openly paraded, with the framed, approved learner's permit from the day I passed my driving test—a genuine fucking *accomplishment*, given that it had taken me three tries. And there, in one corner of the room, was the same bed I had slept in since my boyhood, the same box frame that I had used since I had outgrown my crib, the same antique that I was too ashamed to ask my parents to replace, lest it call any further attention to the incongruous plight of a twenty-two-year-old sleeping in a five-year-old's bed.

But in the days following my return, I began to perceive that certain things were different. My father had gained weight, which made him look more docile than he usually was; he hardly seemed to have any bones in his body, mean-spirited or otherwise. He was also spending considerably more time on the living room couch. That he was on the couch at all wasn't news—since we had moved into the house, he and my mother had stopped sleeping in the same bed. There was no incident or argument that had resulted in this arrangement; it was just something that had become the routine. Besides, it was easier for both of them: She could rest quietly while he slept with the television on all night, another habit he had developed since we left the city.

Now he had expanded his viewing schedule from an already healthy 10.5 hours a day, from the time he got home from work in the evening to when he left for work the following morning, to an even more impressive twenty-three hours, being the full length of a day minus the time he got up to go to the bathroom or the refrigerator. There had also been a significant change in his attire; he had gone from wearing clothing to slogging around the house in ratty undershirts and cotton briefs. In practice there was surely something wrong with this behavior, but to see it set down on paper, it sure does sound like somebody's idea of the American dream.

It was especially sad to see him like this knowing what he had been like in his prime. My father was a furrier, after his father, and after his father's father, and it was not a vocation into which he entered willingly. As he had told me many times before, his line of work was not so much a calling as it was the result of having failed his freshman year of college—twice. Instead of attending his classes, he stayed in his dorm room the whole semester and played poker. Given a second chance, my father instead gambled away another term, at which point my grandfather forcibly removed him from school and drafted him into the family profession.

I must sheepishly confess that, to this day, I don't completely understand how the fur business works. Essentially, it involves the purchase of raw animal skins at a time when they are plentiful and cheap (the buying season), then holding on to them until such time when they are scarce and in demand (the selling season). Sometimes my father would sell the pelts to manufacturers who, through their own particular alchemy, transmuted the greasy hides into coats or handbag trim. Sometimes he would deal them to other merchants from around the globe, and sometimes he'd sell them back to the same people from whom he'd bought them. Divorced from the actual commodity, his work was really the most basic of economic arrangements. In the end, isn't everything a kind of skin trade?

When we were living in our high-rise Manhattan apartment, before my father was commuting to his office diligently, then infrequently, then never, his job was the source of his vitality, an all-consuming engine that was as difficult to start up as it was to shut down. Each morning from our bedroom, my sister and I would hear him carrying on with our mother: "I'm not going in today! You can't make me! Maddy, please don't make me go! *No work today!*"

But each morning he was compelled to venture into the outside world, and after a full day at his warehouse, located amid the remnants of what was once the city's thriving fur district, he would come home restless, with fur on the brain. There wasn't a dinner table conversation that didn't hinge upon fur in some crucial way, and as best as I could tell, the whole business was always hanging by a whisker—he was perpetually trying to persuade someone to pay him the money they owed him or to give him more time to come up with the money he owed them. Then, after my sister and I had been tucked in for the night, we could hear him barking into the telephone to some associate or another, conducting his spasmodic one-sided conversations, cursing and screaming and asserting his mastery of the industry in short bursts of energy that didn't convey any information:

"Now, Leo, listen to me—*listen to me!* If these cocksuckers want red foxes, you know what I mean, they're going to have to come to me. . . . Uh-huh . . . uh-huh . . . that's right, Leo. And I'm not gonna let those sonofabitches have just the five hundred or six hundred best pieces, you know what I mean? They're going to have to take the whole lot, Leo. *The whole fucking lot!* . . . That's right. . . . That's right. . . . Not just the Xs, not just the double Xs, but all of it, Leo, all of it, you know? And I am going to *make them pay.* If they say fifteen a skin, I'm gonna say twenty. If they say twenty, *I'm* gonna say twenty-five. . . . Right . . . right . . . 'Cause where else are they gonna get these goods? From Donnie? From Carl? From those no-good cocksuckers up in Montana? Fuck 'em. They ain't got what I got. We got 'em, Leo, we got 'em. We got 'em by the balls, you know what I mean?"

We heard it every night, and to be honest, we had no idea what he meant.

These were the evenings that he bothered to come home at all. The remaining nights of the week, my father was so high on cocaine that it took all of his resolve to propel himself out of his office chair and into the louse-infested comfort of the nearest motel with hourly rates. When I was especially young, I would lie awake wondering where he had gone, worrying for his physical safety—that is, until I was old enough to understand what he was doing, and then I preferred it if he left me alone to conjure up hypothetical scenarios of what might be happening to him in his drugged-up state, instead of forcing me to confront him as he actually was: manic, wild-eyed, and reeking of musk, his own rotten breath, and the lemon air freshener with which he sprayed himself to conceal the other smells. The same *click-clack* sound of his key turning in the front door that once lulled me to sleep was now an alarm, a call to arms, because it meant that he was home, and he was looking for a fight.

Once he was finished shouting down my mother, he would corner me for hours at a time to proselytize about his progressive attitudes on male-female relations. "Do you understand that sex between a man and a woman is the most beautiful thing in the world?" he'd tell me, nostrils flaring, chest heaving, eyes brimming with chemically induced sincerity. "You should never be afraid of this. My father didn't have the courage to tell me, but I don't want you to be ashamed of sex." At this point in the presentation, he would usually meander from his main thesis to one of three possible digressions: how my mother was the only woman he'd ever had sex with; how lucky he was that my mother would have sex with him; and how difficult it is to convince women to have sex with you. The secrets it had taken him fifty frustrating years to accumulate were mine to benefit from, before I'd even hit puberty. From his perspective, my father must have thought he was doing me a favor.

To my innocent ears it was all nonsense anyway, as incoherent as his midnight chatterings to his business clientele, but there comes a point, even at the age of ten, when you become tired of hearing it. But my father was a man who was strong in his convictions, even more so with a minuscule quantity of cocaine in his bloodstream, and asking him to please stop because, well, *he was scaring the shit out of me*, that was like a dagger in his heart. That's when he'd threaten to cut me off, kick me out of the apartment, and, worst of all, send me to public school. First, to my mother: "He's out of here, Maddy. I don't want you, or your mother, giving him any money, you got that? *You're not to give him one cent!*" Then, to me: "It's public school for you! Do you hear me? *Public school!*" (It should be noted that he did eventually make good on this last threat.)

My upbringing in New York had accustomed me to a certain degree of background noise—the apocalyptic predawn rumblings of newspaper delivery trucks being dispatched onto the streets, of pent-up steam escaping from power plant turbines into the air, of my mother and father screaming slurs like "junkie" and "whore" (two syllables) at each other before I learned what such words meant. Our new rustic existence had brought with it my father's fragile sobriety, but also an eerie, discomforting tranquillity I could never bring myself to accept completely. As I watched my father exercise his dominion over a three-piece sectional sofa and the channels of his TV set, wait for the phone to ring, and otherwise cultivate excuses not to go to his office, I felt only pity—not for him, or for myself, but for all my former classmates, the ones about to embark on their European backpacking adventures or begin their nominal desk jobs in some family friend's firm, the ones now being propelled through life by their faith in the invulnerability of their own fathers, who wouldn't discover the truth about the old man until he was dead from a stroke or indicted for tax evasion—or maybe they'd never find out at all, the poor bastards. I, on the other hand, was more enlightened. I was about to become the only person in my household who was also a contributing member of the American workforce.

TRADITIONALLY, THE SUMMER after college is supposed to be one of repose and personal reflection, of furtive keggers and pot parties in idle high school parking lots, of lying poolside while putting off the shackles of responsibility and having affairs with married women while simultaneously courting their daughters. I wouldn't get to enjoy any of these liberties, because I had allowed myself exactly twelve days between graduation and the commencement of my first full-time job.

I'm not certain what it was that initially attracted me to the trainee program at the William Morris Agency, whether it was the sex appeal of the many celebrities whose salaries they negotiated or the day I came to drop off my employment application and thought I spotted Joel Coen in the lobby. Historically, I knew the company had launched the careers of height-challenged Jews from the Marx Brothers to Michael Ovitz, and I was further distracted by an unduly rigorous hiring process that required me to visit their offices on four separate occasions: first to take a typing test, then to meet with a human resources manager, then to meet with a different human resources manager, and then to meet with a panel of their highest-ranking agents, who would pass final judgment on me before casually tossing their *tallises* over their shoulders and heading off to lunch. I was so overjoyed when at last they offered me a job that I hardly even noticed that the starting wages of $350 a week would render me an Ivy League alum living below the poverty line. Instead, my dwindling days of freedom were spent poring over the training manual they had sent me in the mail, with its capitalized common nouns and its pages upon pages of protocol for correctly conducting telephone calls with the Client, and composing written correspondence for the Agent, and looking for a cheap parking space in the Vicinity of the Building where the Agency was housed, and trying to convince myself that this line of work was a good idea.

As someone who might one day rise to the rank of agent, I was required to arrive at the office in a suit and tie to push a diminutive metal cart that carried the mail for the forty-odd assistants of the forty-odd agents and executives of William Morris, five times a day. In between trips around the agency floor, I was relegated to the mailroom, a cold subterranean space I shared with my fellow trainees. When we weren't attending to our appointed rounds, we were shuttling up and down in the building's service elevator, running errands, reading scripts, or congregating quietly in the mailroom lounge. The mailroom manager, a stringy and excitable man of West Indian descent, spent the day sitting behind a soundproof glass enclosure fielding phone calls from upstairs; when our assistance was needed, he'd press a button that triggered a buzzer in the lounge, point to me or one of my properly attired colleagues, and send us on our way.

How any of this was supposed to transform me into a cutthroat Sammy Glick–type *macher,* I have no fucking clue. What I do know is that I was one of the worst mail carriers in the company's hundred years of operation. I attribute this in part to the thoroughly inadequate preparation I received from another trainee who had been on the job only a few weeks longer than I had, a lanky, soft-spoken Mongoloid with hands bigger than his head, who barely knew the delivery routes himself. The rest of the fault was entirely my own: The burden of carrying the mail made me inordinately nervous — more so — and I couldn't seem to master the arcane system of secret abbreviations the agents used to address their interoffice correspondence. Yet at the end of the summer I was given a promotion out of the mailroom, largely on the strength of a bathroom cleanup checklist I designed for the overnight maintenance crew, a Microsoft Word document so stunning and immaculate that a copy of it remains in my permanent employee file to this day. I had been promoted ahead of the Mongoloid, and I'm told that on the day my good fortune was announced to the mailroom staff, he placed his head inside his colossal hands and cried.

Fifteen stories above, I found myself at the bottom of a very different hierarchy. I was given the title of floating assistant, made an unattached in-house temp who could cover for the permanent assistants who sat at desks placed before each agent's office, filling in whenever they took vacations or called in sick. Except they never took vacations or called in sick, because they knew the day they returned, this little *pisher* would be waiting in their seat, and he wouldn't leave. The full-time assistants were several years older than me, all college graduates, some even with JD and MBA degrees who had given up lucrative legal and business practices for a shot at the very best kind of money—Hollywood money. They were also, mostly, totally defeated before they reached the age of thirty. Each had achieved much before arriving here: One assistant had orchestrated the legendary reunion of a forgotten seventies-era rock band; another had written a spec script for *Sex and the City* that everyone agreed was as good as any episode that had made it on the air, whatever that was worth. But their greatest accomplishments were behind them. Now they shared a job that offered them no responsibility more challenging than the introduction of teabags into boiling water, a job in which they had invested so many of their best years that their only remaining options were to continue to hold out for a promotion to agent or start over in an altogether new field. The single mistake they had made was pursuing a career in which even a single mistake would not be tolerated, where just one error got you sent to the end of a line that had no apparent end in sight.

For people in the business of talent, the agents themselves did not have the slightest interest in cultivating it in the people who worked for them. Each one was a tyrant in a kingdom populated by tyrants, entitled to have his every wish fulfilled even when it conflicted with the wishes of the agent next door, and capable of communicating his orders through the varying intonations of a solitary word he was totally unaccustomed to having said to him: *no.* When not tending to their affairs, the agents were sniffing the air for blood, watching for any sign of weakness in their assistants; a single missed phone call or typographical error would often result in the hurling of epithets or hot beverages in their direction. The agents' entire way of life was predicated on the accumulation and protection of information, information they had no incentive to share with a younger generation who would inevitably use it to surpass them. It was the first time in my life I had encountered adults dedicated to any purpose other than my own self-improvement; the first time in my life when nothing was expected of me—when nothing was *demanded* of me. And I couldn't do nothing.

In the course of applying for the trainee program, in my final

appearance before the agent panel, I had, in an especially glib moment, told my inquisitors that I wanted to work for William Morris
because "in the entertainment industry, we always talk about how
celebrities are thought to have a certain X factor, that they are stars
because they have 'It.' Well, gentlemen, I want to see if I've got It,
too." After eight months on the job, the point had been made abundantly clear: I didn't have It, didn't know where It could be found,
didn't even know anyone who could hazard a guess as to where It
was residing these days. Now I just wanted out of It. Fuck It.

MY NEW JOB, when it was still new, had briefly reinvigorated my
father. During the summer, he had vowed to help me pay for a
place of my own in the city until I could cover the rent myself, and
together we made intermittent weekend trips to New York to search
for apartments. He did his best to keep pace with the indefatigable
real estate brokers who raced him up and down the rickety stair-
cases of dilapidated brownstones, who could barely hide their disdain as my father lagged numerous flights behind the sound of his
own wheezing; but we never did find a property I could reasonably
afford, even with his assistance, and the tenuous economics of his
trade made him a less than desirable sponsor in the eyes of potential landlords who expected him to guarantee my lease. Then one
day I returned home from work to find him stretched out on his favorite couch, his face buried in a pillow.

"What's wrong?" I said. I expected to hear that someone close
to him had died.

"The ruble has been devalued," he said. The Russian market
for his fur had collapsed, and along with it his confidence and any
hope we shared of his financing my independence.

"So what are you going to do now?" I asked. "What's your game
plan?"

"I'm out of gas." That was his answer.

He had never been a man who reacted well to any news, good
or bad. My college years had seen a slow tapering off of our inti-

macy, during which time my most personal milestones—the first girl I laid, the first joint I smoked, the first time I successfully ate soft-boiled eggs, my decision as a rule to stop dating Asian women—went unreported to him, for fear that any one of these revelations could be the one that finally sent him over the edge. What right did I now have to impose upon his delicate equilibrium with my nebulous dilemmas of destiny and personal fulfillment? How could I tell him that the sole decision in my young adult life for which I bore full responsibility had been a complete mistake?

We had both barely recovered from the last instance in which I'd sought my father's guidance: I was thirteen years old, newly made *bar mitzvah*, flush with cash (what a scam!), and in the grip of an unhealthy fixation on comic books. In the free hours I gained following my immediate withdrawal from Hebrew school, I had tracked down a comic book dealer in Texas who was willing to sell me a copy of *Batman #1*, a collectible issued in 1940—the same year as my father, by the way—for the paltry sum of $1,000. But being unable to see the goods for myself, I could not judge if his merchandise was in sufficiently decent shape to merit the price. What to do? On my father's recommendation, the dealer in Texas would find an associate in New York to whom he could send the merchandise on consignment; we would inspect it in this middle-man's care and pay him a commission for his efforts. Consignment! Who had ever heard of such a thing? A genius, my father was! The Jewish Donald Trump! I was practically holding the antique volume in my hands, turning its brittle pages with the tips of my fingers, filling my sinuses with the tantalizing smells of prewar ink and decomposing pulp!

Except that the unscrupulous dealer to whom the Texan consigned the comic book sold it to someone else for twice what I was offering and kept the difference for himself. End of story.

It wasn't until a full ten years had passed that, on one cold morning in February, after much brooding and inflicting considerable damage upon my stomach lining, I concluded it was time once again to confer with the Solomon of the sofa. He was easy enough to locate, stretched out in front of the television, where he'd been since the broadcast of Bill Clinton's impeachment trial had begun. ("Now," he had assured me, "you're going to see *real* democracy in action.") While one hundred histrionic statesmen took turns deliberating the fate of our president on the floor of the Senate, I stood before my father, the elastic collar of his stained T-shirt stretched out in a disapproving scowl and his underpants riddled with revealing holes, and laid out the reasons that I wanted to quit the agent training program: how the monotonous responsibilities and lack of encouragement were hurting my self-esteem, how the career of an agent did not appeal to me, and besides, the women there were stuck-up, status-seeking bitches who would never in a million years go out with me, let alone set me up with their friends. Then I took a breath and waited for his verdict.

"Well," said the man who had been working the singularly most miserable and unrewarding job known to civilization since the day his own father had forcibly drafted him into it, who knew nothing of an era when men were allowed—and *encouraged!*—to seek the paths that provided them with the greatest possible sense of satisfaction, who for the last thirty-five years had not been permitted to go one moment without having to consider the wants and needs of another human being before making any decisions of his own, "it sounds that you've tried as hard as you can with this job, but maybe it just isn't right for you."

"Are you disappointed?" I asked. "Do you want me to wait until I find another job to move on to?"

"I want whatever you want," he said. "Someday, when you have a son of your own, you'll understand. You will only want the best for him. And sometimes he will succeed, and sometimes he will fail, but every pain he suffers, and every time he fails, *you* will feel it a hundred times worse." And with that, he reached around me with his thick arms, pulled me tight against his pudgy chest, and whispered in my ear. "All good things. All good things. All good things," he said over and over, as if simply repeating these words were enough to make them so. It was all he could do.

"Now," my father added as he let go of me, "when do you think you might consider coming to work for me? I could pay you whatever you wanted. Whatever you thought was fair."

"Can I have some time to think about it?" I said. But really, what was there to think about?

My resignation from William Morris had about as much impact as any of my myriad other achievements at the company. When I offered my two weeks' notice, I was told that it wouldn't be required, that I could leave on the spot if I wanted. But I insisted I be allowed to stay, and frittered away my remaining hours on useless chores, though no more useless than the functions I usually performed. On my last day, I e-mailed a terse farewell message to the entire New York staff, this time choosing as my epigram a quotation from one of their oldest surviving agents, a frail octogenarian who held the position of chairman emeritus, reproducing the words I had seen attributed to him in a recent issue of *Variety*: "They come. They go. Who called?" It was as close to a corporate slogan as William Morris possessed.

Once again I consolidated my life into my parents' house, where each passing day was indistinguishable from the one that preceded it. Every twenty-four-hour period was a precise ritual of doors opening and closing, of pets being let out of and into the house, of vacuum cleaners and laundry machines humming, of cookware rattling and toilets flushing, that repeated itself with no deviation. I became hyperaware of my mother's and father's bodily clocks even as I was subjected to similar scrutiny. Surely they must have suspected that not all the hours I logged in my bedroom, behind a locked door and connected to the Internet, were expended in the interests of finding a new job.

While my interactions with my father were limited to fighting over the newspaper we had both come to depend on for our daily dose of groundless inspiration (for me the horoscopes, for him the lottery numbers), I realized I had almost completely forgotten about my mother. She had lately undergone a transition of her own, from a phase in which she dressed in costume jewelry and heavy makeup to a phase in which she wore only my old college sweatshirts and no makeup at all. When she wasn't slipping handwritten inspirational notes under my door (the words *Remember, we love you!!!* trembling on the page in her thin, wavering script), she could often be found on her hands and knees, combing the carpets for stray clumps of cat hair—an impossible task when she was applying herself to it, and now she was hardly trying at all. It was during one of these search-and-destroy missions that I spoke to her for the first time in weeks.

"You know that Dad asked me to come work for him," I said.

"Yes, I know," she said. Though it wasn't within her character to get passionate about things anymore, her advice to me was concise and unambiguous. "Don't do it," she said. "*Don't* do it."

"I'm not going to," I replied. I was surprised to hear myself say these words. It was only then that I realized I meant them.

2

THE PRINCETON RUB

ONE OF MY MOST VIVID MEMORIES OF CHILDHOOD IS a fantasy: the wish that, were my parents ever to die, I too should be struck dead on the spot, so that I would never have to suffer the pain of living without them. At the age of twenty-three, I was seeing my wish belatedly come true. My mother and father were again the only people in my world, and as long as none of us were working, we were all being buried alive in that house, that suburban tomb my father had consigned us to. We spoke only to one another, interacted with no one outside of our social triangle, and we were suffocating.

On an April day that offered no more promise than the months of inactivity that preceded it, I was startled out of my self-loathing by a shrill digital whine that I recognized as the ringing of my telephone. The yellowing device on my bedroom nightstand had become a mystery to me—more often than not it sat disconnected while my computer plugged me into the infinite universe of pornography that commanded my attention from sunrise to sunset and usually to the following sunrise. Whether it was the result of karma or cramped wrists, I was prepared to receive this particular call, accompanied by the blaring electronic sirens and flashing lights that usually announce the payoff of a slot machine—which, in some sense, this would prove to be.

"Hello," said a gentle female voice, the first I'd heard since the winter that was not my mother's. "I'm calling from the human resources department at Condé Nast. You might have heard, there's been a . . . shuffling of the chairs over at *Details* magazine, and they're going to be looking for some new assistants. We were wondering if you might like to interview for one of the positions."

"Great, sure, absolutely," I answered, doing my best to conceal my desperation.

"Excellent," came the reply. Then, more portentously: "Bucky will be in touch with you shortly about a time to meet with the new editors over there." There was a brief pause of realization. "Shouldn't you be at work right now?"

"I—I *am* at work. I have my telephone number set to ring at home and on my cell phone at the same time." Saved, once again, by technology!

The exchange, which couldn't have lasted more than thirty seconds, was the latest link in a chain of events that had started over a year ago. As my college career was winding down, I had haphazardly tossed off a letter of inquiry to the magazine publisher Condé Nast, among the many firms I foolishly thought might compete to hire me. Even before I realized I could earn a living contributing to them, magazines had been present at almost every stage of my development; they had attended to me, cared for me, and nourished me as well as any member of my family had. Like every other astigmatic Jewish kid in New York City, I had spent my boyhood being fed a steady diet of *MAD*, whose knee-jerk cynicism, Yiddish sound effects, and sneering parodies of movies I had never seen nursed me through countless illnesses real and faked. At a certain age I made the transition to *National Lampoon*, when I discovered it printed words like *tits*, cartoon representations of tits, and even photographs of tits. Countless generations of unborn Itzkoff offspring would be forever lost after I spilled them into the pages of *Playboy* pictorials. (Sorry, kids.) And for the years in college when I lived with roommates and had to satisfy myself with surreptitious star fucking, I cherished my subscription to *Rolling Stone* as if each issue were a biweekly installment of the Talmud, with ads for home tanning beds and term paper research services at the end of the scroll. To this day, the very sight of a newsstand, no matter how many I've previously passed by, is enough to reduce me to that same excitable toddler who learned to read from the nutritional information panels on cereal boxes and the tiny subscription stamps that came enclosed with magazine sweepstakes entry forms, a boy who could always be tempted by the possibility of seeing something he'd never seen before.

There really was once a man with the improbable name of Condé Nast, an ad salesman–turned–magazine publisher, a Jazz Age dandy who wasn't above dressing in the occasional monocle or top hat, who lost a fortune in the Great Crash of 1929, and who left this world having gazed deeper into the abyss of destitution than any millionaire ever should. While alive, he specialized in magazines with names like *Vogue* and *Vanity Fair* and *Glamour*, archaic words and expressions that might otherwise have fallen out of usage altogether, had he not preserved them in the cultural lexicon. Now the business he started was just another trophy in the showcase of a privately held media conglomerate, and his periodicals had uniformly become catalogs of middle-class desire, all means to the same end: convincing you that your life as you were currently living it was somehow incomplete and could be remedied only by the products and services offered in their perfume-scented pages. The aspirational and the unattainable were free to mingle without any sense of contradiction; the comparison test of home facial kits could sit side by side with the advertisement for the $2,000 chaise longue, and both were considered to be of equal importance.

Condé Nast the company was not one with a reputation for recruiting my kind, by which I don't mean men. Even in my academic obliviousness in pastoral New Jersey, I was aware of its supposed predilection for dutiful Protestant women, for whom a job there provided not just a launching pad to a career in publishing but a springboard into the arms of dutiful Protestant husbands with whom they could have dutiful Protestant children. So crucial was the notion of lineage to the corporate philosophy of Condé Nast that its employment application form asked if you had any relatives who already belonged to its ranks. The only place I'd previously seen a similar query was on the undergraduate application for Princeton.

The résumé I had sent the company a year ago gave top billing to my scholastic credentials, and my cover letter was unrepentant in dropping the names of my professors who were contributors to their magazines. In any other circumstance, these actions would have constituted professional suicide. Most everyone despises Princeton graduates, with good reason: We are intolerable self-promoters, committed careerists who have come to see the world as our personal feeding trough, and we wear our connections to one another like a bib as we bury our greedy faces deeper in the slop. But I sensed that none of this would be held against me the moment I walked into the office of a hiring manager who was known professionally—it said so right there on her business card—by the decidedly *goyische* nickname of Bucky.

In person, Bucky was a pleasantly puritanical, middle-aged matron with a firm handshake and posture that would make a broomstick jealous. From her navy blue dress that probably never needed ironing to her desk decorated with pictures of her cherubic Benetton- and Abercrombie-clad progeny, the clues to her own ancestry were as subtle as Plymouth Rock.

"So, Dave," she began, "tell me about Princeton." In this sanctuary I was free to take pride in my pedigree, but if she was expecting to be regaled with memories of wintertime cotillions at the Cap and Gown Club and weekend regattas on Lake Carnegie, she was barking up the wrong family tree.

"I have very mixed feelings about the experience," went my canned response. "I mean, I took some classes there that I wouldn't trade for anything in the world, but let's say the social scene is very . . . antiquated."

"Mmmm," Bucky ruminated. "Do you know this girl?" she asked, providing the name of a fellow undergrad, a family friend she had recently hooked up with a summer internship. Rather than reveal her protégée as one more untouchable classmate who'd sooner fellate a beer bottle than give me the time of day—and given the atmosphere at Princeton, such things were not out of the question—I said we'd never met. "Oh, that's too bad," she said. "You should look her up when you get back to campus." I noticed that as she spoke, she had the unusual habit of focusing her gaze at a point slightly above my eye level, which might have been a technique she picked up in a management training course, or maybe she was looking for my horns. Then, as carelessly as one might observe an overcast day, she asked me: "Have you given any thought to which of our magazines you might want to work for?"

I was totally unprepared for the question and rattled off a list of titles, some of which I read regularly and some I simply recalled from the company letterhead. "Gosh, I don't know. *Vanity Fair? GQ? Details?*"

Bucky frowned at the suggestion of the first two publications, but her stern demeanor melted away when I mentioned the third. "Forget about *Vanity Fair* and *GQ*," she advised me. "These magazines are institutions. You don't just walk into either of them and start writing cover stories. But I happen to think you'd be perfect for *Details*." If we were on a first date, this would have been the equivalent of her stopping in midintroduction to invite me back to her place for a spirited session of slap-ass. But that's how these people worked: In the blink of a curled, mascara-encrusted eyelash, they had peered deep within your soul, and either they saw that you were predestined for salvation or else no amount of argument or prayer could redeem you. You were Harvard, you were Vassar, you were Wellesley, you were Princeton; you are *GQ*, you are *Vogue*, you are *Glamour*—and you, my dear, deluded Jewboy, are *Details*.

Except.

"It's just that I don't have any openings over there right now," said Bucky, clearing my anemic employment file from her desk. "But let's stay in touch, and I'll let you know as soon as something becomes available." Maybe I hadn't quite solved Condé Nast.

Maybe this was their polite way of saying, Thanks for coming, and by the way, try not to kill any of our Messiahs on your way out the door.

THIRTEEN MONTHS IS an eternity in publishing time. Many magazine jobs don't last as long, nor do some magazines. In the period between this introductory meeting and the final callback, I had already racked up one entirely failed career, a version of myself that had to be completely scrapped, torn apart at every seam until nothing was left but my name. This made me the perfect candidate to work at *Details*.

In the seven years since it had been purchased by Condé Nast, at which time it was hardly more than a hand-photocopied news-letter about New York City nightlife, *Details* had been reconceived in multiple formats under multiple editorial staffs: as an authoritative compendium of alternative pop culture, a style bible for the downtown scene, a professional guide for today's upwardly mobile young man. By the publishing trade's own Darwinian standards, this lack of identity should have been an outward sign that the beast had outlived its usefulness and was on the verge of extinction. Yet after each metamorphosis, the magazine had managed to retain enough of its core audience to survive to the next evolution, because in each incarnation it never lost sight of a fundamental guiding principle: It was gay. Not because it published pictures of erect penises and aggravated ass-fucking on every page, but because it went after a young male demographic in such a cool, detached manner that it did not alienate men of any orientation. For the straight reader there was just enough celebrity smut and automobile ads to keep him from suspecting that anything was amiss; for the limp-wristed set, there were bare-chested cologne models and high-end fashion spreads intended to foster feelings of admiration and envy and a yearning to possess the things in those photographs—the interior responses that by the industry's standards of armchair psychoanalysis spelled F-A-G—only not so much of this content that heterosexual men would be driven away.

For all the volatility going on behind the scenes, sales of the magazine had remained stagnant through each regime change. This losing streak had been broken—if not broken, then dented slightly—in 1997 with the hiring of a new editor in chief, Michael Caruso. Under Caruso, a seasoned editor who had come up through the ranks of *Vanity Fair*, *Los Angeles* magazine, and *The Village Voice*, the delicate sexual balance that *Details* had maintained was finally toppled, and you didn't have to be Sherlock Holmes or John Holmes to figure out in whose favor: While the queer-friendly fashion stories were retained, the service journalism dedicated itself to manufacturing eight-minute abs, exorcising excess sweat and body odor, and reducing razor burn. Technology and gadgets were fetishized alongside more traditional lust objects: The mix of cover celebrities rotated between easygoing, ambivalent leading men and shapely temptresses draped only in layers of celluloid or gold paint. Every piece of copy within was ladled with a healthy serving of irony, allowing its writer and reader alike an air of sarcastic superiority over any subject matter. Perhaps Caruso had good reason to feel superior: By the end of his first year on the job, *Details* was selling as many as 200,000 copies a month on the newsstand (representing gains of anywhere from 20 to 50 percent over the issues of his predecessors). Upon receiving the information, he couldn't wait to whip it out in public, hastily blabbing to a newspaper reporter that he expected to be rewarded by his bosses at Condé Nast with "a big fat raise." Actually, he was fired.

What had happened in the interim was basically this: *Maxim*. Around the time that Caruso's reign at *Details* began, the first issues of this latest entry in the overcrowded field of men's-interest publications began appearing on American newsstands. *Maxim*'s format, if not its content, was imported from England, where a thriving market had sprung up for magazines that catered to young males who were adults only in age. Like the opulent glossies it strove to compete with, *Maxim* offered the standard mix of narrative features and self-help articles, but wrapped in a tone of self-deprecation; its uniformly casual voice was there to remind you that your fears and anxieties were widespread and universal. In its pages, advice on such cubicle daydreams as how to manage a stock portfolio or write a bestselling novel was mixed with more down-to-earth fare like grilling the perfect steak or measuring yourself for a sport jacket. Their infinitely mutable mother tongue had already given a name to the sorts of guys who read these magazines, who wanted the benefits of maturity without the burdens, the freedoms without the obligations—a diminutive that celebrated their boyish tendencies while derisively denying them their status as grown men. In British slang, they were called *lads*.

The American edition of *Maxim*, which after two years of operation was selling well over one million copies a month, did not tamper much with this formula. Beyond its chest-beating cover boast, proclaiming itself THE BEST THING TO HAPPEN TO MEN SINCE WOMEN, the only significant addition was the prominent space it devoted to teasing, non-nude pictorials of female celebrities. The women on its cover—and its cover subjects were always women—were not stylized goddesses, but slightly unwholesome embodiments of the girl-next-door fantasy, neglected celebrities who had never appeared on magazine covers before—the sexy daughter on that trashy family sitcom, the buff action-adventure star everyone always assumed was a lesbian. The earliest issues were devoid of any fashion photography whatsoever.

Much of *Maxim*'s stateside success could be attributed to its editor in chief, Mark Golin. A former deputy editor of *Cosmopolitan*, he had overseen many of the minor but memorable stories that defined *Maxim*'s character; you'd hardly call them journalism, but they were pieces that had never run before in any mass-market publication and were never likely to run again: an article by an overweight writer who attempts to go about his normal day-to-day existence without wearing a shirt, and Golin's own imaginative first-person account of a tour of hell. His coup de grâce was the real-life story of a guy who, on a bet, got himself fitted with breast implants—then discovered he liked the fake knockers so much, he kept them.

From as far away as New City, I was hearing about Mark Golin more and more frequently, seeing his name in the gossip columns that first predicted, and then confirmed, that Condé Nast had hired him to take over as the editor of *Details*. In the publicity photographs that accompanied these articles, Mark's chubby, elliptical face, with its wild wisps of hair on either side of his balding pate, gave him the look of a *Peanuts* character come to life, a doodle from one of Charles Schulz's final years when his hands weren't so steady, with a quivering smirk that suggested he didn't place much conviction in the celebrity status bestowed on him.

Through a series of whims, caprices, and coincidences, I was on my way to meeting this man. Donning a suit and tie, I drove myself down to the *Details* offices in Manhattan's East Village. While the company's many other titles were confined to a staid corporate headquarters on Madison Avenue, *Details* was one of just two Condé Nast publications allowed the autonomy of its own building (the other being *The New Yorker*). Lodged snugly within the penthouse of an aging loft, the magazine exuded an ostentatious hipness that bled from every crack and knothole in the deteriorating workspace and radiated from the eyes of its receptionist, in the I-could-give-a-shit glance she shot me when I told her I was here to meet the new editor in chief.

"Hey, dude!" shouted a spry, slender woman as she bounded into the reception area and shook my hand. This was Catherine Romano, once Mark Golin's second in command at *Maxim*—his "editrix," as the masthead declared, whom he had brought with him to be one of his executive editors at *Details*; she was a woman on the cusp of forty who thought nothing of showing up to work in a white cotton T-shirt and painted-on leather pants. As she led me down a hallway to Mark's office, trampling an old wood-paneled floor that was filthy with character, it was as if we had time-traveled back to the bygone year of 1995, surrounded by stucco walls that didn't quite reach the ceiling, decorated with old *Details* covers that honored dispensable heroes—Anthony Kiedis! Liv Tyler! Michael Stipe!—from a cultural epoch that already felt as ancient and mythical as the Trojan War.

Seated behind one last door in the farthest corner of the office was Mark Golin himself, appearing exactly as I would see him for the next several months: haggard, worn out from what seemed like forty-eight consecutive hours without sleep, yet looking as if he were raring to go for another seventy-two. He was a tiny man, tinier than me—when seated, his head barely extended above the horizon of his steel desk, currently strewn with receptacles for the dozens of cigarette butts he had accumulated since daybreak. He had a fresh cigarette pressed between each of his ears and the bushy scraps of his hair; one eye was open wide with surprise, while the other was semipermanently locked in a diabolical squint. At present, his decidedly un-*Details*-like attire consisted of a sweatshirt whose sleeves had been ripped off to highlight his startlingly beefy forearms. His personal space was decorated less like a highly paid publishing executive's suite than an excited freshman's first dorm room—it was more square footage than he knew what to do with, containing only a couch, an empty bookshelf, and several six-packs in various stages of completion.

Oblivious to the absolute unimportance of this interview in the grand scheme of putting out a magazine, Catherine sat in on the meeting, joined by Bill Shapiro, her fellow executive editor and another *Maxim* transplant, a tall, gangly man with the posture of a praying mantis and the fatalistic personality to match. Together they formed Mark's ready-made audience for whenever he wanted to put on a show, but he wasn't playing to them this time.

"Did you buy a suit just for this interview?" Mark asked in a rasp that recalled my grandma Edith, were she only so sharp-witted.

"This old thing?" I said. "Nah, it's just left over from my bar mitzvah." All three editors roared with laughter, but none as loud as Mark, who gave up a rapid-fire, hacking cackle, so close to a cough that I was sure a gob of phlegm would soon follow.

"So," he said, clutching in his stubby fingers a copy of the résumé that had brought me this far. "Princeton, eh?" The familiar grin I had already seen in print was now sitting across the desk from me. "Do you happen to know what the Princeton Rub is?"

"It's a sex thing, isn't it?" I answered tentatively, even though I knew the answer.

"Go on," Mark prodded. Clearly he knew the answer, too, but he wanted to see if he could get me to say it out loud. "Tell us about it."

With nothing to lose but my dignity, I continued: "It's when a guy gets off by rubbing . . . himself between the thighs of another guy."

My cross-examiners giggled. "How do you know this?" Mark wondered.

"It's sad to say, but I looked it up in a dictionary." This was true. Your better dictionaries will likely have a definition of the phrase, possibly even an illustration.

"Why do you think they call it the *Princeton* Rub?" he asked, emphasizing the name of my alma mater as if it were Dachau or Belsen.

"I think it was a hazing ritual," I guessed, "something the upperclassmen used to do to the new students. It was an all-male school for over two hundred years, you know."

"When you were there, did anyone try to perform the Princeton Rub on you?"

"Look at me," I pleaded. "I'm barely a hundred and twenty pounds. If anyone had tried that on me, I would have been crushed to death."

There was an obvious chemistry between Mark and me—the two of us had the natural rapport of a Borscht Belt comedy team, two clumsy, bumbling Jerry Lewises mugging for the camera without a dapper, dignified Dean Martin to keep us grounded. He didn't ask to see my clips from the piddling college newspapers I had written for, didn't care about the great men and women of letters I had studied under—or, for that matter, about the gaping two-month hole in my employment history; he just wanted an assistant who could keep him entertained. It was the oddest interview I'd ever participated in, and he was the most unforgettable character I'd met—the first man I knew who had risen to his stature, or at least to his status, by refusing to ever take his job seriously.

"They really put you in charge of this place?" I asked boldly.

The smile on Mark's face faded, and I thought I had just blown my chance. "Listen," he said with sudden gravity, "do you know that two years ago, I tried to get a job here, with Condé Nast, as the editor of one of their websites? They wouldn't even give me an interview! Now here I am, running one of their magazines! The fact is, I may not know what I'm doing. But they came to me. They hired me. So we're going to do whatever the hell we want to do."

"So," I said to Catherine as she escorted me back to the lobby, "*that's* the boss."

"I know!" she said sympathetically. "Isn't he a trip?"

An uncharacteristic feeling of confidence came over me as I left the meeting. I was certain I had nailed it—I would be offered the position, and it would redeem me for the precious year I had just pissed away. But my certainty soon gave way to anxiety, and as each day passed with no answer, my thoughts turned from opportunities presented to opportunities lost, the crushing sense that another chance to reinvent myself had slipped through my fingers. I wandered my parents' house, searching for strong, well-supported protrusions I could hang myself from when *Details* turned me down.

Then I got the blessed call from Bucky: Mark had hired me to be his new assistant. I was about to enter a world where I was trusted enough to fill out my own time sheet, where overtime kicked in after thirty-five hours a week, where I'd be allowed to take off for the High Holidays (only they were referred to as *personal days*). My starting salary of $25,000 a year—a preferential rate because I was the assistant to an editor in chief and not some common editorial assistant—was enough that I could finally move into my own place, a small Upper East Side studio that offered not much more breathing room than my new boss's office. While my mother, who hardly had the strength to raise her voice, let alone heavy objects, offered to help me pack up and move out, my father preferred to sit on the sidelines, searching for strings he could pull on that would cause everything to unravel. "What happens if you lose the job?" he wanted to know. "How will you pay for the apartment then?"

ON THE EVE of my first day at *Details,* I spent several hours exhuming my limited wardrobe, trying to put together the perfect outfit for the following morning—one that made it clear I had put a considerable effort into something that looked effortless. I settled on a pair of khakis and a blue polyester shirt with white trim around its oversize lapel, the adult equivalent of a little boy's sailor suit. The ensemble was not wasted on Mark when he saw me at my desk. "Pret-*ty* gay," he observed.

So began our working relationship. But the carefree, come-on-in-and-take-off-your-pants spirit of our introductory encounter had spoiled me, and it wasn't as easy to recapture that irreverence as we got acclimated to each other. He spent his days working behind closed doors, and on the occasions when his hungover countenance emerged, to order me into the streets in search of aspirin, a pack of cigarettes, or a double cheeseburger, the surprise would often cause one or both of us to recoil in shock, a habit that took several weeks to break. For some time, my only other companion was a fellow editorial assistant, a former phone sex operator with the sugary voice and rippling, overabundant frame of . . . well, a former phone sex worker, and there was no point in getting attached to anyone else, because everyone was leaving. In his inaugural editor's letter, Mark sardonically referred to himself as "#5-in-chief," a reminder that he, like his predecessors, was easily expendable, and perhaps a subconscious reflection of the ominous going-away parties we were throwing for departing staffers on a round-the-clock basis. I grew to cherish the routine errands that

Mark would send me on, to revel in the daily regimen of caffeine, nicotine, and saturated fats that had to be administered to him each day to revive him back to health, as if it were a game. I felt relieved to have someone in my life who actually seemed to need my help—to have someone I was actually capable of helping.

As someone who'd clearly never had an assistant before, Mark came to appreciate the most rudimentary services that I performed for him as sources of delight and astonishment. He loved it that I'd come into work before he arrived (essentially any time before noon) to empty his ashtrays and clear out his beer bottles, loved the freedom that came with having someone to answer his phone calls for him, loved it when I'd demand to rerecord his outgoing voice mail greeting in my own voice. And nothing pleased him more than the afternoon when he emerged from his office to ask for more salt for his French fries, and I summoned up my courage to inform him, "Semen has salt in it." This story was repeated to so many of Mark's friends and acquaintances in subsequent months, you'd think I'd brought him my first report card of straight As.

For as much as he enjoyed a good joke, Mark never let it be forgotten that he was the head prankster in charge. Every business day was that day when some beleaguered parent brings her ill-mannered brat to work and lets him run amok—only in this case, no one could tell the brat to behave himself. When he wasn't chasing editors out of his office with a gigantic, battery-powered water pistol, he was relaxing on our rooftop deck to the sounds of several dozen firecrackers he was setting off in the direction of the Manhattan Bridge. When a veteran *Details* columnist was released from his contract and took a farewell shot at Mark in the press, advising him as he departed to "always make sure you flush the toilet," I was told to drop all my other projects and arrange to order a porcelain throne and have it wrapped in a bow and delivered to the ex-contributor's home. I had nearly completed the task when, days later, Mark calmed down and withdrew the instruction.

At the start of the summer, Mark left for a weeklong pilgrimage to the men's fashion shows in Milan, a semiannual rite of passage for the magazine industry that he had never experienced during his tenure at *Maxim*, and he wasn't looking forward to the trip. Neither was I: Mark's itinerary had been planned and booked long before I was hired, and in his absence, there was nothing for me to do around the office. One evening, answering Mark's phone as I always did, I happened to catch him by accident as he was calling in, and there was a nervous, giddy energy to the conversation as we played catch-up.

"What are you doing?" he asked.

"What are *you* doing?" I demanded in return.

"I was just checking my voice mail," he said. A cheerful glimmer of recognition infiltrated his voice. "You were trying to change my message, weren't you?"

"No, I wasn't," I assured him, "but I'd still like to take care of that."

"It really means a lot to you, doesn't it? We'll do it as soon as I'm back in New York, I promise."

"How's Milan treating you, monsignor?" I asked.

"Aaggghh, it's horrible," he grumbled from his $400-a-night hotel room. "I'm like a trained monkey over here. They let me out for a few hours every day to do my dance for everyone, and then it's back to my cage."

"How bad can that be?" I wondered. "You're eating for free! You're partying for free! You're in Italy, man—live it up a little."

But if Mark's mind worked anything like my old man's, I knew there was no verse in all the librettos of Verdi that could sufficiently summarize his sense of longing—not for his loved ones, not for his wife and his children, but for his livelihood—that the terror of entrusting his business to others, even for a few days, could make the most spacious suite feel as claustrophobic as a crypt. "If you want to know the truth," he said, "I'd rather be sitting at home, watching TV and eating a hamburger. They've got me double- and sometimes triple-booked for dinners with all these fashion big shots. Most of the time I don't even know who these people are—I just know that we need their advertising."

"So at least you're kissing some quality ass?"

"Oh, I'm puckering up good. How's the office these days?"

"Eh, you know how it is." I shrugged. "Kinda slow, actually."

Mark could hear the boredom from four thousand miles away. "What, the rough-and-tumble world of magazines isn't exciting enough for you?" he teased.

"Well, the place pretty much runs itself, y'know? It's awfully quiet around here without you." There was no other way to explain it. "I think . . . I think I *miss* you."

For a moment Mark seemed genuinely touched by the sentiment. "Aww, isn't that sweet? I'll bring you back something nice."

The cost of a bullshit phone call from Milan to New York finally struck us both as too excessive, even if someone else was picking up the tab, and with the sun setting over the Hudson River, I concluded the call the only way that seemed appropriate.

"Good night, Dad," I kidded him.

"Good night, son," Mark joked back. "You get all your homework done, and then it's off to bed with you. Kiss your mother for me. No tongue this time, okay?"

Mark was back in the office the following week. I waited a few futile days for my gift, until my disappointment and the memory of the original promise were both forgotten.

3

INTO THE FOLD

THE FUTURE TENANTS OF THE SKYSCRAPER LOCATED AT 4 Times Square had taken to calling it the Death Star long before it was fully operational. The unflattering appellation probably dated back to an incident during the building's construction, when one of the massive cranes used in erecting the thirty-five-story colossus toppled over and killed an elderly resident in a hotel across the street. As one of the original staffs relocated to the fortress that would soon house the complete collection of Condé Nast publications— including, yes, *The New Yorker*—the *Details* crew was treated to an early taste of the structure's persistent morbidity. From the uncaring metallic exterior to the blindingly white sterile lobbies that greeted visitors on each floor; from the smell of melted plastic that followed us down the colorless corridors to the hollow silence associated with the utter and unmistakable absence of human souls anywhere else in the building, the first days of our occupancy felt as if we had wandered into a no-longer-hot zone still recovering from a devastating epidemic, and we were somehow invulnerable to the toxic effects around us, having amputated most of the gangrenous limbs from earlier embodiments of *Details* in the previous months. The last to go was Bill Shapiro's assistant, a holdover from an earlier administration, who was fired right after he finished packing up Bill's belongings in preparation for the move.

"Are we going to have to dress differently when we're in the new building?" I asked Mark just before the transition, an innocuous remark that became an immediate addition to his growing repertoire of stories about his beloved assistant. He never surrendered his muscle shirts and jeans for cardigans and capri pants, but the work environment was having a noticeable effect on his demeanor. His latest office was so spacious and criminally indulgent, it had its own private bathroom, where no one would have to suffer the embarrassment of crossing streams with the boss at a urinal trough—no one would ever have to know that the man in charge excreted human waste. He was now sharing an address, not to mention a floor plan, with the company's pantheon of celebrity editors, the ones who made headlines simply for attending yoga classes or getting doused with paint by animal-rights activists, whose magazines were barely concealed amplifications of their own unimpeachable psyches. Each morning Mark was greeted with another newspaper profile of himself, inevitably titled "The Devil Is in the *Details*," another gossip item about him wantonly lighting up cigarettes in an allegedly smoke-free environment.

This was a long way from Allentown, Pennsylvania, where Mark was educated, where he had most recently lived, and where he probably assumed he'd be buried. In his media appearances, he gleefully characterized his former homestead as a backwater sticks strewn with broken-down cars balanced on cinder blocks and populated by porch-sitting, chaw-chewing yokels—a group from which he didn't exclude himself. He didn't merit much attention during the ten years he toiled anonymously at nearby Rodale Press, a publisher of exercise-related offerings, where he edited short-lived titles with names like *Muscle* and *Exec*; but his fortunes changed dramatically when Rodale created *Men's Health*, a frenzied, fitness-conscious magazine that was singularly responsible for reintroducing the macho male market to the concept of shame. With covers that shunned portraits of famous people in favor of black-and-white pictures of bare-chested studs with toned abs, surrounded by sell lines that offered you 25 SECRET SEX TIPS! and demanded you BURN

OFF THAT BELLY!, *Men's Health* soon doubled the sales of its closest competitor; it was shaping up to be the success story of the 1990s until *Maxim* head-butted it from its perch. Still, it was his work at *Men's Health* that had catapulted Mark to *Cosmopolitan* and eventually into the public eye. Now the same endearingly self-hating hayseed, who had openly referred to himself as a "troll" in the pages of his last publication, merited a corner office with a panoramic view of Broadway, costly Le Corbusier furniture, and its own Princeton graduate to answer the telephones. The troll had finally arrived.

The physical components of my new cubicle seemed designed to reinforce the menial aspects of my job: a lengthy desk with an imposing marble countertop on which to pile papers; a small partition over which I could peer snidely at anyone who approached; a location directly in front of Mark's office, from which I could throw myself upon any trespasser who tried to bolt into his inner sanctum. But our increased proximity did not bring us any closer, and I was aggravated to find that he still spent the entirety of his day locked behind his gray steel door. While he worked so nearby and yet in such secrecy—sometimes alone, but more often with his loyal confidants Catherine and Bill—I found myself overwhelmed with jealousy, certain that they were cooking up magnificent plans for the magazine that I had every right to be part of. Then one day I thought I heard them through the door, huddled together, shouting racial slurs at one another, and I could hardly hold back my rage. I grabbed my keys to Mark's office and forced my way inside, but I was too late to stop them.

"Knickers!" Catherine shouted in a pompous English accent.

"*Knickers!*" Bill cried in turn, his fake inflection slightly more exaggerated.

"*KNICK-AAAAHHHHS!*" Mark screamed in the loudest and most grotesque voice yet, resulting in the largest peal of laughter so far.

What I had barged in on was a running joke, a one-word impersonation of their former employer and continued nemesis, Felix Dennis, the British publishing baron who had brought *Maxim* to

America. Mark was surely a surrogate father to *Maxim*, but Felix, as founder and chairman of its eponymous parent company, Dennis Publishing, was the magazine's true patriarch: This mad dog of an Englishman, already a millionaire innumerable times over in his native land, had taken the gamble of importing *Maxim* into the States, and he wasn't humble about claiming his share of the payoff. Though Mark enjoyed a certain independence in determining the magazine's contents, Felix still held veto power over every vowel, consonant, and punctuation mark, demanding final approval of even the cover lines. As *Maxim*'s astronomical ascent became apparent to the industry, Felix was loath to single out Mark for his role in its success; when Mark ultimately departed for *Details*, he was thrown a heartfelt farewell party by the staff he was forsaking at *Maxim*—only to find that Felix wouldn't let him out of the remaining months on his contract. While Mark spent the time between jobs in limbo, unable to fully contribute to either title, an editor's letter in *Maxim* declared that control of the magazine had been ceded to a small rodent named Sammy the Hamster, complete with a photograph of the puffy-cheeked varmint. For once, Mark had been outpranked, and the gag had Felix's pudgy fingerprints all over it.

But Mark was determined to have the last cancerous, cigarette-smoke-saturated laugh. When he left *Maxim* he took almost all of its top editors along with him; the promises of substantially increased salaries, company cars, and clothing allowances were all enticing, but not as irresistible as being granted free rein to redesign *Details* in any way they saw fit. It was a power they wasted no time in exercising: The changes their predecessor had introduced over the previous year were abruptly jettisoned—everything from the health advice section to the horoscopes was dumped in the span of a single issue. Trademark writers had their contracts canceled, including *Details*'s female sex columnist, a woman whose body of work looked downright prudish next to the musings of the foul-mouthed maids who contributed far more explicit stories in *Maxim* each month. Besides, Mark reasoned, "Who wants to read dirty talk from some ugly broad you'd never fuck?"

As he settled into his new job, his imperial proclamations became more assured. His edict that no other editor but himself could write on a manuscript in red pen made little difference, since most copy came back awash with his jagged, childlike scrawl—everything from headlines to punch lines to whole paragraphs to entire articles would be rewritten on the dark side of his office door, and the bright bloody ink made it easier to make out the carnage he had wrought. But when one of his first issues of *Details*, whose cover featured the comedian Jon Stewart clutching a bloated frog, bombed at the newsstand, the effects were far more drastic: Mark decreed that no man would ever again grace the cover of the magazine. His fickle predilections held full sway at our weekly pitch meetings, where any story idea that seemed too exclusionary or sophisticated for our readership was rejected as being "too old *Details*," whereas any concept that struck him as being too prurient, too crude, or too stupid was refused for being "too *Maxim*." He was determined to show the world that it wasn't the brand name or the selection of famous personalities or some nebulous, of-the-moment sensibility that had made *Maxim* a hit—it was Mark Golin. To prove this point, it wouldn't be enough for him to make *Details* prosperous again; with the same stroke, he would have to destroy *Maxim*, the magazine he had helped to create.

To an unrepentant opportunist such as myself, the chaos was good for my career. When I first showed up at *Details*, I hoped I'd have a solitary byline by the end of my first year. Instead, I was being published on a regular basis, writing front-of-book blurbs and wacky charticles, faking my way through roundups of breakfast cereals from around the world and interviews with nubile starlets who'd bared their breasts in obvious Oscar bait, copying tropes and lifting jokes I'd seen in the two strikingly similar magazines Mark had edited. By engineering my ideas to appeal to his impulsive tastes, I could ensure that—in an organization where every idea was rigorously scrutinized, considered, reconsidered, and shelved for future consideration—my stories would go straight onto the page, unfiltered, with minimal debate. I would like to believe that as the lone member of the editorial staff who fit the magazine's demographic, my cultural pronouncements carried special weight, but no: My authority derived from the fact that I was the boss's assistant. And where did his authority derive from? The fact that he was the boss. All this authority, however, did not come without risk—the risk of being called upon to use it. If this process continued for much longer, it was just a matter of time before everyone realized I had no idea what I was doing and no right to be doing it.

Then I was offered another job.

ANY FRIENDSHIP FORGED on the Princeton campus is in and of itself a miracle, but the connection between myself and Parker was even more improbable. He was my polar opposite in many respects, tall and imposing, descended from strapping, Scandinavian stock, Paul Bunyan without the pickax. While I spent my Saturday nights at home scanning the pictures in the freshman facebook, Parker was actually out there, meeting—and sometimes fucking—the people depicted in those photographs. After we bonded over our shared appreciation for an obscure punk rock band (which turned to revulsion when we learned its lead singer was gay), Parker became the only consistent element in my otherwise erratic life; he was my classmate, my shift supervisor when I washed dishes at the dining hall, my editor at the university's struggling humor magazine, and it was impossible not to befriend him. I admired him for his confidence, for having rejected the school's social elite long before it surely would have accepted him. Though he was a year ahead of me in his studies, I was three days older than him, and I sometimes wondered if, had it not been for the difference of those few days and a few strands of DNA, I could have ended up with his life.

To even his pals, Parker was known as a personable, pathologi-

cal procrastinator and a master fabulist who would claim Civil War
heroes and Revolutionary War scoundrels as his ancestors; he alternately hailed from Atlanta, Boston, Canada, or Norway whenever
it suited his storytelling needs. Most of his anecdotes began, "You
see that girl over there?," and when his tales of getting it on with a
girlfriend in the cafeteria's industrial-size soup cauldron, or turning
on the two coeds from Bryn Mawr—and then turning them on to
each other—seemed hyperbolic beyond belief, I found it easier
to focus on the trifling details that changed with each telling than
to contemplate the possibility that the legends might be grounded
in truth. I shouldn't have been surprised he ended up working at
Maxim.

We hadn't spoken much since Parker graduated, when he told
me he was going to work for some start-up men's magazine, and
though I never made good on my promise to subscribe to it, I'd occasionally thumb through copies I found at bookstores or in gas stations, to see if he was still listed on the masthead. With each issue I
kept expecting to find that his name had dropped off, but instead it
rose steadily through the ranks, from editorial assistant to associate
editor, a title that meant he didn't have to answer anyone's phones
but his own. He had worked with Mark Golin for nearly two years,
and after my interview with the former *Maxim* chief, I had contemplated asking Parker to put in a good word for me; but I spent
so many hours agonizing over the decision that by the time I was offered the job, it had become a moot point. It was Parker who at last
reached out to me when our worlds unexpectedly collided again,
inviting me to catch up with him at a popular barbecue restaurant
where *New York Times* editors and *New York Times* readers could
cross paths without ever having to speak to one another.

Success hadn't spoiled him—he was a little fuller around the
face and the waist, but he was still dressed in shorts and a ratty concert T-shirt from a show we had seen in my sophomore year, as if he
had just come bounding back from a professor's office after dropping off a term paper. As we sat down to eat, I thought there was
something exactly right about this meeting. We were friends above

all, and that connection meant more than any petty rivalry that existed between our publications.

"How does it feel to have sold out?" Parker crowed in his booming, gregarious voice.

So that's how it was going to be. "Hey, last time I checked, you and I were both in the same line of work," I fired back.

"Take it easy," Parker said. "I was only kidding you. I was going to ask you how the job was treating you so far, but I guess I got my answer."

"How are things at your place?" I said. "Is it like the Wild Wild West over there or what?"

"They just hired us a new editor, but it was getting crazy for a while there. They were pretty much letting us do whatever we wanted. If you suggested a story, they'd print it. In a way, it was kind of fun, you know?" I was incredulous: a magazine where everyone had a stake in the final product, where decisions were made without ever pausing to consider how they might reflect on the perceived coolness of the people behind them? It had to be another of Parker's tall tales.

I tried to change the subject. "I suppose congratulations are in order," I said. "You just got promoted again?"

"Thanks, man," he replied softly, so that only the tables adjacent to ours could hear him. "Actually, that's what I wanted to talk to you about. They're going to let me focus on more features, and they're looking for a new person to bring on as an assistant editor, to take over the section I used to edit." Parker paused for effect and stared me directly in the eye, with the intensity of an exasperated amateur magician who was sure he had my card. "I think that person should be you."

"Are you kidding?" I blurted out through a mouthful of collard greens. "How can you be sure I'll even get the job?"

"Trust me—so far, no one we've spoken to has your qualifications. All I'd have to do is recommend you. What do you think?"

"I don't know, Parker. They've been good to me at *Details*. It's hard to walk away from that. I'll have to think about it." But I didn't plan to waste so much as a single neuron on the idea.

"So how's Golin?" he asked with a knowing smile on his face.

"It's like working for the Tasmanian Devil," I replied. "I have to say, I'm stunned at how easily you guys forgave him for leaving you. If it happened to me, I'd be pissed."

"Well, it was kind of a dick maneuver, but we still miss him. Threw him one hell of a going-away bash, too. You know, I got so drunk that night, I accidentally pegged the editor in chief of GQ in the head with a stuffed hamster." Of course I knew—this wasn't the first time Parker had told me the story, and it certainly wouldn't be the last. "I think a bunch of us are going to get together to go drinking with Mark. You should come with us."

"I don't know," I said hesitantly. "I think it would be weird to see him like that. Besides, there's no way I'd be able to keep up with him."

"Yeah, for a little guy he sure can pack it in. That man's appetites are insatiable."

I put down my silverware. Generally there are few words possessed of enough concentrated power to frighten me—*biopsy* is one exception to this rule; *colostomy* is another—but the terminal end of Parker's observation stopped me cold. It made me think not only of Mark, but of another, considerably larger man, one with more hair and less restraint, who at this hour of the evening was almost certainly fast asleep on his couch, whose life alternated from periods of superhuman productivity to epochs of total inertia and existed nowhere in between. His essence kept forcing its way into everything and everyone I came into contact with. Was there no refuge sufficiently distant, no barrier dense enough to keep his signature scent, that blending of fur and narcotics and flannel and fatigue, from reaching my nose? The inevitability of it all was enough to make you sick. Or me.

I could sense an unfamiliar feeling emanating from my stomach. To this point in my life, I had experienced enough anxiety to render it powerless over me—to let the wave wash past me without carrying me out to sea. What I was now experiencing was not a wave. This was a tremor, one whose fault line began in my belly, extended to my esophagus, and terminated in my throat; once started, its destructive force could not be stopped. I vomited my entire meal onto the table, spraying my plate with a putrid array of chewed-up bits of pink pork and green vegetables that came up exactly as they had gone down.

"Parker," I said, a dollop of my undigested dinner still dangling from my chin, "please don't tell anyone about this."

BY THE TIME I arrived at work the next morning, I expected that Parker would have related the previous night's debacle to Mark, and that Mark, in turn, would have a fresh plate of ribs and a can of Lysol waiting at my desk. Fortunately the boss was away in Los Angeles, power lunching with publicists, trying to secure more of their famous clients for the cover of the magazine. A few months into his tenure this was proving to be his biggest stumbling block: The cover of *Details*'s first redesigned issue, soon to be appearing on newsstands, would feature a female celebrity who had been loaned to us by *Vanity Fair*, whose editors had booked her for that same month. Our prospective cover star for the very next issue had refused to be photographed in anything more revealing than a sweater, and Mark had deemed the shoot unusable; instead, the marquee position went to an untried actress who was about to play the love interest in Arnold Schwarzenegger's latest cinematic comeback vehicle. From there, the celebrity well seemed to run dry. The drought was made more complicated by Mark's refusal to consider any personality for the cover whom he could not have first, before anyone else had discovered her—to him, any woman who had already been spotlighted by another publication was impure, unclean. But perhaps it was not the women who needed to be concerned about their taints.

I kept busy by organizing Mark's mail, setting out the magazine's most recent circulation reports for him to read, teeming with figures printed in bright red and preceded by minus signs, and seeking out participants for yet another in a series of focus groups we had been holding with increasing frequency. It was a tremendous relief when Mark came back to New York. "How did it go?" I asked him.

"Awesome!" he bragged. "I told them that from here on out, when a woman appears on the cover of *Maxim*, it's basically the equivalent of her getting fucked by the entire football team! I think they're going to start coming around to our way of thinking."

Although lately we had to ask ourselves: What was Mark thinking? When he wasn't sending out staffwide e-mails enthusing about the newest hit novelty single of the latest dispensable pop music act (the earliest radio broadcasts of which were just now reverberating off the rings of Saturn), he was barging in late to his own editorial meetings, to unveil his latest brainstorm. "I've got it!" he had once announced. "I know what the next issue of *Details* is going to be! *Robots!* We're going to do an all-robot issue! The entire magazine has been taken over by robots, and we humans will acknowledge them as our superior masters!" He paused for adulation. There was some clapping, but mostly quiet confusion; maybe, we thought, he was just worked up about the *Details* launch party that was only days away.

It is no simple matter to explain the industry tradition of the launch party, but I shall do my best: It is a custom by which a magazine spends large sums of money in hopes of obtaining free publicity; where celebrities are invited to tacitly endorse a periodical they would never appear in, let alone read; where a publication attempts to introduce readers to the lifestyle it purveys by excluding them from it. The coordination of these various elements is naturally too complicated for the people who put out the magazine and is therefore entrusted to phalanxes of bottle-blond professional *yentas* who, if they cannot produce actual famous people, at least know how to fill a room with enough out-of-work models and actors to make it look attractive.

For our coming-out party, we had spent our money on a posh studio space in Chelsea, on the demarcation line between the city's straight and gay cultures, and a private performance by the rock musician Moby. What we got in return was the presence of boxing announcers and balding former teen heartthrobs, and—I swear on Conrad Bain's eternal soul—the runty *Diff'rent Strokes* star Gary Coleman. Madonna and Gwyneth Paltrow made a cameo appearance to watch Moby's set, but in less than ten minutes the pair were so enveloped by gawkers that they were forced to flee through the studio's rear exit. Our cover girl declined to appear in person, having been displeased by a reference in her story to her father's criminal past, but she was nevertheless represented throughout the room by oversize blowups of her likeness, airbrushed beyond recognition and flanked by such inelegant sell lines as WELL HUNG (advertising a feature about wall decorations) and THE SECRET INGREDIENT MEN ARE STICKING DOWN THEIR PANTS (it turned out to be Gold Bond Powder). For everything that had been subtracted from this particular incarnation of the magazine, there had been one notable addition: Just beneath the *Details* title appeared the words FOR MEN.

And there, mingling up a storm, was Mark, looking a total wreck, his formal wear a maze of wrinkles held together by sheer willpower and his brow gushing geysers of sweat from every gland. His eyes were redder than I'd ever seen on even his most exhausted day at the office, and his chest was heaving, but his mouth folded into a thin smile when he saw me. He grabbed me by the collar and pinned me against a column. "You," he said hoarsely, "you've really got something, you know that? You've got the talent, the ability . . ." The sentiment was there, but the words were failing him. He kept gasping for air, and his breath was falling directly on my face. "You're . . . you're going somewhere, don't forget that. You could take this thing . . . take it anywhere you want it to go. You're somebody to watch, I can tell that. You know that, don't you?" Before I could answer, he let me go and disappeared into the human wallpaper.

I had just been held hostage by a man six inches shorter than me. He had paid me the kindest compliment I had ever received in my career or would ever likely receive again, and I couldn't remember the last time I felt more intimidated. No, actually, I could, and that's what made it so frightening.

It was around this time that I decided to quit.

PARKER'S COURTSHIP OF me had continued unabated: He had taken me to dinner, taken me out for drinks, taken me to see *Fight Club*, where we had watched Brad Pitt and Edward Norton strip to their waists and beat each other senseless. Now it was time for me to put out. It took a phone call to Parker, followed by a cover letter and résumé, followed by a battery of surreptitious interviews with the magazine's editors, followed by a handsomely bound presentation dossier produced at Kinko's at a cost of $150 (and charged to my Condé Nast corporate card), before the opening at *Maxim* was offered to me. That was the easy part. Now I had to tell Mark that I was leaving him—leaving him for the magazine he had left in the most public and irreparable manner possible.

Conventional wisdom dictates that employee terminations should be conducted on Fridays, so that the recipients of the bad tidings have the minimal amount of time to stew in their own indignation—and therefore the minimal amount of time to enact a retaliation—and a weekend in which to ponder what the fuck just happened. The day on which I had chosen to do the deed was the Friday before Thanksgiving, when Mark was more likely preparing to watch the Macy's parade with his wife and kids from his office vista than to be stabbed in the back by his assistant.

With one inconsequential resignation already under my belt, I assumed this next one would be equally uneventful, right up until the moment I had to enter Mark's private suite and deliver the news to him. Then I became an epileptic marionette, twisting and jittering in unnatural directions from every joint. This was a conversation I was totally unprepared for, yet it was a conversation I had been preparing for my whole life. But there was no way Mark could possibly be ready for what I was about to tell him.

"I wanted you to hear this directly from me, before word got back to you," I said with as much composure as I could feign. "I've been offered a job as an assistant editor at *Maxim*." Even to my ears I sounded nothing like a man who'd just quit his job.

Mark took a drag from what was likely his ninth or tenth cigarette of the morning. "You're not going to blackmail me into giving you a promotion," he said. "You've been working for me for, what, six months now? Come back to me when it's been a full year and then we'll talk."

That was the end of that conversation.

I returned to my seat, did my day's work, went home for the weekend, and collected my thoughts. I had promised my new employers that I would start with them in two weeks. If I didn't resign the following Monday, I wouldn't be giving Mark sufficient notice, and that would be awkward. I resolved to do better on my next attempt. And when the weekend was over I returned to his office, about ten or twelve cigarettes into the morning, to deliver a modified version of my earlier statement.

"I've been offered a job as an assistant editor at *Maxim*," I repeated, this time adding, "And I've decided to accept it."

Mark remained unfazed. His eyes narrowed wistfully, and he began to reminisce. "See, this is the problem with the magazine industry," he said, exhaling a plume of smoke that lingered in the air between us. "Do you know that when I started out, the only job I could get was answering reader mail at Rodale? Can you imagine? Every single letter they received had to receive a response! And I had to write them! I spent a year in that job before I even got to work on a magazine, and it took years more before they let me *run* one. Now everybody wants everything right away. Everything is going to come to you, in time. But for now, you've got to be patient."

"I don't think you understand, Mark," I said. "Things don't work like that anymore. Besides, I've already proven myself to you repeatedly."

"You're an assistant!" he shouted. *"That's what you're supposed to do!"*

"The people at *Maxim* seem to think I'm worth more than that."

He pondered the comment for a moment. "So what would it take for you to stay? I don't want to lose you." I could swear I heard something I had never heard in Mark's voice before: remorse.

I could have said anything here. I could have calmly and considerately worked out a compromise solution with Mark that would have been acceptable to both of us and kept me at *Details*. I could have countered with some impossibly grandiose terms he couldn't meet, just to see what he'd say. I could have told him that he reminded me too much of my father and that no amount of compensation was enough to make me endure him a second time. I could have tried to extort him for a raise or pleaded with him to seek professional help. But I'd never before had the upper hand in any negotiation, however fleetingly, and I choked. "You already said you couldn't be swayed," I said, "so what's the point? *Maxim* has made me a really good offer, and I'd be a fool to walk away from it."

Mark was squinting at me through both eyes instead of just one as he labored to make sure that each word of his response revealed no emotion whatsoever. "Well then, it sounds like your mind is made up. But understand something: You've crossed sides. You've defected to the enemy. And I'd appreciate it if you cleared out your desk and left by the end of the day."

And that is how a relationship that had taken months to build, and one I thought would last me a lifetime, was undone in minutes. And part of me was actually shocked by the severity of Mark's response. Hadn't I followed his example perfectly? Hadn't I jumped ship as soon as a better opportunity presented itself, without any regard to what my colleagues might think? Didn't anyone wish me well in my new endeavor? Where was my goddamn going-away party?

Instead, as word of my departure made its way around the floor and I conspicuously packed up the few possessions I could truly call my own, I was made to revisit the three people who had first welcomed me into the *Details* fold. First, Bill called me into his office to offer me his ominous portents of the future. "They have no idea what they're doing over there," he said of the *Maxim* staff that still regarded him as a friend and mentor. He opened up a copy of the magazine and pointed to a byline printed within it. "I hired *him* right out of grad school a year ago. Now he's a senior editor. Do you really think he's ready to be a senior editor? These are the guys you're going to be learning from. It's a magazine run by people who have absolutely no experience running a magazine."

"Don't you find that exciting?" I asked him.

"I find that dangerous. I hope you're ready to work lots of long hours, because all I can say is you're making a tremendous mistake."

When I saw Catherine next, she had a far more succinct assessment of my decision: "Dude, you're *such* an asshole." I clumsily tried to explain the situation in a light that portrayed me as the victim, but there wasn't any.

The last stop on my involuntary farewell tour before that long walk out the door was a return visit with Mark. I thought it might be my opportunity to say a proper good-bye, but instead he used it to take one last parting shot. "I always take care of the people who have stayed loyal to me," he said, "and by the same token, I don't look kindly on the people who desert me. As far as I'm concerned, you can lose my phone number. And I promise you, you'll never work for this company again." I was twenty-three years old.

I cracked a valedictory joke. "I hope that if I ever find myself caught in your headlights, you'll at least have the courtesy to tap the brakes."

"I'll honk the horn," Mark joked back. He had enough dignity to shake my hand and flash that smile one more time.

Exiting the Condé Nast building alone, mercifully without a security escort, I contented myself with thoughts of Mark's teeth, the bad ones scattered along his jawline like busted posts on a weather-beaten picket fence, the canines filed down to daggers and the incisors like shattered windowpanes. They were a permanent record of all his defects, a display of his mortality uncovered whenever he so much as opened his mouth. Perhaps there was a time when they had shone like some marble temple built in honor of an ancient pagan god, but after two decades in this industry, wearing them down an imperceptible amount each time he had clenched them in anger, rattled them against one another in a fiendish cackle, or gritted them in a moment of self-doubt, all that remained of them was rubble.

Only later did it occur to me that there might exist an altogether different interpretation of these events: that this was a man who had done as best as he could to nurture me, in an environment where such encouragement was rare and wholly unrequired; that my rejection of this support might be upsetting to the man who offered it, even traumatic; that the pride I felt for being competed over, and the wicked pleasure of having abandoned someone before he had a chance to abandon me, might prove to be as transitory as a puff of cigarette smoke.

There would be plenty of time to consider this in the days ahead, plenty of free hours to sit around at home and play video games, to rehearse my account of these events for the Thanksgiving dinner table, to jerk off in frustration, to enjoy those few seconds of release that preceded the minutes spent contemplating the trail of goo left on my chest. But when I wasn't hovering over the toilet bowl with dry heaves or wondering what my future colleagues might be like, I kept coming back to the same thought: How could I ever have heroes in my life if I couldn't stop thinking I was better than everybody else?

4

BITCHKOFF

WISH I WERE THE SORT OF PERSON WHOSE DREAMS
have subtext, that my nightly visions were lavishly surreal produc-
tions full of public nudity, falls from infinite heights, lustful trysts
with my blood relatives, trains hammering their way through tun-
nels, and conversations with dead presidents in which the late
James K. Polk is portrayed by Christopher Walken. But my subconscious is so simple and stratified that my dreams, when I can remember them at all, are only literal manifestations of the same
problems my waking mind is fixated on. In the days before I began
my job at *Maxim*, all I dreamed about was *Details*, and in every fantasy I happily found myself at my station in front of Mark's office,
until he appeared from behind his door and reminded me that I no
longer worked for him, at which point I'd wake up, afraid.

I was sitting in the reception area of my latest employer, waiting
for my first working day to begin and contemplating how the rippling effects of my treachery might still resonate later in my life,
when it hit me: The fluorescent light directly overhead collapsed,
leaving bunches of wires dangling millimeters away from my
skull and dumping a pile of unknown powder onto the lapel of
my freshly dry-cleaned sport coat. It had been a lovely vacation at
4 Times Square, but now I was going to learn what it meant to work
for a company whose headquarters hadn't been assembled from the

ground up, where the luxuries I once enjoyed—a custom-designed cafeteria, smoothly accelerating elevators, a steady supply of pencils and paper on demand, electrical fixtures that wouldn't capriciously try to kill me—could no longer be expected. The *Maxim* office was only three blocks away from the Condé Nast tower but miles and miles away in spirit: It occupied the fourteenth floor (technically the thirteenth story) of an unremarkable building in the city's old garment district, where the other tenants were mostly textile wholesalers. The walls were painted discordant shades of blue and gray, and the last time the floors had been varnished, the Du Mont network was still on the air. All that distinguished this place of business from those on neighboring floors were the framed *Maxim* cover blowups hanging in the lobby, the peek-a-boo proportions of the cover girls grown to even more gargantuan heights, and the sell lines screaming EXPERT SEX! and HOT LOVE! in three-inch type to frighten away any prudes who might wander onto the wrong floor. The uncomplicated decoration was a bold declaration of purpose: This is what we do here, and fuck you if you don't like it.

Presented with another opportunity to make myself over, I was determined to do it correctly this time. That meant dressing in a blazer, slacks, and loafers; applying cologne liberally to my wrists, neck, earlobes, armpits, chin, forehead, and anywhere else I assumed it was supposed to be affixed; and getting to work so compulsively early that I preceded even the receptionist. After several minutes of waiting, the editor's assistant, a raven-haired rocker chick in a white cotton tank top and suede boots that seemed to come up to her calves, appeared to escort me inside. "Come on, let me take you back to your cage." She smiled before pausing to wrinkle her nose. "Hey, do you smell something?"

Even in moments of emptiness a workplace tends to reveal its true nature, but in its present vacant state the editorial bullpen of *Maxim* looked less like a factory of male fantasy than simply a factory. It did not resemble a fraternity house so much as it did that other close-quartered crucible of masculinity, a barracks. The magazine was not the first business to have inhabited this space, nor was it the fifth or even the fifteenth — there were no signs that any roots had been put down, no tangible assets that couldn't be packed up and moved in a day, except maybe the accumulation of dust. Nor were there any palpable manifestations of its spring break sensibility, no inflatable clowns set up for punching, no sex toys lying in plain view, no soiled lingerie dangling from drawers, just row after row of tiny, tidy desks separated by partitions too low to have disguised a beer gut. No photographs of family members or significant others (aside from a *Dukes of Hazzard* poster) decorated anyone's personal space, and no clock hung on any wall. The bookshelves were lined with volumes on foreign travel, sports statistics, and giant pictures of insects. Truly, this was the workplace of men.

The only man to be seen at this hour was *Maxim*'s editor in chief and my new boss, Mike Soutar, staring intently into his computer screen. In this egalitarian setup, even the highest-ranking member of the organization was denied a corner office and instead worked at a three-walled enclosure no different from one assigned to the lowliest underling — he was on display at all times to his entire crew. The only outward sign of his authority was the suit and tie he wore today, and every day, and which he wore for the same reason I had come to work wearing the most imposing items in my wardrobe: He wanted to be taken seriously. Mike — never Michael — was just thirty-two years old, with big round eyes and dimpled cheeks and a bald spot you could see only if you tried really hard to find it, and even in clothes that may well have been his own, he looked every bit the boy who'd just raided his father's closet. He was barely older — and in some instances younger — than the men he had been placed in charge of, and though he appeared to be the kind of guy you could pal around with, I had to remind myself that the days of goofing off with bosses were over, that this man was simply my manager and nothing more. I approached Mike's desk and said a polite good morning.

He glanced up from his monitor. "Ow's 'er wee kin?" he asked. Mike wasn't from around here.

"I—I'm sorry?"

"How was your weekend?" he repeated. It may have sounded like an idle pleasantry, but to Mike it was a question of supreme importance. His native Scotland and, by extension, the United Kingdom had given birth to the world's most vibrant weekend culture, where every second you were away from your office or mine shaft or mill was spent at the corner pub, in the company of familiar faces, where lives depended on nothing more drastic than an afternoon's football match, a throw of the darts, and your bartender's ability to pour out pints of the room-temperature brew of your choice. As a man, you didn't need a magazine to tell you how to live, and all you were likely to find at your local newsstand were the British editions of American fashion titles like the sixty-six-year-old *Esquire* and its forty-two-year-old spin-off-turned-nemesis *GQ*, or periodicals that came in black vinyl bags heralding the number of open poses in that month's issue.

Mike Soutar's great innovation, achieved at the age of twenty-eight, was creating a magazine for men who weren't buying magazines at all—one that, instead of condemning them for failing to meet impossible materialistic standards, celebrated them for the modest lives they were leading. In 1994, Mike gave up his editor's chair at *Smash Hits*, a popular teenybopper music publication, to take over *FHM*, a struggling men's title whose content and monogram—an unattractive abbreviation for the even clumsier *For Him Magazine*—owed an obvious debt to its transatlantic ancestor, *GQ*. By dumping the highbrow material and reinventing the book as an embodiment of pub culture, full of sports heroes, sixties-era cinema stars, trivia quizzes, sex advice, poke-yer-ribs bar humor, and plenty of nearly-though-not-naked flesh, Mike was single-handedly able to turn *FHM* into Britain's biggest-selling men's magazine. Or so his press release would read.

Months before Mike assumed control of *FHM*, the philosophical revolution in England's men's magazines was well under way. When it launched in that same fateful year of 1994, little attention was paid to *Loaded*, an uncharacteristically cheeky entry in the category edited by a savvy young Londoner named James Brown, who also happened to be twenty-eight years old. He claimed the title had been suggested to him by a girlfriend in a postcoital embrace following a victory by his favorite football team—and that said pretty much all you need to know about *Loaded*. Its name, and its slogan, "For Men Who Should Know Better," were triple or possibly quadruple entendres, puns on man's many hungers and winking references to the magazine's own playful stupidity. *Loaded* was surely where Mike had turned for his inspiration in redesigning *FHM*, and despite being direct competitors, both publications thrived. At its peak in the 1990s, *FHM* was selling as many as 800,000 copies a month in a country with a total male population of 28 million.

But Mike hadn't entirely overseen that hot streak—when Felix Dennis recruited him to take over for Mark Golin in 1999, he had since left *FHM* to become the program director for a dance music radio station in London. Mike's hiring seemed contrary to Dennis Publishing's anticelebrity sentiment, and it meant he was the first editor to come into the company with any real sense of duty: *Maxim*'s American circulation had recently broken the 1.5 million barrier and was sure as hell expected to get better. Mike proved himself a good enough salesman to convince his wife and two wee bairns to relocate to New York so he could take the job. And he had sold me, too.

When we had been negotiating the terms of my employment and I was frequently unsure of myself, Mike always resorted to the same stock catchphrase: "What do I have to do to put you in this car today?" To him, the choice of one job opportunity versus another was no more consequential than deciding between cloth or leather interior.

What I hoped to hear from Mike today was how happy he was to have me on his team, how much he appreciated the sacrifices I had made, and how much he thought I could add to the magazine's mix. Only when he said it, it sounded like "There's where you'll be working." And then he went back to peering into his monitor.

Though no one at *Maxim* was allowed his own office, I had the next closest thing—a closet at a far corner of the floor with a desk and a computer. I checked to make sure the door could be locked only from the inside, then spent the rest of my morning sending e-mails to old coworkers and waiting for Parker, my sponsor and my savior, to arrive. "Hey, Parker," I eventually heard Mike's assistant call out. "Your frosty-haired friend is here." She was talking about me.

There is an awful secret about myself I have been waiting for this moment to reveal: My hair was once blond. Except for a brief period during my infancy when it was cute and curly and jet black, my hair has been (and remains) straight and brown. The only other era when it deviated from this genetic, Semitic certainty began in the summer before my final year of college, when I gave myself bleached-blond highlights. It was on a trip to London, during which I also gave up my contact lenses for glasses, got my left ear pierced, and had a caricature of Sid Vicious tattooed on my right bicep. I ended up liking my new platinum look so much that I had the blond streaks professionally retouched every few months; by the time I reached *Maxim*, I had been committed to this routine for about two years. To my superiors at *Details*, the artificial coloring may have made me appear hip, edgy, alternative. But in the eyes of the *Maxim* staff, who knew? Maybe I was a homo.

My new colleagues couldn't have been too intimidated by my presence, because they had already coined a nickname for me. "Bitchkoff!" Parker said as he appeared in the doorway of my closet. "You ready to get to work?" As he began showing me around the office, acquainting me with another set of names I nervously forgot, I thought these people might be eager to meet me, to congratulate me on my move, or to hear about how their old allies were faring. But as the editors clocked in, they hardly said hello to one another—an infinitesimal nod of the head or a grunted "Hey" was all they were likely to yield before making a beeline to their cubicles. Instead of being welcomed with open arms, I was viewed with suspicion—perhaps I was a double agent, sent to steal *Maxim*'s ideas for my shrewd masters at *Details*. To them I was "Blondie," "What's with the hair?," "Bitchkoff," or, most frequently, "Parker's assistant."

And really, I was Parker's bitch. My sole assignment for the foreseeable future was to do whatever Parker told me to do. He, in turn, was responsible for editing the magazine's front section, called "Circus Maximus," which was regarded even by the people who worked there as *Maxim*'s junk drawer. Each month "Circus Maximus" was meant to provide our audience with an introduction to the magazine's punchy, episodic format; it consisted of miniature articles about weird and unusual artifacts pilfered from other publications or the Internet—prosthetic testicles for neutered dogs, sex-fetish playing cards depicting women clad in horses' saddles and bridles, a German-made soda brewed from hemp leaves. In case the subject of, say, an insurance company that specialized in policies against alien abduction was not inherently funny enough, it was up to Parker and me to rewrite these items as they came in from our freelance writers to make them funnier. It was modest work, but I congratulated myself whenever I came up with a clever caption for a picture of a human skull encased within a bowling ball ("Get your mind out of the gutter") or a gag that connected Burger King with Stephen King (they both give you the shakes). I hoped the jokes might provoke the laughter of a few readers before they flipped ahead to the content intended for other stimulative purposes and wondered how profuse an apology it would take to get me back in Mark Golin's good graces.

I hoped I would get better acquainted with my office mates at the two company Christmas parties scheduled for the same week in December. The first of these was, like the *Details* launch party, an event intended to generate media attention for *Maxim*, and it followed the same press-friendly blueprint, with its own opulent studio space and its own exclusive guest list. Stripped of even the most inoffensive religious symbolism, the function seemed little more than a celebration of cold weather: The room was lavishly decorated to evoke an arctic paradise, with fully stocked bars carved out of blocks of ice, private igloos for guests to sneak in and out of, and go-go dancers in snow white bikinis and fur boots dancing in crystalline cages. The contingent of editors I had tagged along with was overwhelmed by the excess of it all; in a moment of lightheadedness induced by the omnipresent artificial fog, everyone had to agree it was the most extravagant affair the magazine had ever thrown or, at any rate, the most extravagant affair they had been permitted to attend.

I still could not distinguish my colleagues by name, nor by the sound of their voices, but as our group gathered around a bar made of ice to drink a round of vodka shots from glasses made of ice, I discovered something: In conversation, these men spoke like no other men I had ever met before. They talked openly of how much they disliked their jobs and despised their boss, and instead of excluding competing speakers from their debate, this peculiar form of one-upmanship encouraged more people to participate—each depressing disclosure elicited another more dejected than the one before it. While I wished I'd known they felt this way before I came to work with them, I was content to sit and listen to the cacophonous shooting gallery of complaints and grievances until the individual, unfamiliar voices melded into one magnificent chorus of discontent.

"Hey, who's that beast that Soutar brought in with him?"

"That's his *wife*—haven't you ever met her before?"

"My God, she's a more convincing man than he is!"

"I guess we know who wears the kilt in *that* family."

"Did you happen to catch the look on his face when he was giving out the year-end bonuses?"

"What look?"

"Oh man, it was priceless. He just looked so uncomfortable—like he'd sooner circumcise himself than say something complimentary about any of us."

"Have you noticed how restless he gets in any one-on-one situation?"

"I was too busy noticing how crappy our bonuses were this year."

"I'd still rather have a crappy bonus than that ridiculous gift they gave us last year."

"You mean those remaindered poetry books Felix sent to us?"

"Right—the ones that came with the note to his business manager that said it was cheaper to give us the books than to have them destroyed."

"I swear, if we didn't get a bonus this year, I was going straight to the gossip columnists."

"Like who?"

"We could tell 'Page Six.' We could tell *The Observer.*"

"And what would we say to them? That we just threw this awesome party and now we're deprived because there wasn't money left over for bonuses?"

"Who wants to read about a bunch of magazine people complaining about their jobs?"

"Especially when they don't even think of us as a real magazine."

"I think you guys are scaring the new kid. Look at him—he hasn't said a word yet."

"Hey, Bitchkoff, what did you get for your Christmas bonus? A giant-screen TV for your personal office?"

I was about to say that I hadn't been given anything at all, that as he was passing out the bonus checks, Mike had taken me aside to explain that I hadn't been working at *Maxim* long enough to qualify for one, but the discussion was interrupted by Mike's assistant. "I told him he's not allowed to touch me like that anymore," she said of some unseen assailant, tears welling up in her eyes. "He's doing it again." A general rumble of consternation made its way around the ice table; she was clearly referring to another member of the staff, and there was consensus that someone would get up and explain to this person that he'd keep his hands to himself if he knew what was good for him. I looked to see who might be missing from the scene. Then we ordered another round of vodka shots.

When he was conducting his search for *Maxim*'s new editor in chief, Felix Dennis found three candidates he liked so much that he hired them all. And at the end of the night, in a downstairs bathroom, I met the first of these two consolation-prize winners standing at a sink, next to a man who would later be identified in the papers as an Antonio Banderas impersonator. This was Lester W., and he, too, had come out of Rodale Press, the small-town Pennsylvania publisher that yielded Mark Golin, but he had come out *weird*—so weird, even Mark thought he was weird. Lester W. was a serpentine little man with scaly, jaundiced skin, an intense gaze, and an imperceptible pucker of a mouth from which the most vulgar and repugnant expressions escaped. His sartorial tastes favored dour turtlenecks with sinuous, tendril-like sleeves, and though he was nominally responsible for overseeing half the magazine's contents, he often spent his days seated at his desk, concocting complicated story proposals of questionable merit (his latest inspiration was a self-explanatory feature called "The Great *Maxim* Wife Swap"). Our interns tended to stay away from him, and I was shocked to find out Lester W. was not only married, but also the father of two young daughters—I thought surely such a man would be permitted to marry only on the condition that he not reproduce.

Through his reflection in a bathroom mirror, he had caught me spying on him. "What do you think of our little soiree so far?" he asked in a voice that was all nose and no throat.

"Gosh," I answered in my uncharmingly innocent manner. "I'm not sure I'm worthy to call myself a *Maxim* man yet. I can only aspire to party like you guys can!"

Lester W. turned around to face me, his eyes wobbling in his head like two stale olives floating in a pair of tepid martinis. "*This* is what you aspire to?" he said incredulously. Then he spat a huge gob of phlegm into the sink. That was Holiday Party Number One.

Holiday Party Number Two was the traditional year-end employee-only affair, and I thought it was indicative of Dennis

Publishing's attitude toward its labor that the event was held at an indoor amusement park, where the main attractions other than the open bar were Skee-Ball ramps, bumper pool tables, and a go-kart course. But no one else was bothered by the surfeit of chintz: Dennis was still an organization small enough that each employee could remember that he or she was the company's seventeenth or thirty-first or eighty-fourth American hire, and simply having the whole gang in one room, where the *Maxim* editors could mingle with the administrators from Human Resources and the circulation director could carouse with the girls in Accounts Payable, would have been occasion enough to celebrate, regardless of the location.

The most populist gesture of the evening was the presentation of the "Employee of the Year" awards, an annual contest in which the winners were determined solely by the votes of the staff and for which they were compensated with not only the comforting but unquantifiable esteem of their peers, but also the very substantial reward of a weeklong vacation at Felix Dennis's private residence on the Caribbean island of Mustique. Indeed, the honorees called up one at a time to accept the distinction at a makeshift stage were a true cross section of the corporate payrolls: an ad sales rep, a receptionist, even a mailroom assistant, and finally Parker, who choked back his emotions long enough to lean into the microphone and announce, "You guys are like a family to me." It may have sounded like a corny sentiment, but he meant every word of it: This was the only stable unit of human beings he had known in his whole adult life.

As the bar closed down for the night, the president of Dennis Publishing's American office, a sprightly Northern Irishman whose bright voice belied no sign of troubles (or the Troubles), got on the public-address system to make his closing remarks to the assembled staff. "Hello, all you beautiful people!" he began cheerfully. "And what a year it's been for *Maxim*! Only two years ago, no one had ever heard of us—you ask Lance Ford there in advertising, he'll tell you, he couldn't even get media buyers to return his phone calls—and now here we are, 1999, two million circulation, well on our way to becoming the biggest North American general-interest men's publication, you'd better believe our phone calls are getting returned!" There was a burst of applause mixed with hoots and hollers from the crowd. "As you all know, we had some very public departures this year," he continued, and the applause died down. "A few people—I'm not going to mention them by name—seemed to think Dennis wasn't good enough for them, and so they went to Condé Nast." Here, some listeners started to boo. "But this month, a certain Mr. Itzkoff decided that Condé Nast wasn't good enough for him! And so Mr. Itzkoff left his job over there to come work for us! And I think Mr. Itzkoff made the right decision." This remark was met with the most rapturous cheers of the entire speech.

I found it strange that I was the only *Maxim* employee singled out in the brief oration—stranger still that he kept referring to me as "Mr. Itzkoff," as if he couldn't remember my first name—but I was flattered that at least he got my last name right. I felt a meaty paw park itself on my shoulder with all the force of a passenger plane landing on a runway. "Boy, the way he tells it, you'd think *you* were running the entire magazine."

Jim Kaminsky was the other runner-up in Felix Dennis's hiring contest. By the spartan topology of the *Maxim* offices, Jim and Lester W. were confined to identical cookie-cutter cubicles flanking Mike Soutar's own on either side, about as far apart as the two men could possibly be, which was probably how they preferred it. Jim was, to use someone else's words, a real grizzer—a brawny bear of a man with eyes so deeply set that they revealed nothing about him, not even their own color. But the shade most closely associated with him was gray, the color of his bushy hair and his wild eyebrows, the color of the rumpled dress shirts and wrinkled pants he wore each day without fail, the color of his perpetually skeptical disposition. His career had taken him from the heights of *Men's Journal* to the depths of *Women's Sports & Fitness*, and the accumulated weariness in his face let you know he had spent many a late night wrestling with untamed copy until it sat down, behaved itself, and brought him his morning paper. His relentless, self-imposed work schedule had endured even after his wife delivered him their first child.

Jim's desk was an inextricable mess, a war zone whose boundaries were determined by piles of back issues of *Maxim* and *Playboy* and *Esquire* and the original set of cardboard boxes he had moved in with. But when Jim wasn't beating up on prose or the writers who composed it for him, that desk was surrounded with chairs, where fellow editors gathered to verbally spar with him over metaphysical dilemmas whose resolutions could never be objectively attained: whether the young Fernando Valenzuela had made a greater contribution to the Los Angeles Dodgers than the young Michael Jordan made to the Chicago Bulls; whether Norman Mailer had better seats for the Rumble in the Jungle than George Plimpton; whether Martin Scorsese's *Mean Streets* was a greater accomplishment than the Rolling Stones's *Sticky Fingers*; whether *Taxi* was a greater sitcom than John McCain was a senator; whether or not all organized religions were total frauds. But his favorite subject of all was magazines—the ones he read (all of them), the ones he hated (most of them), and what he'd change about them (almost everything) to make them better.

Unlike Lester W.'s unwelcome affection, Jim's attention was desirable, even fought over. I wasn't yet allowed into that circle of chairs, and the more it was denied to me, the more I wanted into it. But my invitation wasn't coming any time soon: Jim already disliked me because I was the only editor who had his own office, such as it was, and now I had inadvertently stolen his thunder in a screwed-up speech I didn't write or deliver. I calmly reminded myself that with patience and persistence, I would eventually put these early gaffes behind me and earn my coworkers' acceptance.

MY FIRST APPEARANCE in *Maxim* occurred on page twenty of the February 2000 issue. There, in the upper-left-hand corner of the letters column, is a photograph of me shaving with a Schick razor and a healthy layer of peanut butter on my cheek, to illustrate a suggestion sent in by a reader on how one should handle an unanticipated shortage of shaving cream (but not sandwich spreads, apparently). It is not a great likeness of me. The picture is cropped so that you can see only the lower-right quarter of my face—a nostril, an ear, and my lips glowing red against the golden brown condiment whose aromatic oils took three days to completely wash out of my skin. If you squint closely enough, you can even spot a few lonely wisps of facial hair peeking out around my jawline, looking in vain for companionship.

My inability to grow a beard—I mean, a really lush and convincing beard, the kind that can be seen both at close range and from a distance—has always been my most humiliating personal defect. Long ago I accepted that there was nothing I could do about being short; whether it's the result of genetics or all those formative years spent drinking soda with every meal or some combination of the two, there are no latent growth spurts waiting in my future. I realize this means that there are certain roller coasters I'll never be allowed to ride and certain women (anyone with a whiff of poise or maturity or taller than five feet nine) I'll never be able to date. I have made my peace with this. So it goes.

But somehow, I suspect that when I get carded for buying liquor, or cigarettes, or tickets to an R-rated movie, it's not my meager height that has thrown off another vigilant cash register attendant—it's the fact that they're seeing the same face I've had since I was thirteen years old. Don't get me wrong: The hair on my chest, on my back, and out my nose grows free and unabated, but above the neck it's a wasteland. Nothing I have tried, be it shaving more or shaving less, deep-tissue massages or applications of Rogaine, will coax those precious strands from their follicles any farther or any faster. Even now, my whiskers require only a light servicing every couple of days, and I prefer to shave at night—this gives me a much needed chance to grow some stubble by the following morning, because when my face is completely bare, shorn of all its character, it just looks bizarre.

I'm not the only person who feels this way. At least one reader was so perplexed by my hot buttered visage that it prompted her—yes, her—to write a letter to the magazine, questioning the effectiveness of my shaving tactics ("Where does he put the jelly?" she asked) and insisting that the photograph she had seen was surely that of a woman's mouth superimposed on a man's face. My stubble was genuine, even "manly," "but that mouth, those lips and teeth—the expression was just dripping female sexuality."

This assessment caught me by surprise. I'll be the first to admit there are qualities about me that are decidedly androgynous. My voice, for example, operates in a high register, and the condition is sadly exacerbated when it's heard from the other end of a telephone. But after a while, it becomes comfortably amusing when a telemarketer repeatedly calls me "ma'am," then has to apologize when I tell her my first name. I'm also aware that my eyelids have an unusual purple tint, like permanent eye shadow, and the dark, curly lashes flowing from them have grown thicker than *payess*. And sure, I've been addressed as "miss" in public, by a waiter or bartender who, upon closer inspection, immediately apologized and corrected himself. But the response of this reader—and not just any *Maxim* reader, but a *female* reader—was pure gestalt. Based on what little information was visible, she had concluded that she must be gazing at a woman's face, or perhaps parts of a woman grafted onto a man, and felt so strongly in her convictions that she was compelled to write in to the magazine about it. The fact that she found me attractive, whatever gender I was, brought me little consolation.

What surprised me even more was reading this message for the first time, published in the subsequent month's letters column, with the following postscript from the editors:

> That's our very own senior editor James Heidenry. After reading your letter, James exclaimed: "Hey, we're not going to print that, are we?"

None of this was true, of course. To the readership this was nothing more than one of the magazine's trademark defense mechanisms: Insult a *Maxim* man and all he can do by way of retaliation is insult himself some more. But my colleagues, who had seen to it that we did print the letter and the reply, knew exactly who was depicted in that freakish piece of photography. I couldn't tell if, by swapping my name out of the punch line for that of another editor (and one who, even by the most European standards, would never pass for a woman), they were trying to protect my ego—or just reminding me that they were as acutely aware of my shortcomings as I was.

Patience and persistence, sure, but for how much goddamn longer?

5

AT LAST, SOME FUCKING

L OOK, ANY FAIR-HAIRED BOY WITH A PROFESSIONALLY bonded smile on his face and a Carpenters song in his heart can be an optimist. Being a pessimist—now *that* requires faith in one's convictions, a negative capability that would make Keats stand on tiptoes, and, above all else, creativity. Optimism is a simple, single-minded philosophy; it concerns itself with only one state of affairs: events turning out exactly as you'd hoped. The thing happens. The discipline of pessimism, however, takes into account the infinite variety of the universe—it demands that you keep a careful record of all the ways in which things have gone wrong in the past, so that you can predict the circumstances by which things could potentially go wrong in the future. Then you can hardly be surprised when those events come to pass.

Anyone who has spent time living among the female inhabitants of New York should understand exactly what I'm talking about. A *Maxim* colleague—one who was engaged in a healthy, long-term relationship at the time—once explained it to me like this: "Any woman who has lived in this city for more than three years goes crazy." As a guiding principle it was a bit cursory, but it neatly accounted for the two years' worth of accumulated rejections that were causing me to question my own sanity. Since graduating to this pool of more assured and thoughtful prospective partners, so-called, I had only seen my romantic advances shot down with the flimsiest, most contrived excuses: *I want to keep my options open. I'll have to ask my father what he thinks. I didn't realize that when you took me to the movies and bought me dinner, we were on a date. I forgot to mention I have a secret boyfriend in Italy. I was attracted to you at first, but now I'm feeling moody. I think I might be gay. I think you might be gay.* How could a town so conflicted ever have become so overpopulated?

For leaving behind my (relatively) free-ejaculating college days, for turning my sights from the haze of liquor fumes and marijuana smoke that made them possible, I thought surely I would be rewarded with a steady supply of women comfortable in their bodies and honest in their expressions. Instead I found a city of single girls so shell-shocked that they could not bear to be appreciated, could not stand to think they were that good or special. They would sooner avoid making eye contact than look to see you looking back at them and would reach for their keys—in preparation to *stab you!*—if you stood too close to them at a bus stop or a rock concert. The very thought of asking out one such woman was an act of violation, tantamount to crying "blow job" in a crowded theater.

With their unconvincing explanations and their undisguised grimaces, these women accused me: By plying them with compliments and my devoted attention, in hopes of getting to know them, being alone with them, and yes, quite possibly, sticking my dick in them, I had misrepresented myself. But wasn't I the one taking the risk here? Was I not exposing myself to an equal, if not greater, danger? Behind those delicate, disapproving faces, who knew what twisted lattice of insecurities, of abusive ex-boyfriends and thwarted assaults and body image issues, awaited the next unlucky suitor who tried to untangle them? I have never made mental health a prerequisite for compatibility, but at this point I would have gladly settled for a Sylvia Plath wannabe with abandonment issues and an eating disorder.

I couldn't remember how new people were supposed to enter into my life. When it did occur, it was always an event of pure chance, uncontrollable and irreproducible, like an alien crash-landing on the outskirts of civilization, who slowly conforms to your customs and adapts to your culture without your realizing it, and it isn't until months have gone by that you think to yourself, *Who is this creature? How did you come to completely infiltrate my existence?*

There had once been a girl who voluntarily struck up a conversation with me, who turned to me in an elevator in the Condé Nast building and said, "They don't like it when you use their soda machine." Not that it bothered her much. I had known our bachelorhood at *Details* was over as soon as the women showed up — when half our floor was given over to a mob of scribbling females from a shelter magazine for readers less embarrassed by themselves than by their homes. Their arrival heralded the end of our late nights racing our thousand-dollar ergonomic chairs through the hallways, and a start to sharing copiers, conference rooms, and refrigerators with our new neighbors, the ones with the tortoiseshell glasses and the apartments full of cats. She was more amused than annoyed that she had been chosen to deliver this message to me, as a representative of the unruly *Details* staff. "You wouldn't believe the controversy that you guys have set off," she said, sighing. "They want to complain to Si Newhouse." With her mangy dark brown hair, her wide eyes, her thrift-store fashion sense, and her blissful aversion to makeup, she was evidently the black sheep of her magazine, like Little Orphan Annie delivered to the doorstep of the Golden Girls. We e-mailed each other to argue who had the more unstable editor in chief and shared with each other the modest milestones we had achieved in our careers. I showed her a star-shaped paperweight I had been given by the company's CEO; she showed me the potted plant they awarded her on the one-year anniversary of her hiring. I was older than her, and somehow taller, but she far outmatched me with her intensity and determination to pull herself up by her army-surplus bootstraps. She had moved to New York from the rural Midwest, had no special affection for the city, no connection to anyone within a thousand miles of here, and she belonged to no one. Hence, the Orphan.

And such a cool, liberated Orphan, too, who lived with male roommates and who used to hang out at a library where Tom Waits was once employed as a clerk. This made it impossible for her to resist the offer of tickets to an upcoming Tom Waits show (doubly impossible to pass up, given that the man goes on tour only once every decade), and my feelings for her were assured when I turned to see tears streaming down her cheeks during his second encore of "Innocent When You Dream."

As we left the performance to return home on different subways, I stepped into the gutter while the Orphan stood on the curb, so that our heads would be at about the same height. Then I leaned in and kissed her, a move she received by tentatively clasping her arms around me. But as I pulled away, the look on her face was one of puzzlement. "I don't really date people," she said. It hardly made a difference to me—it was the world's loss if no one else had taken note of her nuanced beauty until now, and if she lacked experience, she couldn't have picked a more patient and less judgmental companion than myself.

Sitting on the steps of the New York Public Library one week later, the Orphan explained it to me again. "I don't really date people," she repeated, this time in a weary tone that made me understand it was by choice, not by accident. "You think you have feelings for me, but you don't. That's just the city talking. It makes people lonely." It was the silliest, most succinct rebuke I had ever received, but it was also sincere; it was all the explanation I was going to get from her, and there was no hope of talking her out of this position. Then she said I could take some consolation in being her very dear friend, and I didn't believe that for a second.

TRY TO IMAGINE the hopeless routine of extending yourself as you are, in all your flawed, frantic, unretouched glory, to the hordes of apathetic and overly critical women, clinging the whole time to some hoary superstition that in your heart of hearts you know to be a lie, that says there is one and only one girl who can fully meet your needs, when really the first one to say yes will do just fine — only now, try to imagine having to subject yourself to this brutality every single month, having to come up with one answer in the affirmative each and every thirty days from now until the end of time, and you will have a small sense of what it is like to publish a men's magazine at the turn of the twenty-first century.

In my earliest months at *Maxim*, there were many, many, many, many, many problems that threatened to derail the publication on a daily basis, but none so daunting or endlessly frustrating as trying to find some goddamned girl to appear on our cover each month. It's not as if our standards were unattainably high. As best as I could determine, the criteria for choosing a cover subject were as follows: The subject must be female and must be willing to appear in a state of undress. She should be famous enough to sell magazines yet obscure enough to consent to a photo shoot that might depict her cupping her bare breasts in her own hands. She should seem innocent but corruptible — ineffable yet totally f-able. It goes without saying that she should be white. And if possible, she should be blond.

Yet the process of getting a woman into that space inevitably proved more byzantine and regimented than obtaining her home phone number: Our editor in chief would consult privately with his deputies, and occasionally with other trusted colleagues, to compose a wish list of women *Maxim* might want in a given month. The candidates were then conveyed to our West Coast editor, an employee in Los Angeles who was our liaison to the publicists and talent wranglers who represented the personalities we wanted so badly to see in their underwear; this editor would then report back on which women were realistically within our grasp. The list had been revised and rerevised numerous times since Mike Soutar took charge, and at a glance it provided an instantaneous measurement of the magazine's self-esteem: Where his predecessor had favored slightly tarnished stars who at least maintained the illusion that an average reader could score with them, Mike's list initially read like an index of the entertainment industry's A-list actresses and super-models, who are the lifeblood of any celebrity glossy. After those first few months of refusals, the roll was expanded to incorporate rising but unproven ingenues from adolescent sex comedies and teen soap operas, then expanded again to include only the most respectable cast members of *Baywatch* and women whose singular claim to fame was their pinup status attained through appearing on the cover of *Maxim*.

Not one of the cover selections I had witnessed so far had transpired without some element of controversy: There was the swim-suit model so titanically buxom that you hardly noticed she was only sixteen years old. She was followed by the former *Playboy* Playmate who ended up on our cover when no one more famous could be procured (our timely justification for the story was that she had dyed her famous blond locks black). There was the sickly-thin television star whose *Maxim* pictorial was quite possibly the first in which its subject had to be airbrushed to look fatter. Next in turn was the teen actress whom we had victoriously snatched away from *Details* after a furious bidding war; we had to photograph the poor girl twice, and let's just say she could have taken some dietary lessons from the previous month's subject.

This is what happened when things theoretically went right. In the dating scene, the worst thing a girl can do is turn you down; the magazine industry has no such code of chivalry. Publicists don't just say no on behalf of their clients, they say no with a vengeance—they tell your West Coast editor that there is no fuck-ing way on fucking earth that their client is going to appear in your sleazy, semen-stained skin rag, and if you ever fucking ask about that fucking client again, they'll see to it that you won't even be able to find work booking celebrity panelists for the fucking *Holly-wood Squares*, you useless hag. Or they have their assistant tell you they're on the other line or out to lunch or gone for the day every time you call, and then they return your calls only at six a.m.

or eleven p.m. or any hour you are guaranteed to be out of the office, and if you still haven't gotten the picture after a month of these grade school games, they simply stop calling back altogether. And then sometimes the worst thing a girl can do is say yes.

We were engaged in the fastidious pursuit of a young actress whose most memorable credit to date was her on-screen portrayal of a fictional nymphet who, had she existed in real life, would surely have made the ideal *Maxim* cover girl. (You can always count on a masturbator for a fancy prose style.) This actress also happened to be a rising star whose credibility exceeded her cup size, and when she consented to appear in our magazine, I let it slip to some of my superiors that I had a close friend who was well acquainted with her—which is to say, he had once met her at a film festival and diddled her. I thought I could only benefit from the association.

While work on the rest of the issue proceeded at a pace that made Zeno's paradox look grueling, I was spending another afternoon confined to my closet when Jim Kaminsky took the unusual step of entering my workspace and addressing me directly. I knew something must have been wrong.

"How are you enjoying your nice new office?" he asked.

"Oh, it's *great*," I replied. "It's so great, you can have it."

"No, no, you earned it—you keep it," Jim said as he closed the door behind him. "What I'm about to tell you cannot leave this room," he said, a request that was easy enough to respect since we could barely leave the cramped quarters ourselves. "Today was the day we were supposed to photograph you-know-who for the cover. The problem is, she never showed up for the shoot. From what we understand, she's locked herself in her hotel room and she won't come out. We've tried going through her publicist, but she's basically useless at this point."

"Where do I fit into this?" I asked.

"Well, you said you had a friend who knew her, right?"

"Yes?" In the biblical sense, but how did that help?

"We were hoping that you could get him to call her, maybe

coax her out of her room and get her to do this. I know it sounds ridiculous, but we're desperate. This could be your big moment to save the day."

This friend of mine was, of course, a Princeton graduate, who like myself had majored in Delusions of Grandeur with a minor in Entitlement. When I started at *Maxim*, he had asked me to petition the magazine's publishers to pay for his trip to the very same festival where he and our coquette had first become entwined; I had laughed off his request. Now I expected him to return the favor.

"I don't think I'm going to be any help here," he confessed. "I still have her cell number around here somewhere, but she and I haven't spoken in weeks. I could give her a call, but I wouldn't get your hopes up." I doubt if he even did that much.

I can only assume our little bobby-soxer spent the day wrapped up in a bathrobe, engrossed in pay-per-view movies, because she never did emerge from that hotel room, and the photo session was scrapped. Technically, the magazine had legal recourse against her and her representatives, but is there anything less sexy than a shoot in which your subject is flanked by court-appointed officers? She became yet another name added to the list of lovers who had jilted *Maxim* at the altar, and we dejectedly handed the cover to a big-bosomed also-ran whose midseason replacement sitcom would be canceled weeks before our issue hit newsstands.

I later apologized to Jim for failing to salvage the story. "Don't worry about it," he consoled me. "The longer you work in this industry, the more experiences like this you're going to have. There's no point in getting attached to any one particular thing. You'll only end up being disappointed."

MAXIM WAS STILL too young a magazine to have many traditions, but one incipient institution we had was a sort of trophy wall directly behind Mike Soutar's desk, a collection of relics paying tribute to other emerging men's titles that *Maxim* had vanquished in its two years of existence, those valiant but ultimately futile competitors drowned in our inescapable wake. Stapled to the wall was a wristband bearing the logo of the defunct *Icon: Thoughtstyle,* an erudite offering that favored words over pictures and was naturally the first to go down; a portion of a T-shirt from *P.O.V.,* a mixture of cheesecake and career advice that had seen its advertising run out as *Maxim*'s prosperity increased; and a baseball cap from *Bikini,* a hip Los Angeles tome that had merely gone on hiatus and remains so to this day. But most of these memorials had been accumulated in my earliest weeks on the job, and the wall was practically crying out for fresh blood.

It had been almost as long since I'd had contact with any of my old *Details* associates, either; on one overcast Monday in March 2000, I was supposed to have lunch with an editorial assistant who was one of my few former colleagues with whom I was still on speaking terms. But when I called him that morning to pick a meeting place, he abruptly called off our plans. "I just can't do it today," he said. "I can't explain why. Don't ask me to explain. Trust me, by the end of the day, I'm sure you'll understand."

The secret was out in a matter of hours. At first there were the speculative e-mails bouncing around the office, then uncertain phone calls, and then, by noon, a companywide memo confirming it: *Details* had been canceled. Only a couple of hours earlier, their whole staff had been herded into a surprise meeting with Condé Nast's chief executive, who informed them that every single one of them—the editors, the design and photo people, the copy and re-search teams, the advertising staff, everyone from Mark Golin to a newly recruited art director who wasn't scheduled to start work until the following week—was fired. Everyone would be given the opportunity to meet with Human Resources for possible reassign-ment elsewhere in the company; those who did not find new work would have until the end of the week to pack up their belong-ings and be gone. When an impertinent ex–promotions assistant complained that *Details* had a celebrity-studded pre-Oscars party scheduled for that same day, the CEO reportedly barked back,

"No, you don't. You don't have an event. *You don't have a magazine.*"

Even we, in our media-free vacuum, had heard rumors that *Details* was in trouble, but you didn't have to be a publishing insider to comprehend this—you only had to look at any recent copy of the magazine. Simply to hold an emaciated issue in your hands—so gaunt that if you turned it on its side, it disappeared—was to recognize a periodical suffering through its death throes. Mark had made good on his threat that no male personalities would again appear on its cover, yet the women he was choosing in their place were obscure, bordering on unrecognizable. On the inside, readers were greeted with self-help features bearing such guilt-inducing titles as "Why Aren't You Famous Yet?" and "Have You Annoyed Your Boss Lately?," all of them sounding as if they had sprung straight from Mark's peculiar imagination and onto the page and expressing ideas that were entirely incompatible with the magazine's fundamental values. A *Details* man was not supposed to worry that his rebellious actions were alienating his employer or denying him the notoriety he never sought—he was supposed to be confidently cool and self-assured. Even the most loyal reader who had stuck with the magazine through all of its previous identity crises would have been driven away. But it wasn't the lost readers or the lost advertising pages that did *Details* in; at this time Condé Nast was putting out plenty of other publications that bled millions of dollars a year more. It was a third and final deficiency—a loss of prestige—that the executive powers could no longer tolerate. The lad-ization of *Details* had been smothered in its infancy.

The announcement of this bloodbath was naturally the cause of much gloating around the *Maxim* offices. "Don't you feel validated now?" someone asked me. But I didn't. What I felt primarily was a tremendous sense of relief—relief that I had so narrowly missed this mass termination, because it most certainly would have sent me scrambling for the nearest open window. And as he was assuring reporters that if he'd just been given a few more issues, he could have turned things around, I thought of Mark, and it broke my heart. Not because he was out of a job—by all accounts, he still had a year left on his contract and would be paid a large sum of money to go away—but because he had stumbled while chasing his own muse. *Details* was the first magazine he had been allowed to run without any outside interference, the most accurate reflection of his own tastes and sensibilities he had yet presided over. To have that opportunity rescinded—only a man who had succeeded as he had could know what that rejection felt like.

Though we hardly needed the additional incentive to celebrate, we were already planning to throw ourselves another party that same night. The occasion this time was that *Maxim* had been named "Magazine of the Year" by a trade publication that covered the advertising industry. It was a noteworthy distinction for which we were being honored alongside—and above—enduring institutions like *Time* and *The New Yorker* and breathlessly hyped ephemera like *Talk* and *The Industry Standard,* an invaluable shot of credibility we needed in a category where our competitors still refused to acknowledge *Maxim*'s existence. And while it was an honor predicated entirely on the magazine's financial success, having nothing to do with the quality of the editorial content, that didn't stop us from trumpeting the award with a bright red banner emblazoned across the cover of our next issue—as if any of our readers could give a shit.

That was the prevailing mood at the dimly lit get-together, held at a private club in a neighborhood I knew too well: Around one corner from the bar was my father's fur warehouse, with its cracking paint job, incomprehensible bale-making machines, and inside-out pelts stacked to the ceiling; around the other was the apartment of the Orphan. She had accepted my invitation to meet me at this party, because she was excited—maybe a little too excited—to finally see the faces of the men I worked with. Whatever her expectations, the scene that awaited her must have looked like a high school dance: editorial staff on one side of the room, advertising on the other, a cover band playing to a completely empty dance floor, and everyone holding beverages laced with booze.

"Start drinking," I told her. "It's going to be a long night."

The Orphan's first words to me were the same I had been hearing from everyone else that day: "You know about *Details*, right?" From her vantage point across the floor, she had an eyewitness view of the day's devastation. "My God, Dave, they were drinking all morning and all afternoon," she said as she sipped a glass of wine. "Nobody knew where the alcohol was even coming from. I went by Mark's office and he was by far the drunkest of all of them. It looked like a day care center in there."

"I think they're taking the news better than I am," I said. If I needed further proof that the demise of *Details* had hardly affected its own employees, I could look to the end of the bar, to see its ex–deputy editor Bill Shapiro. Instead of spending his first night of unemployment with the men he took down, or even with his wife and infant son, he was here carousing with his old *Maxim* crew, the same people he had so openly disparaged in his parting words to me.

Stepping away from his disciples, Bill shepherded me aside and leaned into my ear. "I gotta tell you," he said quietly, "*Maxim* looks *so bad* these days." I didn't realize it at the time, but in the publishing business this is a salutation as commonplace as "hello," an everyday greeting a former editor will often address to a current one, often because it is the truth. "The articles—they're so pointless. They make no sense. I don't know what you guys are thinking anymore."

"You've sure got a lot of advice for someone who just lost his job," I snapped at him. "*This* magazine's going to be just fine."

"Of course it is," he said.

I grabbed the Orphan by the arm. "Come on," I said to her. "Let's go stand somewhere else."

So we drank, and drank some more, and we wandered through a darkened hallway that we thought would lead to an even more exclusive back room but took us only to a kitchen. And I introduced the Orphan to Parker, whom she had heard so much about when I was still contemplating the *Maxim* job offer. "This is my boss," I said, indicating the man three days my junior.

"Yeah, but only when he listens to me," he replied.

When our British executives shooed away the house band so they could serenade the crowd with their own rousing rendition of "American Pie," the party was truly over. A gentle, tickling rain had started to fall outside, and the Orphan and I took our time walking from the club to the entrance of her walk-up. "I'm having trouble believing that those are the people you work with," she said, still buzzed from the wine.

"What do you mean?" I wanted to know. I was drunk, too, past the point where I am pleasantly festive and well into my introspective mode.

"I mean, you don't look like a *Maxim* guy."

"Does anybody?" I said. "You wouldn't know it, but every single guy in that room was either married, engaged, or committed to somebody."

"Except for you." She giggled. "You should just *be* committed."

"Very funny," I said. "I'm sorry I pulled you out of there, but I couldn't take it anymore. I don't really feel like there's much worth celebrating tonight. How can they have the balls to throw a party when these people they used to work with just got fired? Everyone is telling me that I should be grateful. I'm miserable."

By now we had reached her front door. She looked up at me, squinting slightly, and said, "You're a really good person." With that, she pulled my head to hers, pressed her lips against mine, and forced her tongue past my teeth and into my mouth. It was awfully forward for a good-night gesture, but I decided to allow it. So we stood there, pawing and probing and taking each other in, more fully than I had ever been permitted to when I was actively pursuing her.

"Would you like me to come upstairs?" I asked.

"If that's what you want." And I wanted.

The steep ascent to her apartment was made more perilous as we stopped at every landing to make out with fevered intensity. I was instructed to behave myself as she unlocked her door and sneaked me past her sleeping roommates into her bedroom. By the streetlights shining through a single window that lacked blinds or curtains, I could see that it wasn't much of a boudoir: clothes piled everywhere; framed record jackets and magazine perfume inserts hanging on the walls; and the Orphan sprawled across her bed, ready and willing for whatever I was going to do next.

"Why are men so obsessed with breasts?" she asked as I groped my way beneath her shirt.

"We have to discuss this right now?"

"Yes!" she insisted, crossing her arms across her chest for emphasis.

"How should I know? We don't have any of our own. We spend the first year of our lives nuzzling at them, and then we spend the rest of our lives trying to get them back in our mouths." And then I sated myself, however briefly.

My mind kept flashing a line I had inexplicably retained from an old biology textbook: "The revelation of erogenous zones may be a source of stimulation for both partners." And it was. It was comforting to be pressed up against a normal, naked human body again—the freckled skin, the occasional pockmark from a popped pimple, the floppy, unevenly sized tits, the wide, curvy hips, the matted, overgrown pubic hair. I exposed myself eagerly and without embarrassment, and though she swatted away any further attempt at foreplay, she was perfectly happy to take me directly inside her, and I was equally happy to comply.

It is my first fuck since college, and I can hardly believe that anyone outside of Hollywood really does this—that there was ever a time when men did this solely for their own enjoyment. It is also my first time working with a condom since who can remember, so I have to rely on the gentle, gasping grunts she occasionally emits to be certain that I'm still doing it correctly, because for all I know I am thrusting a wrapped cigar into a jar of mayonnaise, and it occurs to me that maybe I have spent so many of the intervening years engaged in chronic masturbation that I have stripped the underside of my penis of any ability to register stimulation, and all this empty pounding has exhausted me in minutes, and it's impossible to work up a decent rhythm because her idea of gender equality is lying completely still, and I'm feeling wet where I shouldn't be wet, and something smells like stale iced tea, and I'm praying to God, O Blessed are You, O Lord our God, King of the Universe, who has been so merciful to us except for a brief period in the 1940s, I promise to give up the *chazerai* and visit my family plot once a week if You would see fit to create some friction between myself and a millimeter's layer of latex so I can *just feel something*, when I realize the panting and moaning has ceased and the Orphan is looking straight up at me.

"I'm not sure how I feel about this," she says.

"Do you want to try a different position?"

"No, I mean about *me and you*. I'm not sure that I want to keep doing this."

And, really, what can you do in a situation like this? What is the accepted protocol when a woman decides she wants to stop screwing in midscrew? As I saw it, I could either grab her firmly at the wrists and keep pumping away, over her protests, until I got what I came for and her screams woke up the roommates and landed me in a court of law, or I could take one last stroke for posterity, accept that this was how it was really going to end, and grit my teeth as the blood that had built up in my erection begrudgingly redistributed itself throughout my body.

"I'm sorry," she said as I rolled onto my back, and I was, too—sorry that decades of intimidation had yielded a man so completely deferential that he had no choice but to capitulate to a single instance of denial even in the face of all the previous, repeated acts of consent. Had there ever been a more difficult period in human history to get laid than right this very moment? If *no* had meant *no* every time my father heard it, would I even be here today?

I pulled on my pants and made my way to her bathroom, where

I prepared to finish myself off as I had every night, and the occasional morning, and four to seven times every weekend, since the day I discovered I could do it alone. And as I sat on a fetid toilet, my gaze drifted past the clumps of hair and dirt visible even against the black porcelain of her bathtub, to the rows of prescription bottles lining her sink, identified by aggregations of letters so linguistically valueless that I found their names dizzying to read, and I had to go back to bed.

The Orphan let me sleep silently next to her, but when I woke up the next morning she was gone, confident that I'd show myself out without stealing her underwear or setting something on fire. I showered in that same horrible cesspool I had surveyed the previous night, then got dressed and headed straight back to work, where Parker was waiting for me.

"Aren't those the same clothes you were wearing yesterday?" he said, proudly rubbing my head in his expansive palm.

I made myself grin in reply. I was glad someone around here still had fantasies.

6

ALWAYS BE CLOSING

IF YOU IGNORED THE LETTERS IN WHICH READERS SHARED their favorite dirty jokes, and overlooked the envelopes containing blurry photographs of kindhearted girls in burlesque poses stapled to handwritten notes that begged us to publish these pictures as a reward to their devoted boyfriends, the most frequent piece of fan mail we received at *Maxim* could be reduced to the same simple question: Why does your magazine come out only once every month? And in response, among ourselves, we offered a simple, unprinted answer: *Only?*

After working at *Maxim* for long enough, you had to accept that there was an intelligent design to the universe, because what you discovered was that the thirty days it takes for the moon to revolve around the earth is precisely the least amount of time in which the combined efforts of you and your colleagues could produce a single issue. No matter how hard you worked, you were told that you had completed your task at The. Last. Possible. Second. To understand why, consider the torturous path that any piece of copy had to follow before it ever appeared in print.

First the text came to you from your writer, raw and unfocused, and you poked at it, prodded it, and mostly rewrote it, then passed it along to your boss, who passed it along to his boss, who passed it back to you. Once everyone had signed off, its next stop was the

copy department, where sentences were inspected for petty offenses like dangling modifiers and subject-verb agreement, under
the guidance of an agreeable, bespectacled den mother who had
once worked at *Penthouse* yet implored editors to eliminate ob-
scene words like *clusterfuck* in favor of more acceptable equivalents
like *gangbang*. From there, the story was forwarded to the research
department, which bore the burden of checking facts and corrobo-
rating sources, for preserving accuracy and averting liability, and
was therefore staffed by recent college grads even younger than myself who possessed no previous journalism training. Meanwhile,
the layout for your article was being designed by a skeleton crew of
Brits imported from Dennis Publishing's London office, who believed that any quantity of words could be fitted into a box measuring five inches by three inches, and you didn't dare complain to
them because to do so would necessitate a trip to the far corner
where the Brits resided, a dank cavity clouded with the stench of
their constant belching and farting and cigarette smoking. So you
cut your copy-edited, fact-checked text, and you cut some more,
and you reviewed the page two additional times, recognizing that at
any step in the sequence the magazine's lawyers could cry foul,
contending that a reference within your story to "being buggered
with a size-9 Gucci loafer" was not merely of questionable taste but
legally indefensible, and needed to be rewritten. If you could avoid
that, you were done—with that page, anyway.

We lived our lives in constant fear of the Close, that portion of
the production schedule when we reviewed our pages one final
time and the state of our office metastasized from mere delirium to
outright hysteria. The Close should have lasted for only one week
every month, but soon the Close stretched to two weeks and then
three, until finally we were working in a state of perpetual Close.
The Close took precedence over all matters, and the Close denied
all other aspects of your existence until the Close was complete.
The Close tried you on, the Close wore you out, the Close shrank
you to fit. The Close made the man, and the Close made him miserable; you'd hear the Close invoked in every telephone Close

around six or seven o'Close each Close: "Sorry, I can't. We're closing."

Days and nights, weekdays and weekends, were spent at our
desks, poring over copy, waiting for pages, surfing the Web to check
stock quotes, sneaking onto the fire escape for clandestine bong
hits, and engaging in computer games that allowed our alter egos to
run through fantastically complex labyrinths while toting imaginary weaponry designed to kill one another on sight. The cathartic
release we derived from seeing someone blown to bits was no reflection of what we felt toward one another—we were too depen-
dent on our fellow editors to wish them dead. When a comrade
needed assistance with a photo caption or a wacky headline for his
winter sports feature, we sprang into action and gathered around
his computer, batting around innuendoes, awful puns, and allitera-
tion, until "Ice Holes" gave way to "Snow Jobs," which yielded
"Snow Means Yes!" and everyone was satisfied. Each evening we
gathered in a conference room furnished with mismatched chairs
of varying sizes and degrees of comfort, a television set that wasn't
connected to anything, and a lacquered wooden table where we ate
our catered dinners in communal quiet, raising our voices only to
mock the one guy who inevitably didn't get his order.

Once a week we'd assemble around the same table, still littered
with plates of half-eaten egg rolls and quarter-finished pizza pies,
still sticky from spilled sodas and prepackaged honey mustard
sauce, and ten of us—nine men and one woman who was perfectly
at ease referring to her own genitals as her "cooch"—would determine the contents of a periodical that would be consumed by some
two million people. At the age of twenty-four, Parker and I were the
youngest of the team and the only members who fit its target demographic. True to Bill Shapiro's ominous warnings, most of these
people had never worked a full-time publishing job in their lives—
and it was to their advantage. Uncorrupted by the rigors of the
trade, not yet indoctrinated into believing that a magazine had to
look or read a certain way, they had mastered the ability to spin the
mundane afflictions and curiosities from their own lives into arti-

cles a casual reader could find compelling. If you had ever wondered why you were perpetually picked on by bank tellers, toll collectors, and meter maids; in what order you should remove your clothes when undressing in front of a woman; or how to escape from a stuck elevator—and if there was enough consent around that filthy table—then that idea became an article.

It was an unusual approach that almost entirely shunned submissions from outsiders: The pitches we seldom received from professional magazine writers read like pitches from professional magazine writers, and the ideas that came from our readers were usually pleas to pay for their road trip to Mardi Gras or Burning Man. Jim Kaminsky and Lester W. would offer their counsel, and Mike Soutar would occasionally chime in to remind us that an element was missing from the formula he had long ago perfected. "Where is this month's personal benefit story?" he would inquire, reciting from an imaginary checklist he knew better than "The Flower of Scotland." "Where is the gritty read?" Otherwise, the fate of the book was ours to decide, the magazine's reputation ours to enhance or to ruin.

Unable to leave the premises except to sleep in our beds, we became the only people in one another's lives. Were this a rational work environment, discerning employees might have started quitting, but by now it wasn't just Parker who had come to see the squad as his surrogate family—it was all of us: We had no say in who the other members of our household were, and no matter how oppressive circumstances became, our sense of obligation to the group prevented us from walking away. It might as well have been in our blood.

But like any modern family, we were exhibiting symptoms of dysfunction, and ours could be largely attributed to an absentee parent. Mike had never fully embraced his role as editor in chief, nor had his subordinates ever completely accepted him, and it all started with that accent of his. In his very first meeting with his inherited staff, he had declared that he could "edit the *fook* out of this magazine," a bold proclamation that yielded more open laughter than the hushed obeisance he was hoping for. Little by little, his linguistic tics burrowed into our brains—the way his palate tortured vowel sounds until they emerged from his lips so mangled that they couldn't be recognized without their dental records; how his burr stretched out frequently used superlatives like "great" into "grrrrrrrrrreat"; his preference for comical Britishisms, wishing us good night with a courteous "Ta-ta!," labeling deceitful behavior as "under-the-table form," or sending us on our way with the untranslatable exclamation "Bob's your uncle!"—until we couldn't stop ourselves from lashing out. Everyone had perfected an impression of Mike they could perform on command, each keyed to a different mannerism or catchphrase of his—even the Brits in the art department, with their guttural northern accents that marked them as the progeny of England's working class.

Our satire wasn't affectionate, and it wasn't discreet. And it wasn't long before Mike simply stopped coming in to work. Not all at once—a missed day here, another couple of days there, and every time a different excuse: He had to run down the pub to watch his football club's championship match; the wife and kids had insisted he take them on a sightseeing tour around the city or a really grrrrrrrrrreat ski trip; he had to fly back to London for an old friend's bachelor party. So we did what any group of Americans would do when faced with an underperforming teammate: We covered for him, finding ways to run a magazine without a warm body in the single most important seat, redistributing his duties throughout the office; even his editor's letter, the few hundred introductory words at the front of every issue that no one ever—ever—reads, was being ghostwritten for him. Without Mike to inform us about the outside world, to demand that we increase productivity because our print run was going up or our production plant was fining us for missed deadlines, we had no one to enforce the motto we had each resiliently adopted: "We will work harder." Without his authoritative presence, without the fear of being chastised, we had lost any sense of right and wrong.

Sometimes, when Parker was away from his desk and I was allowed to sit in his chair, I would spend my idle hours watching Harold, another assistant editor, who sat in an adjoining cubicle. Harold was a fellow Hebe, also short and also with glasses, approaching the magical, perfect, halfway age of thirty, with a hairline that could no longer be described as receding—it was in full retreat. ("With the amount of hair we tear out here, we should all be bald," he explained.) By his own admission, he had first caught the attention of the magazine by pitching a story in which he claimed to have, at one time or another, contracted every sexually transmitted disease known to man (except HIV, of course); it was a blatant lie, but the sort of lie that editors love to harmlessly perpetuate on their readership, one in which the semblance of truth made it true enough. This literary persona contrasted sharply with what I took to be his authentic one: an unassuming guy with no more going on beneath his meek exterior than perhaps a deviated septum, though I'm sure if you asked him, he'd have described me the same way. He liked to make crank phone calls to escort agencies; he would sing himself imaginary show tunes using the name Slobodan Milošević as his only lyric; he'd jam his finger in his nose, and when I caught him in the act, he'd just jam it in there deeper.

"Harold," I would say, "I can't stand you."

"That makes two of us," he would answer. "I can't stand me either."

When Parker was around, he and I fought incessantly, over deadlines and edits and missing assignments, and "Circus Maximus" was routinely the last portion of the magazine to be completed every month. When we both appealed to shifty, suspicious Lester W. to mediate our dispute, I fully expected that he would put me in charge of the section and be done with it. Instead, when the three of us met privately to hear his verdict, Parker sat speechlessly to the side as Lester W. directed his comments entirely at me. "I don't want to hear any more complaints from you," he snarled. "Parker is the editor of 'Circus Maximus,' and you are his assistant. That means you do whatever he tells you to do. Are we clear about this?"

I gave no answer, so Lester W. got right up in my personal space, his face so close to mine that I could taste the bile in his words. "Are we *clear?*" he repeated. "Because if you don't like it, there's the door."

The following morning I awoke to find that my arms and waist had erupted with clusters of yellow purple pustules, itchy and painful to the touch. Shingles, I was told by my doctor, can be brought on by anything from a common cold to an episode of intense stress. *Wonderful,* I thought, *now it's coming out through my skin.* After a few days of recuperation, I returned to work to find a sign with the word QUARANTINE handwritten on it, taped to my closet door. I didn't know how much longer I could put up with this.

AT LEAST I LASTED longer than Mike Soutar. With the onset of spring, as I was about to celebrate my first year of continuous employment, he requested that we gather in the conference room that doubled as our dining hall and family den. He let us stare at one another for a minute, the room silent except for the sounds of people peeling their arms from the squalid table surface, and then he went into action: "Thank you all for coomin' this morning," he said, looking at no one in particular. In the measured tones of a man who had obviously rehearsed this speech for maximum clarity, he continued, "While I consider it a privilege to have worked with each and every one of you this past year, I have decided to accept a job that requires that I return to England, and so I am resigning as editor of *Maxim.*"

None of us had agreed on much these past months, but in that instant it was safe to say we were all thinking the same thing: *You son of a bitch.* Too late, we understood that there had been no ski trips, no bachelor parties for friends, no friends; Mike had been shopping himself around, going on job interviews, seeking someone to pull him out of the rut he'd dug for himself. Now it looked as though *Maxim* would be without an editor in chief for the second time in as many years. The last time around, it had taken nearly three months to fill the vacancy. Who would take care of us now?

But Mike wasn't finished with us. "I'm 'appy to report," he said, "that my replacement has already been chosen." At this moment he could have held aloft a brick and designated it his heir, and we all would have worshipped it like a god. But his revelation was slightly more surprising: "It gives me *grrrrrrreat* pleasure to introduce the next editor in chief of *Maxim*, a name I'm sure you're quite familiar with, a titan in the field of men's magazines . . . Keith Blanchard."

It was true, Keith's name was one I knew well, and one I might have taken greater notice of if I had been able to conceive of a situation when the man behind it might someday be put in charge of me. Even I am appalled to report he was yet another Princeton graduate, from the class ten years ahead of mine, an era when the eating clubs hadn't yet been mandated by law to admit female members. In his day, he had also worked for the *Tiger*, the school's struggling anthology of humor, inside jokes, and crudely drawn cartoons. From our tiny berth in the student publication office, as we compiled lists of campus buildings that sounded vaguely like euphemisms for the male and female genitalia, Parker and I were watched over by press clippings bearing Keith's byline. Torn from the pages of tossable women's monthlies like *YM* and *Redbook*, with titles that asked "Is Your Man a Liar?" and revealed "Your Husband's Secret Sex Wish," the articles hung from the bare walls like motivational posters, reminding us that there was hope outside Old Nassau's gates for those of us who didn't want to become investment bankers or middle managers, urging us to surpass these modest accomplishments even though we knew we never would. Keith would occasionally show up at our alumni functions to graciously donate a few bucks to the magazine's coffers or buy a round of drinks for us struggling undergrads, then dissolve into the background without even making a clumsy attempt to hit on the few female students in our ranks.

More recently, he had hooked up with Dennis Publishing

when it set up shop in America; he'd had his name on the *Maxim* masthead since issue number one, and his status as a company man was sealed when he took the reins after the magazine's first editor in chief, a woman and self-described "hot chick" named Clare McHugh, departed after barely six months. But the editorship was just a temp gig, a humble act of keeping the seat warm until Mark Golin came along, at which point Keith was asked to oversee the launch of a *Maxim* spin-off called *Stuff*. That position, too, lasted as long as it took for Dennis to import another editor from the United Kingdom to supplant him. Through it all, Keith remained the highest-ranking editor at *Maxim* who opted not to follow Mark on his trail of tears to *Details*; for his fidelity, Keith was made Dennis's creative director, a job that entailed . . . well, who could say for sure? It was rumored that he occupied a corner office on our floor, a room that might have lacked electricity since it was always dark and its computer sat perpetually idle. The few who claimed to have seen him in the halls lately reported that, when approached directly, he addressed you in soft, mumbled sentences, with a tendency to jiggle his hunched shoulders up and down in tandem as he spoke, or else he scurried away like a cockroach suddenly caught in the light. Despite my intimate knowledge of his career, I had almost no familiarity with Keith as a person, but I understood what his latest promotion meant to those of us who spelled *honor* without the letter *u*.

When Keith stood up at the meeting to accept his commission, it was as if he'd appeared out of nowhere. He still sported that generically clean look from years ago—clean-cut hairdo cropped at perfect right angles, doughy face, winning smile, the same crew shirt and khakis that he might as well have worn underneath his graduation gown. Though he must have known about the decision for days, his remarks were hasty and off-the-cuff. "I, ah, I just wanted to tell everybody what a great job I think you're all doing with the magazine, and, ah, I'm really excited to start working with you. I've got a lot of ideas for what I want to do in the future— I want to do a *Maxim* salary survey, a car feature . . ." His voice trailed off. He started again. "I, ah, I know it's been tough around here lately, but I want you to know that they're going to be addressed, and we're going to make this magazine a fun place to work." Everyone cheered. He may not have known how to make things better, but at least he knew enough to recognize that things were bad. He may have been a brick, but he was *our* brick.

We ended the day early with a celebratory drink at our preferred corner bar, a mock-Irish pub with the coincidental name of Blaggard's (coincidental in that *blackguard* happens to be English slang for a boorish lout, which is what each of us turned into when we drank there, and *blaggard* a sound that many of us had made on its bathroom floor on one night or another). While Mike nursed a warm Bass and waited for someone to compliment him on his good fortune, the rest of us congregated around Keith and toasted his success. Keith thanked us for our kind gesture, reiterated that he had a lot of great ideas for the future, including a *Maxim* salary survey and a car feature, and then excused himself to make a phone call. "I promised my wife I would check in with her," he explained. "If she hears bar sounds in the background, she's going to kill me." He never came back.

Mike retreated soon after, leaving behind the editorial underclass to neurotically obsess over what might lie ahead. Only Parker was unrestrained in his enthusiasm for Keith's impending takeover; it was Keith, after all, who had gotten Parker hired at *Maxim*, just as Parker had done for me, and he had a great deal of faith in the man he regarded as his mentor. The rest of us couldn't see things with his clarity, and it wasn't solely because of the alcohol.

"I can't believe it! Keith's going to be our new editor!"

"Thanks, Parker. We were all at the meeting."

"What I want to know is, how did Mike get out of his contract? I heard he had a whole year left."

"Do you think he told them he was quitting, or did they finally wise up and fire his sorry ass?"

"I can't believe it! I mean, I can't believe it!"

"Okay, Parker, you made your point."

"I wonder why they didn't hire an editor from outside the company again?"

"I wonder if they even had the chance to look for one this time."

"You know, there was a moment in there when I could have *sworn* he was going to say they were bringing Golin back."

"I bet you were relieved when he didn't. That would've been *your* ass."

"I can't believe it! I just can't believe it!"

"Shut *up*, Parker!"

"Is Keith going to fire Lester?"

"What's going to happen to Kaminsky?"

"What's going to happen to *us*?"

I had been down this road before. The arrival of a new editor in chief is simultaneously the most stabilizing and the most tumultuous event in the life of a magazine. A new editor has the omnipotence to wipe a roster clean as well as the potential to right a sinking ship, but rarely the practical experience to use one to achieve the other. The occasion means that everyone's job is at risk—in the ensuing confusion, the playing field is momentarily leveled, and an entry-level minion can find himself as powerful as a seasoned veteran. It was a situation that I intended to fully exploit.

THEY SAY, ALTHOUGH I cannot confirm this, that one of the effects of hallucinogenic drugs is that your senses become confused— that tastes acquire texture, and sounds take on shape and pigment, and you can better appreciate that Jimi Hendrix guitar solo because you can *see* it, man. I wasn't on anything at the time, but as I was led through the offices of *Glamour*, I was certain I could smell the color pink. It was the smell of molded plastic workspace dividers and aerosol spray, of vinyl dry-cleaning garment bags and fresh-cut lilacs in vases of bottled water, of chamomile tea in the afternoon and leather spaghetti-strapped high-heeled pumps with matching purses. It was the smell of women.

Mark's assertion that I would never work for Condé Nast again had held true for about six months; while he continued to live off the severance package they had granted him, I had been invited back to their Times Square tower to interview for an associate editor post at the most profitable magazine they published, whose single-copy sales could give even the mighty *Maxim* a case of circulation envy. Much had changed since the day I was last asked to leave the building and never return: *Details* was gone for good, replaced by a monthly shopping guide whose editorial pages consisted of product photography and stickers to help readers avoid losing their place. A company cafeteria, created by the same architect who was redesigning the Guggenheim Museum, had recently opened for business. And now that all the titles in the Condé Nast pantheon had moved into the building, there were women everywhere. In every hallway and elevator car I was surrounded by maids of all shapes, cup sizes, and sexual orientations, who worked and gossiped, answered phones and pushed clothing carts, edited copy and endured their own late night closes together in beautiful, menstrual-cycle-synchronizing harmony. It was an empire built entirely on a principle my father had drilled into my head long ago: Women will buy anything. From the pimple-faced teenager ashamed of her acne, to the soon-to-be bride who fantasized about an extravagant Hollywood wedding, to the dowager who yearned for gossipy tales of romantic and financial strife among the global aristocracy, they had an offering for every age and every inadequacy.

Someone once told me that when she worked for *Cosmopolitan*, *Glamour*'s archrival and the granny-pantied progenitor of the women's-interest titles we now know, she had one particularly undesirable responsibility: cleaning the encrusted snot off the chair of Helen Gurley Brown, the wizened former advertising copywriter whose book *Sex and the Single Girl* made her a living embodiment of the sixties spirit of sexual emancipation. If you want to believe the legends, it was Brown who, as *Cosmopolitan*'s editor in chief, transformed it from a doddering compendium of needlecraft projects and Bundt cake recipes into a powerful, positive force in women's lives. In actuality, *Cosmo* was a pretty damn good magazine without her help, and while she was filling her armrests with mucus, her periodical was filling its readers' heads with the writing of Nat Hentoff and Tom Wolfe—before she even got there, *Cosmopolitan* was publishing J. D. Salinger and Philip fucking Roth—the magazine had a *fiction editor*, for chrissakes.

Today these publications specialized in a different kind of fiction but didn't advertise it as such. I had certainly profited from writing my share of it; for a time, my most lucrative payday was a *Glamour* assignment that allegedly consisted of transcripts from secretly recorded bull sessions between me and my male friends but was made up entirely off the top of my head and then entirely rewritten by my editor. (In my defense, let me point out that I was paid $2 a word.)

Today the pages of these magazines were female empowerment run amok—the freedom of feminism without all the pesky politics, the moral consciousness, or, y'know, *ideas*. These were publications progressive enough to publish advice columns by pseudonymous male writers who didn't actually exist, licentious enough to describe the male organ in all its contorted manifestations, but too tame to actually print the word *penis*. The women creating these magazines were far better than the material they were producing: They didn't need the fashion guidance or beauty tips because they could buy their name-brand clothing and makeup at sample sales that were closed to the general public or receive it for free from the designers; they had no need for coy sex counseling since they got their own lustful leanings out of their systems long ago and could tell you to within a margin of error of one millimeter where their G-spots were located; and they didn't have to rely upon the inspirational tales of the real-life women their magazines commended because they already were the liberated, self-actualized people their readers aspired to be.

In a previous conversation I had sufficiently impressed one of *Glamour*'s deputy editors, who told me, apropos of nothing, that she was in the midst of changing her last name from Brietzke to

Brooks, because, in her words, "you don't get put in charge of a magazine with a name like Brietzke." I had also submitted a set of feature story proposals about couples who'd found each other after one-night stands, warning signs for women that a man is stalking you, and a tribute to a popular line of vibrators that was being discontinued by its manufacturer—this was as much as I understood about the opposite sex at the time—but they had somehow satisfied *Glamour*'s editor in chief, and I was invited back to talk to her one-on-one, to jump through one last satin-trimmed, bateau-necked hoop.

Bonnie Fuller was the real deal. She was a proven achiever who'd worked her Midas touch during triumphant—which is to say profitable—terms as the editor in chief of *YM* (where her disciples included a newly graduated Keith Blanchard), then *Marie Claire*, and then as Helen Gurley Brown's appointed successor at *Cosmopolitan* (where she had passed along a portion of her accumulated wisdom to Mark Golin). But Mark had learned all the wrong lessons from Bonnie: Her flair was for reverse-engineering feature articles from the cover lines that would sell them, for rewriting stories on the fly, even when no rewrites were needed. As I sat at the desk she maintained in the midst of her editorial bullpen (in addition to the traditional corner office she merited), she was busy marking up a manuscript and instructing an assistant to find out the names of current celebrities who owned and flaunted diamond rings. She was a true multitasker, with a couple of small kids and their nanny sitting a few cubicles away and seven months pregnant with what would be her fourth child, not counting the ones she'd previously devoured.

In person, she reminded me of *The Wizard of Oz*'s Margaret Hamilton—a perfectly reasonable-looking woman without all the stage makeup and the prosthetic nose, even handsome, but looking at her, you could never completely shake the feeling that this was a woman with the will to do grievous harm to small dogs. "So you're Dave," she said. It was the only time during the conversation that she made eye contact with me.

"Yes," I answered. This was the only time during the conversation that I told the truth.

"You come very highly recommended to us," she claimed as she scribbled away, though I couldn't imagine by whom. "Why are you interested in working at *Glamour*?"

"Well," I said, "I've been looking for a change of pace, and I really like what you've been doing here." I waited for her to say something. "All of my experience so far has been at men's titles." I waited again. "So maybe working for a women's magazine would be a, uh . . . a good change. Of pace."

"Oh. Do you have any questions for me?" Traditionally, job interviews work the other way around, but as it happened, I did have one concern:

"Could you tell me exactly what my job here would entail?"

"Hmm. As you might have noticed, most of the people who work here are women." I had. "So we were thinking maybe you could be our token guy." She corrected herself: "Token *straight* guy. You are straight, aren't you?" I was in spirit, although lately not in practice. "You could edit some stories, write some pieces yourself, sit in on planning sessions, help bring a male perspective to things. So do you think you'd want to work here?"

"Certainly," I said. "I'm not interested in jerking you around or playing games. I'm not going to go back to my bosses at *Maxim* and ask them to make a counteroffer. If you decide to offer me the job, then, well, that's that."

Bonnie called out to the assistant whom only minutes ago she had assigned a most aimless and impossible task. "Are you done yet?" she grumbled. I'm pretty sure the comment was directed at both of us.

I don't mind admitting that by the end of this encounter, I was thoroughly intimidated. I couldn't see what Bonnie needed me for—her dick was bigger than mine. But I could easily imagine what my life working for her would be like: languishing in a corner during editorial meetings, chiming in with a double entendre whenever they needed a bit of authentic-sounding dirty talk, sitting alone at the cafeteria during lunch while all the gals went out for salads, cracking wise to stay in my boss's good graces, and, despite the enticing sexual mathematics, whacking off in a bathroom I'd never have to share. It was a job I was not the least bit interested in. So, naturally, they offered it to me.

ON HIS FINAL DAY at *Maxim*, Mike Soutar spent the morning approaching each member of the staff individually to make sure they would be attending his going-away party that night. "Ye coomin' oot tonight?" went his sad, shrill refrain, over and over, as he expectantly rocked back and forth on his feet. Though each of us had vowed at one time or another that we wouldn't allow him the dignity of seeing us at his farewell event, we were all in attendance at the somber affair, wisely held at the restaurant within shortest walking distance of our office. There were no tearful good-byes or impassioned retaliatory tell-offs, and when it was over, he and his family boarded a plane back to England. As far as we were concerned, they could keep him. Say no more, Bob's your uncle.

We hadn't prepared any special event for Keith to welcome him back to active duty, but there was a palpable energy on what was to be his first morning as permanent editor in chief, a sense that a momentous transition would soon be upon us, and a feeling that anything could happen. Perhaps no one felt this more acutely than I did, with a job offer from *Glamour* burning a hole in my back pocket and some very vivid memories of the last time I had tried to bargain with my boss. But as we waited for Keith to walk in and clear the last of Mike's possessions off what was now his desk, the hours ticked by, from ten to eleven to noon, without any sign of him. Then, as we were about to call off the search party and break for lunch, Parker had an announcement for us.

"I just called Keith at home," he told us. "He won't be coming in today."

"He's not coming in?" someone said in disbelief.

"His wife said he's recovering from hernia surgery, but he's hoping to be back in the office by Tuesday or Wednesday."

Having undergone two such operations myself, I knew a couple of things about the process: I knew that a hernia, while uncomfortable, was not so life threatening that a man would need to forgo his first day of work. I also knew that after having this most sensitive area of your body tinkered with, it took several days just to regain the ability to walk and that we'd be unlikely to see Keith and his healthy, hernia-free groin in the office any sooner than next week.

By the third day of his convalescence, my patience had run out. I swiped Keith's number from Parker's Rolodex and determinedly dialed him up from the privacy of my closet.

"Huh—hello?" he answered. He sounded dazed, probably still in the gentle, prescription-only grasp of Percodan when I roused him out of his stupor.

"Keith, it's me—it's Dave," I said in a hushed tone. "I need to talk to you about something."

"Are you sure this can't wait until I come into work?" he said, sounding eager to get back to an afternoon of game shows and soap operas.

"When is that going to be?"

"I don't know, another day or two?" he guessed.

"No, no, it can't. Keith, they've offered me a job at *Glamour*. They said they would make me an associate editor."

This, as I had learned the hard way, was the accepted industry approach to haggling for a raise: You obtained an outside offer behind your employer's back, then used that leverage to beat them into submission—and that was if you wanted to *stay*. If you didn't receive a counteroffer, you'd better be prepared to work for the other magazine, the one in which you feigned interest. In all probability, there had to be entire offices out there populated entirely by people laboring for their second- or third-choice publication. I hoped I wouldn't soon find myself working at one of them.

Keith hardly knew how to answer. "You know that we've been

talking about promoting all of you, don't you?" he said. "And there's a bunch of stories coming up that I hoped you would work on. I want to do a *Maxim* salary survey . . . and a car feature. . . ."

"I know, I've heard the rumors. But I can't wait any longer."

"I'm not going to be able to give you an answer right this second. There are other people I'll have to discuss this with."

"Do you think you can get back to me by the end of the day?"

"Okay," he said, exasperated, and hung up. Within seconds, my phone was ringing. It was Keith again. "Look, I just realized, there's no way I'm going to have an answer for you by the end of the day."

"So when will you know?" I said, my voice a register or two below a whine. "I can't make these people wait forever."

"Hey," he said, finally asserting himself, "if you're in such a big hurry to write Harlequin romances for Bonnie Fuller, be my guest, okay?"

"Do you think that's what I want?" I said, working myself into a frenzy. "Do you think I *want* to work for *Glamour*? Do you think I *want* to quit? Of *course* I want to stay here and work with you!"

We had each pushed the other too far, and now we were racing to see who could backpedal faster. "You have to understand, I just started here. *I just started.* I don't know what's going on. I don't know who's staying. I don't know who's leaving. I can't have people quitting on me already. I need people like you. I need you to stay." He sounded genuinely hurt.

Now I was crying, too. "It would be nice," I said between sobs, "to hear people say things like that more often around here." It was a pathetic performance, but it worked.

"I know, I know," he reassured me. "We'll work this out, okay? I promise, we'll work this out."

I had my answer from Keith that afternoon: I was promoted to associate editor and given a raise that was almost enough to make up for the overtime hours I lost when I quit *Details*. I was so thrilled by the news that I gathered up the interns and took them out to a movie. (Unfortunately, the movie starred Jim Carrey.) Keith finally showed up for work the following Monday, and when we spotted each other in the halls for the first time since our argument, there was an awkward moment of improvisational dancing, an exchange of moves half considered and half executed before they could be withdrawn, as we tried to decide how to react. He gradually extended his arm to shake my hand, a gesture I received by circumspectly reaching around his back and giving him a hug. Negotiation was not a skill that came naturally to either of us.

7.

COMPANY INK

Years later, when I was older and all of this was over, I was at a bar where I ran into a former industry colleague of mine. (I would hesitate to call him a friend.) This colleague had recently suffered a significant humiliation for writing a profile of a toothsome female celebrity, in which she supposedly scolded an equally famous, no less toothy ex-boyfriend for being an unimpressive lover. The starlet publicly denied the report, protesting that she had never uttered such words, and the magazine in which this article was published could not find the statement on the author's interview tapes. The quotation had been fabricated.

When I asked the writer why he had done this, he answered, "Oh, she's just mad because we fucked and now she's trying to get back at me."

Let me repeat this for anyone who may have missed it: This writer genuinely wanted me to believe that he and his subject had sex.

This, it turns out, is the best and only acceptable reason why anyone should want to write about celebrities: because it's better than stalking them. It allows a writer an alarming degree of access to illustrious figures, to ask the questions he's yearned to ask them for years, to tour their homes and sort through their garbage, and to then distill the encounter into an open love letter for the world to see—to do all the things that, were they not performed under the auspices of a sanctioning publication, would surely see him dragged away in handcuffs or a straitjacket.

I enjoyed writing about celebrities for *Maxim* for all the reasons you'd suspect. I liked having the proximity to famous people, confirming firsthand that they were exactly the people their work or their reputations suggested and convincing myself that outside the artifice of the interview, we could really be friends. I liked talking to rock stars about their pinup calendar girlfriends and smoking dope with country music legends; I loved it when a renowned director would completely disavow his last film or a happily married leading man would confess a secret crush on his highly desirable female costar. All that stood between me and a successful story was a little homework—all I had to do was prepare a sufficient number of questions that would provide my subjects ample occasion to talk at length about the people they knew best: themselves. With the proper balance of compliments and controversy, of witty rebuttals and outright ass-kissery, these were conversations I could control from start to finish.

When my subjects were female—the models, the actresses, the models-turned-actresses—all rules were discarded. Then I was encouraged to be as sleazy as the situation would allow, to talk with as much swagger in my voice and as much lechery in my language as I could convincingly summon up. Because when the thrust of our conversation turned to sex, everyone—from the mousy forty-something star of that cerebral network sitcom to the token lust object on that sexless science-fiction series—was always willing to open up. Whether they inherently understood the nature of *Maxim* going into the interview or had an itch for talking dirty that had never before been scratched, they gave up the goods: favorite positions, numbers of partners (both single session and career statistics), disposition on undergarments (panties, thongs, or none at all), preferences on where and how they liked to be touched, and how often they shaved—there was no question too prurient, too probing, too undignified, that it did not warrant an answer.

These women knew it was part of the process, that I was merely playing the role of the verbally dexterous Don Juan I didn't dare imagine myself to be, capable of seducing them with nothing more than the breadth of my vocabulary, and that when our conversation was over, my words were the only thing I'd be putting in their mouths. If a minuscule amount of transcript tinkering after the fact was necessary to make their language more entertaining or more coherent, so be it. As one of my editors would often opine, "Nobody will ever complain for making them look smarter in print." It was all fun and games until a publicist wanted to know why you had asked her client if she was a lesbian or why you printed her imprudent comments about her new vibrator that almost cost her that lucrative cosmetics endorsement deal.

And if my *Maxim* cohorts laughed each time my hand too eagerly shot up to volunteer for one of these assignments, the joke was on them. They were the ones missing out on the verbal dry-humping of a lifetime.

THE OPPORTUNITIES TO PLY my peculiar trade had increased dramatically in the time since I—and everyone else along with me—was promoted, in those heady days following Keith Blanchard's installation as editor in chief, when the editorial assistants were made assistant editors, the assistant editors were made associate editors, and Parker was sent upstairs to oversee the *Maxim* website. That's how things operated at Dennis Publishing: If you were doing exemplary work, you were relocated to a different part of the company altogether, and you smiled and said thank you. Or else you quit.

At the suburban New Jersey residence he shared with his girlfriend of two years, Parker lived a life of total transparency. Sometimes the house was clean, and other times it was filthy; sometimes he and the girlfriend were in a state of simmering, silent hostility, and other times they were broken up altogether, but he never attempted to hide any of this from his coworkers when we visited.

Everyone at *Maxim* knew everyone's business, and there was no reason to pretend otherwise.

A group of us were barbecuing in Parker's backyard one Sunday afternoon, taste-testing steaks made from the flesh of alligators, rattlesnakes, and ostriches, while his girlfriend cloistered herself in the house and watched us from a second-story window, when Douglas, one of our senior editors, called for everyone's attention. "I have an announcement to make," he said humbly. "I got a book deal." Then he braced himself and awaited our response. The disclosure shouldn't have shocked anyone: Douglas was already the magazine's success story, with a master's degree in journalism and a career trajectory that should never have intersected with *Maxim* to begin with. But he had good reason to fear our collective reaction: As he politely received our congratulations and deflected our inquiries on the size of the advance he'd scored, he knew the news that he had sold his proposal—a sprawling investigative work based on an article he had written for the magazine—using the same limited resources we all possessed could have just as easily gotten him beaten to death.

Then Max gave her resignation, and hers may have been the more hurtful of the two. When she was on duty, she was Maxine, an associate editor who oversaw all our features that addressed love and sexual relations—how to find a girlfriend, how to keep a girlfriend, how to talk your girlfriend into having a threesome—the sorts of stories that benefited from a woman's touch, where we didn't ask whom the bylines belonged to or where the reporting was coming from. When she was off the clock, she was just plain Max, with her pageboy haircut and modestly unimposing breasts, who didn't mind the nonstop trash talk that went on around her and who each morning willingly recited the graphic details of her previous evening's date, of who, and where, and for how long, to the delight of the exclusively male ears that pricked up. Unlike Douglas, who'd gotten his bad tidings over with all at once, she approached us around the office one by one, sharing her information surreptitiously, letting each editor believe he was the only one who knew her secret. As the newest hire at a leading women's magazine she'd likely be making more money than the rest of us combined, but as Max had confided to each of us, "There was no amount of money that could have convinced me to stay here." I had been working for *Maxim* for only six months compared to her many years, but I couldn't understand how anyone could become so fed up with an employer in so short a period of time.

I wasn't disappointed with my job, exactly, but I was lonely. With Parker gone I could now take his seat among the grown-ups, except that there never seemed to be any around. Keith had earned the right to work from home when he chose to, and he chose to frequently, whenever he felt like hacking away at a novel he'd been writing in his free time or helping his wife look after their children. Jim Kaminsky had recently upgraded his wardrobe from gray dress shirts and gray pants to gray suits, a sure sign that he was interviewing for work outside the company. And Lester W. had discovered that if you said the words *new direction* just right, it sounded like the phrase *nude erection*, and, had taken to randomly approaching people in the office to ask them, "How do you like my new direction?" To my left was Harold, playing absently with a pocketknife or rehearsing lines from *Taxi Driver* to himself ("You should see what a forty-four Magnum will do to a woman's pussy"). To my right was Max's cubicle, soon to be vacated, and beyond it sat Alicia, the only woman left on our editorial team.

Through coincidences of gender and geography, Alicia and Max were often mistaken for each other by visitors to our floor, but if you ask me, there was no comparison between them. It's true, Alicia also had a short haircut and a tomboyish figure and a fashion sense that favored the torn and frayed over the taut and frilly, but when our bullpen bull sessions got too heated, she was less likely to join in than to strap on a pair of headphones and immerse herself in the collection of CDs she kept at her desk. It was only under extreme duress that she would perform her wicked impersonation of Mike Soutar, one that hinged upon his agonizing pronunciation of her name—a salacious flash of the tongue, a predatory pursing of the lips, a vulgar exhibition of the teeth, an expectant opening of the mouth. In her homage to Mike, one could see how cruel he'd been to her; the reenactment was a living record of every homework assignment he'd ever asked her to complete for his children, every editorial meeting to which he'd denied her entrance, every sincere request to be her mentor that he'd rebuffed—all stories I had learned by heart in the era when Alicia's face was the only one I could see from my old isolation booth and she was the only person in the office who didn't regard me as a leper.

Eventually I came to appreciate Alicia's gentler qualities, too, as if each one were an outward sign she had been put on this planet to serve my needs: the way she could always be counted on to accompany me to rock shows when I didn't have a date, which was all the time; the way she knew the obscure origin story behind every song in the Pixies' catalog and would unself-consciously sing bits of them to me as she explained them; the way she had forced her whole life to fit into an Alphabet City tenement that offered her barely enough room for an old videotape copy of *River's Edge*, a dog-eared biography of Malcolm McLaren, and a hirsute women's studies major with whom she shared the apartment, all for the sake of a career opportunity she could hardly tolerate.

If you're going to tell me that I fall in love with people too easily, then may I politely suggest you tell me something about myself I don't already know?

I could conceive of a universe in which each interaction between Alicia and me, each increasingly intimate exchange of favorite records and misplaced aggression and personal disappointments we shared, brought us inexorably closer until we fell into each other's arms, and because we had paced ourselves, because we had so carefully established our friendship first, our expectations would be realistic, and even when we fought, our arguments would always serve to deepen our understanding of each other as caring human beings. At the risk of overselling it, ours would be the greatest, most satisfying relationship in the history of humanity.

I just couldn't think of myself fucking her. I mean, I knew, anatomically, what lurked beneath those pleated miniskirts and what it was meant for—I just couldn't imagine she wanted what I had, respectively, to offer her or that she'd know what to do with it if I did. I didn't think she entertained sexual thoughts of any nature, didn't even know she'd had a boyfriend until she broke up with him, and her newly regained independence brought her such joy that it seemed unfair to ask her to surrender it so soon.

And I certainly did not want to risk her rejection—no, her *revulsion*—at the idea that this person with whom she had been sharing a workplace was having these thoughts about her and—who knows?—maybe staying after hours to sit at her desk and pull on his pud with her image in his mind, because this failure would stain me so irrevocably and resonate so fully around the company until the sense of discomfort in our office was so stifling that I'd either be shamed into resigning or fired outright, and I'd end up on the street. And then, probably, in the fur business. So I did nothing. I told myself that if she and I were meant to be together, the force of gravity would somehow attract her to my side. How long could that take?

FOR A PARTY whose primary purpose was to send two much loved and irreplaceable editors on their way in spirits of appreciation and goodwill, the collective mood leading up to the event was more like fear. There were perfectly reasonable concerns that the combination of finality and free alcohol, of long-repressed feelings and the lack of anything else worth celebrating lately, would lead not only to excessive bar tabs, but to some spectacular Monday morning recriminations, and soon this fateful Friday night would reveal who would be starring in them. Adding to the gloom was Jim Kaminsky, who had been actively denying that he was in any way affected by the loss of Douglas, his most dedicated listener and the closest he'd had to a disciple at *Maxim*, while simultaneously spreading the word that Douglas was throwing away his career. "I'm not going to tell him what to do," Jim had grumbled to anyone who'd listen. "All I'm going to say is that he's making the biggest mistake of his life."

My personal sense of trepidation stemmed from having to spend yet another night in the company of people whose interest and attention I had completely exhausted—from having nothing left in my depleted conversational repertoire that I thought anyone would want to hear. Each time I circled the room, it looked as though everyone else had already found a more ideal mate: Parker was busy entertaining his predecessor, a plump man with a shaven head who had quit his job at *Maxim* to become a legal secretary; together they were parroting old pieces of copy from memory. Keith was briefly making time with Max, his shoulders aflutter as he spoke, before he waved a wobbly good night and went home. There were Douglas and Jim, locked in an impenetrable huddle, swigging drinks and engaged in intense debate. There was sullen Lester W., who didn't want to talk to me any more than I wanted to talk to him. And there was one of the Brits from the art department, muscular, with flowing hair like Samson, regaling listeners with a tale of how he had once rescued a girl from being raped in the restroom of a London pub. *Right*, I thought to myself, *that story must make you a huge hit with the ladies.* With each futile lap I stopped at the bar for another drink, until I had progressed so far on the spectrum of drunkenness, I was approaching sobriety from the opposite direction.

When I found Alicia, slumped deeply in an armchair big enough for two, she was pretty far gone herself, doing her best to look surly and unapproachable. "They want me to start editing all the sex stories that Max used to do," she told me. "It's because I'm a woman, isn't it? Is that all you think I'm capable of?"

I was going to say something witty and reassuring when we were interrupted by the sound of a spoon being rung against an empty glass and the sight of Parker standing on a bar stool, like King Kong atop the Empire State Building. "Listen up, everybody!" he roared. The ceremony had begun.

I was about to witness a long-standing ritual I had heard of but never seen firsthand, one that in and of itself may have accounted for why people were so reluctant to leave the magazine. If you happened to be an especially revered employee, then, as a parting gift, the editors got together and created an imitation *Maxim* cover in your honor, suitable for framing, on which they had replaced the familiar underdressed female celebrity with the most mortifying photograph of you they could find and on which they had written cover lines that were all inside jokes and abbreviated exposés on the embarrassing details about you that your peers had been quietly accumulating during your tenure. If you thought nobody paid attention to the fact that you sat on your chair in an unusual position, that you had been browbeaten by your wife into giving your baby boy a distinctly feminine name, or that you were getting blow jobs on the side from an intern so inexperienced that you had to teach *her* how to do it, believe me, everyone noticed—they had simply been waiting for the latest possible opportunity to ridicule you for it. And then they got the loudest mouth in the company to read the parody in front of the assembled staff, while you stood there and smiled.

GLAMOURPUSS! read the headline on Max's memorial cover, a sly nod to her new job as well as the accompanying picture of her from some Halloween past, dressed appallingly in pigtails and a parochial school uniform. In designing her tribute, we pledged to ourselves that we'd show restraint to avoid hurting her feelings, and aside from a few cover lines that knowingly referenced her distinct tastes in fashion, we made good on the promise. Max laughed a loud laugh as each joke was read to her. I thought she got off easy.

No such self-control had been exercised in creating Douglas's cover, which bore a smirking portrait of him alongside the large-type legend HEY, JIM! (the first utterance from Douglas's mouth each morning as he greeted his favorite superior) and, beneath that, a smaller secondary line that read: CAN I BLOW YOU? Jim cringed as much as Douglas did while the remaining cover lines were broadcast, more crude attacks that lampooned the volatile nature of his relationship with his on-again, off-again girlfriend and questioned his sexuality for daring to live in Chelsea, rounded out by more overt taunts that he would never finish the book he was leaving to write.

His degradation complete, Douglas remained staring at the barroom floor and withstood several slaps to his back. He waited for Parker to climb down from his tower and the partygoers to resume their drinking before approaching me alone at the bar. He was completely unencumbered of any obligation to the magazine now—there was no one here he would ever have to see again unless he chose to, and he was free to speak to anyone in any manner he saw fit, to dispense his departing pearls of wisdom, no matter how rough and misshapen they might seem, no matter how difficult they might be for others to swallow.

"You want to know why nobody talks to you?" he told me confidently. "Look at yourself! You're always standing there with your arms across your chest—you're telling people to stay away!"

I glanced down at myself and saw that I was posed exactly as he'd described me. Douglas moved on to demolish someone else's self-esteem.

I realize that there are people who equate introversion with a kind of arrogance, who believe that a sometimes distant expression and a pattern of uncommunicative behavior stem from a fundamental sense of superiority, an unwillingness to interact with those I consider beneath me, which is everybody. Well, that's part of it.

There is also the part that comes from having a tiny voice and a plain, forgettable face and an uninterrupted chain of experiences in which you always get the seat at the table that's opposite an empty chair, and you can never get a shirt collar to hang evenly around your neck, and you always break up a conversation when you attempt to inject yourself into it. You can never find someone to pick up the phone when you feel like talking, and you never take a photograph that's as good as you think you look in the mirror. You start out by standing in the center of a room full of people, and by doing nothing for long enough, you end up in the corner with your arms across your chest. It's not because you're persecuted or being punished for some past action. There are just people in the world that this happens to, and you happen to be one of them.

No matter where I stood in this room, there was one direction in which everyone was trying to avoid looking—something they were trying to look at without looking and without looking as though they were looking, and at a glance I caught a fraction of the illicit sight for myself: It was Alicia, sitting in the chair where I had left her, next to that Brit with the long, flowing locks—or, rather, sitting on top of him, straddling one of his mighty, sequoia-size thighs while furiously making out with him. When my own legs did not drop out from underneath me as I expected them to, I looked directly at the two lovers, just in time to see lips pulling away from lips, and then, as the Brit beckoned her back with a wagging, come-hither finger, the whole sordid sequence started over again.

She had been ready to go off like a firecracker, and I couldn't recognize the signs. But there was no mistaking the spectacle of two people who were incontrovertibly going to go somewhere and fuck each other's brains out; on some God-Save-the-Queen-size bed or maybe in a bathroom stall, he'd actually be performing all those actual acts I could never think about, on her, and she'd be enjoying it. How did this happen? Had he also been waging some careful campaign of courtship and finally broken through her defenses tonight? Or did he possess, along with that swoon-inducing accent and those charmingly crooked teeth, some innate ability to identify a woman who was primed to put out? Either way, she was ruined for me—even if, on some distant day, I did get into her pants, I'd only be the guy who gave it to her after he did. But more likely I'd never again have a chance at that sensitive, understated girl with the adorable New England accent who still cried at the end of *The Breakfast Club*. And that wasn't even what bothered me.

It wasn't failure; it wasn't having come this close to succeeding and still failing. It was the certainty with which I felt I would never have the one thing I truly wanted, which was for my life to have meaning to someone else, to love and be loved in return, and that without that, my life wasn't worth living anymore. The frustration made me want to commit an act of supreme and conclusive violence—not upon her for spurning me, which was her right, and not upon him for winning out, which was his privilege. It made me want to hurt the only person responsible for this ceaseless spiral of passivity and indecision. The world wanted me gone, and I wanted so badly to comply.

IN THE LITIGIOUS SOCIETY we inhabit, one might expect that if, at an exceptionally late hour, a customer were to walk into a metropolitan location of a national drugstore chain, visibly inebriated and his eyes ruddy from crying, that drugstore would have either an explicit or an informal policy against allowing him to purchase as many bottles of sleeping pills as he could carry. I can assure you, however, that the practice, while humiliating, is not prevented or even discouraged.

Simple as it is to obtain a potentially lethal quantity of over-the-counter sedatives, it is a considerably more challenging proposition to consume them. The degree of difficulty is heightened significantly if you do it in the dark, while drunk and whimpering, because several pills are inevitably going to fall from your unsteady hands and into the void, where they will be lost forever, and that's no good, because you want to make sure you take enough of them to end up dead, not comatose or brain-damaged. At a certain point, the bland, chalky taste of the pills will be enough to force you to retch up more of them, which is a setback, and beyond that point, the reflexive act of swallowing, repeated some forty or fifty times, will become so painful that not even a sip of water will soothe the raw and overworked muscles in your throat.

By then, though, your head will have acquired an irresistible attraction to any flat, horizontal surface on which you can lay it, your joints will have surrendered all functionality, and your consciousness will have begun to swirl slowly like the contents of a snow globe. And as you shut your eyes in preparation for whatever comes next, your last thoughts will be that you've neglected to compose a suicide note that might perhaps explain your drastic, enigmatic deed to the very people whose emotions you were trying to arouse, and it will be days before your body is discovered by family members, who will suppress the circumstances of your death, and you've forgotten to delete the most incriminating pieces of pornography from your computer's hard drive.

WHEN I WOKE UP, there was a moment where I thought I had been stirred by the sting of a full bladder, a familiar symptom after a long night of drinking. But as I struggled to make any part of my body obey my mental commands, I remembered I had gone to bed the previous night with the resolute intention of never waking up again, and I was scared.

To this point in my life, I'd already had two near-death experiences that, as near-death experiences go, were pretty trivial: The first was when I'd accidentally put my hand through a window and sliced my wrist so deeply that I could see down to the fatty deposits that seeped out like cottage cheese, yet as I watched the wound spill more vital materials than I thought I contained, it hardly seemed to hurt at all. The other was an acute case of appendicitis that my parents had helpfully dismissed as a stomach flu. This time was different; given the choice, it seemed a petty and hypocritical way to come to an end, but it also seemed as if it were really going to happen. I felt ashamed of myself for having acted so impulsively. And, also, nauseated.

I crawled to my toilet and expelled the contents of my stomach, dozens and dozens of the pills, still solid and perfectly preserved, like miniature eggs adrift in a sea of yolk, most of which ended up in the bowl. Then I dragged myself back to bed and attempted to obey my body's orders to sleep, until they were interrupted by a far more vehement command to vomit again. Somewhere else, two very content people would be discovering themselves in each other's arms, while I darted between my bed and my bathroom, waking up and falling down and throwing up and lying down until the sun rose.

A few hours into Saturday morning, while I was still passed out on the twilight line between wakefulness and slumber, between regaining my composure and puking my guts out, I heard my phone ring, and I foolishly answered it.

"Bitchkoff," said a voice.

"Parker?" I asked.

It was indeed. "Get your sorry ass out of bed, man," he said with far too much exuberance for a man who had drunk twice my weight the previous night. "We're going to play paintball!"

"Huh?"

"We're all driving out to the Poconos to play paintball. It's only a three-hour trip. Keith rented us a van and everything."

I could envision the words I wanted to say but could not make myself say them. Brain damage! I knew it! *Brain damage!* With intense and careful concentration, I was able to summon a response: "I just can't do it today. I can't."

"C'mon, man," he pleaded. "Keith's coming. It's going to be fun."

"Sorry, but I can't. I'm too hung over."

"Whatever, dude. You're letting me down."

"Fuck. Off." I hung up. Maybe last night I'd had the right idea after all.

As a sort of penance, I made myself leave the apartment to buy a new bathroom mat, to replace the one I had ruined. Then I slept through the rest of the weekend and was back at my desk Monday morning.

FOR ALL THE LESS appealing thoughts he was known to articulate, Lester W. had an irresistibly compact theory on mortality: "Every time the magazine I'm working for runs a story about Kevin Bacon," he had said, "I wind up losing my job." And sure enough, an interview with the lanky actor was on the lineup for our August 2000 issue. The message implied by this coincidence should have been obvious to Lester W. by now, because it was the same subtle suggestion we had been trying to communicate to him for months: It was time for him to go. Keith's takeover had made him obsolete, and we kept waiting for the day when our editor in chief would take him aside and explain—whether courteously or curtly, it didn't matter—that his services were no longer required. Yet the gradual elimination of his few remaining responsibilities at the magazine had taught Lester W. only that he could stay on as long as he wanted, doing as little as he wanted. When he did, at last, leave *Maxim*, we were discouraged to find that it was of his own volition, to work at another magazine with an even more desirable title at an even more inflated salary. "At my next job," he bragged to us, "I'm doing as little as possible."

With a groan and a shudder, our party-planning machinery began warming up for yet another going-away affair. Despite the widespread farewell fatigue, Lester W.'s send-off achieved a respectable turnout, attracting those who wanted to make sure this really was his last stand and those who had come just to see the dominatrix who had been hired to appear at the event. Once disposing of her trench coat camouflage, the mighty mistress paced methodically around the room in a leather bustier and lace garter, before homing in on the guest of honor, who gamely allowed himself to be bent over a table, whereupon the dominatrix took a paddle to his fully clothed posterior, delivering a series of loud, rhythmic slaps that resonated throughout the bar. Then the paddle was handed around to anyone else who wanted to take a turn.

"Go on," Parker encouraged me. "You have as much right as anybody." Some editors had already vented their rage on his ass two or three times, but I couldn't bring myself to do it even once.

Through every blow to his backside, Lester W. gritted his teeth and grinned with uncharacteristic good humor. But the remaining color drained from his pallid face when Parker assumed his own traditional position at the top of a bar stool and began to read from the satirical *Maxim* cover we had been composing for Lester W. over the last several days. At the center of the page was a picture of him, digitally retouched so that he appeared to have a black eye, a missing tooth, and cuts and scrapes all over his face. The most prominent cover line blared CAT SCRATCH FEVER!, our cleverly worded wisecrack about the nicks and bruises we had inflicted upon his photographic effigy, a beating we surely would have administered to the man himself if we had been allowed. TURTLE-NECK SECRETS!, cried another line, suggesting the same; there were four or five more similar gags waiting to be read, taking aim at every possible characteristic we could criticize about him: his wife, his children, his professional competence, his sexuality. The last of these put-downs simply read AU REVOIR, YOU BASTARD, a line that seemed to reference a story Lester W. had edited so long ago that even he'd forgotten what it was about, but which essentially meant exactly what it said. If he had any uncertainty about how his fellow editors regarded him, he could hardly plead ignorance now. He looked into a crowd consisting of twenty or thirty people he'd worked alongside for nearly two years, and one professional sex worker, and saw only strangers.

But the reading of the charges was never finished, because the accused walked out in midpresentation, leaving his souvenir cover behind. Not knowing what to do, we asked Keith to retrieve him; he found Lester W. standing just outside the bar, staring absently into the distance. "C'mon," Keith prodded him gently. "Come back inside."

Lester W. would not even turn to face him. "What's that yapping sound I keep hearing?" he said. "Oh, wait—it's *you.*" Then he walked off into the night and was gone.

8

THE SUMMER OF LOVE

THE MYTH AND THE MISUNDERSTANDING ABOUT THE ritual of the bachelor party is that it is a party for the bachelor—that before a man can fully commit himself to the obligation of marriage, to the don'ts and the no-longers and the why-can't-Is of that glorious institution, he must fully immerse himself in the opposite experience; before he can surrender himself to a life governed entirely by laws, he must know what it means to live in lawlessness one last time. But that's incorrect: The bachelor party is for *the bachelor's party*, for the friends and the hangers-on, for them to celebrate their enduring freedom in the presence of one who is about to give it up, to provide an acceptable setting for them to explore their most depraved flights of fancy behind a veneer of history and tradition. The intrepid souls who were America's first settlers understood this so well that they had the foresight to establish a sanctuary for these very ideals, and they named it New Orleans.

Were it up to Parker, there would have been no bachelor party in his honor, a transgression almost as unthinkable as his getting married. None of us could quite understand why, at twenty-five years old, he was so eager to settle for monogamy, least of all me, having seen how many eligible women came his way when he wasn't even trying to attract them. Yet for all the Ivy League tail that had chased him in days gone by, there was a high school sweetheart even further in his past, a demure Catholic girl who was now—could it be any better?—a schoolteacher herself, with whom he had made a promise: If, by the end of college, neither of them had found true love, they would marry each other. And who was to say this silly and simple-minded pact would not yield a lasting and more perfect union? He liked to watch movies in which NHL stars made cameo appearances; she liked to go on nature walks. How much more compatibility did a couple need?

While Parker made his own wedding arrangements from his desk, the rest of us were swept up in a maelstrom of instinct none of us had encountered since the onset of puberty, as word of the impending nuptials had everyone reflexively envisaging a final all-nighter in some foreign locale. Jim Kaminsky, who was busy taking bets on how many months the marriage would last and offering odds that the prospective groom wouldn't even make it to the altar, was also generous enough to approve our proposal for a service feature on airline travel, a story that by the way just happened to require several editors to fly to New Orleans on *Maxim*'s dime. Sadly, Jim's wife and infant son prevented him from making the journey himself. "Have a good time," he implored us. "Think of me, all alone, in the office." He could take comfort knowing he wasn't the only one denied passage, since we had told Max and Alicia that they couldn't attend, either. It didn't matter how cool and tolerant the women thought they were—they just weren't prepared for the debauched mayhem the men were about to cause. Hold back the edges of your gowns, ladies, we are going through hell.

Hell, I discovered on arrival, features its share of spectacular architecture, suspended in such a state of decay that you hardly feel guilty for urinating on it at two in the morning. With Mardi Gras long over, it was hard to predict how the natives might react to sharing their living space with a bunch of publishing hotshots from New York, a suspicion that was reinforced by the constant reminders from the airline attendants, baggage handlers, and cabdrivers that our party had arrived on "the hottest day in the month of *Jew*-lie."

Well, if the locals didn't like it, they could suck my circumcised *schlong*, because my people had roots here, too: This was the town where my father had set aside his aspirations of higher learning for the lure of backroom poker matches, where my grandfather was among the first fur traders to deal in the hides of the nutria, a South American rodent that was the city's second-biggest pestilence after frat boys. Here was a man who had figured out how to sell an unwanted animal's skin onto your good ol' boy backs, filthy though they were with the mud of the Mississippi Delta and baked by the heat of the Gulf Coast swamp gas — you didn't have to be Theodor Herzl to figure out what religion *he* was, people! But even he wasn't the most mistrusted minority in town: Before dying of a subdural hematoma similar to the one that will do me in someday, my grandfather was assisted in his business by a woman he would have unhesitatingly referred to as "colored." Now, so fate ordained, this woman's daughter was the director of guest services at the same hotel we were crashing, and had already delivered a fruit basket to my room when I checked in. Would she be so gracious, I wondered, when she was standing atop a stepladder, using a toothbrush to scrub my puke off a crystal chandelier?

Such concerns were soon to be washed away as our group assembled for a ceremonial first beer at a Bourbon Street bar that was not so much a bar as a burnt-out heap of stones, one of a dozen different taverns that claimed to be founded by the entrepreneurial swashbuckler Jean Lafitte. There were nine of us in total, all *Maxim* staffers except for Douglas, who had enthusiastically set aside his book project to reunite with us, and a disheveled writer friend he had brought along for the ride, but none of Parker's childhood pals, no gym partners, no neighborly acquaintances, no one he knew in a nonprofessional context. Yet there was a genuine joy as each one of us arrived in our Hawaiian shirts and Bermuda shorts, as we raised our glasses in Parker's honor, in sincere gratitude for the opportunity to share an adventure outside of work, to affirm that in some parallel universe, we might have all ended up friends if it hadn't been for our goddamned job.

"I really need to cut back on my intake," Parker said, belching as he patted his round belly.

"Yeah," one of his companions shouted back. "Of oxygen."

"Gomez," Parker answered, "has a man ever hit you?"

Gomez was one of the few editors among us who'd actually been employed at another magazine before coming to work for *Maxim*. His father had been in publishing for longer than any of us had been alive, and he had bequeathed to his son a job at *Penthouse Forum*, where Gomez was editing its breathtakingly filthy reader mail at the age of twenty-one. ("I didn't know if the stories were ever true," he said, "but the letters were real. All we did was correct the grammar.") When he grew tired of this vocation and felt the grip of wanderlust, he traveled to Japan, where he met a skinny waiter named Hiroki, who spoke no English but wanted to live in America. When Gomez resumed his magazine training at *Maxim*, he arranged for Hiroki to come to New York to work as an assistant in the art department, where his lack of language skills would pose no barrier. At work, Gomez was not particularly chatty himself and rarely jumped into conversations unless he had something significant to contribute to the discussion; but with one failed marriage already to his credit, he knew better than anyone at the table about the subject we were about to broach.

"Tell me, Mr. Divorcé," Parker continued to taunt him, "what wisdom can you offer me? Any advice so that I don't end up paying alimony before I'm thirty?"

"The most important thing to remember," Gomez expounded, demonstrating the same subdued bravado with which he could sometimes be seen marching around the bullpen in a pair of fleece slippers, "is that there's no such thing as a well-adjusted wife. Even the most stable woman is going to freak out on you twice a day."

"I can't believe I'm about to give this all up," Parker said. "Do you know that the other day"—and here he gave the name of an executive assistant who would never need a flotation device in the event of an emergency water landing—"she pulled me aside into the conference room and pulled up her shirt for me? She told me it was my wedding present."

"But come on, Parker," Gomez prodded him, "you've done better than that."

And indeed he had. Apparently, *Maxim* was a much wilder place in its earliest days, because Parker proceeded to rattle off an impressive list of employees past and present who, he claimed, had spent many a late night finessing more than his copy: the ex–photo editor with the butter-face ("great body—*but her face* . . ."); the ad sales rep who had appeared in *Girls Gone Wild* and was into the kind of snorkeling that didn't require any breathing apparatus; and the frigid former receptionist who had, behind her back, been nicknamed the Iceberg. "*She*," we were told, "was into some deviant shit."

"Oh, yeah," Gomez said approvingly, "but you've gotta go along with that. You've gotta punish her for desiring you."

A couple of times it looked as if Parker had run out of tall tales and the mechanical key in his back had come unwound, but then he'd remember another repressed tryst, and when he was through, there was not a single female staff member—not even the magazine's first editor in chief—who, by his recollection, was not guilty of at least being attracted to him. The confessional spirit was contagious, and each person around the table began to recite their inventories of in-house honeys, lists that began with the same names that appeared at the ends of others. And as we went around, it seemed as if everyone in our incestuous circle had once scored, or had the chance to score, with someone who drew a salary from Felix Dennis. Everyone, with a single exception.

"Nobody?" Gomez asked me in disbelief. "What the fuck is wrong with you?" The tension froze in his face for a moment, then dissipated. "I'm just kidding you, dude. You stick around here long enough, you'll get your turn."

"Okay," said Parker. "What next?"

Not to impugn the rich cultural heritage of an entire city or anything, but there are really only two things to do in New Orleans: look at gorgeous strippers and look at ugly strippers. The gorgeous strippers work at clubs with names like Maiden Voyage or Tempta- tions or Night of Joy; their physiques are so buffed and bronzed from the many hours they spend outside the clubs, at weight ma- chines and in tanning beds, that it would be criminal for them *not* to share their bodies with the world, and they smell like perfume, and though they'll take off only their tops, they have so perfected that technique where they straddle your waist and wriggle them- selves out of their panties to the point where you think you're going to see something, but then yank them back up before you do, that you completely believe $20 is a bargain for three minutes of their time. The ugly strippers work at clubs that don't have names at all, and they have rolls of fat, and bruises, and cigarette burns, and they reek of beer, but they'll take it all off and splay themselves in open poses that say, "Here it is," and they don't care if you slap them too hard or if your fingers slip where they're not supposed to go, and for a hundred bucks they'll take you to a back room where there's a brass bed and a half ounce of blow waiting for you, and whatever happens, happens. Despite my appeals to the contrary, we were going to start our night with the gorgeous strippers.

Everybody knows what happens inside strip clubs: Women are paid to take off their clothes. But just because you understand that you're meant to shove your dollar bills down their G-strings, will you be able to execute the maneuver when called upon to do so? To anyone entering such an establishment for the first time, or any- one so dumbfounded by the sheer simplicity of the basic transac- tion that every visit might as well *be* their first time, the experience can be frightening. Within no more than five minutes of settling down in our first venue—deemed classy because it had mechanical mannequin's legs flexing in its windows—Douglas's friend walked out in defeat, feeling oppressed by the constant barrage of bare- chested dancers who wanted his money. "I don't see why I should have to give her a dollar every time she comes up to me," he protested. None of us offered to lend him any of our own cash, and even if we had, he probably wouldn't have taken it.

But in every group there is always one guy who feels as comfortable in the company of exposed female breasts as he does sitting in his easy chair watching *SportsCenter*, and here, Gomez—a man who up until this point had never exhibited any skills, hobbies, talents, or particular interests—was in his element. While the rest of us were shuffling in our seats, trying awkwardly to hide the unmistakable boners in our pants, he was putting on a virtuoso display of all the skills necessary to make the most of one's strip club experience: He knew how to stand at the edge of a stage and command the attention of a girl without looking pushy or overeager; he could coax out a bonus nipple or ass-crack in the face in exchange for a single dollar bill; he could juggle two or three girls at a time and send them all away smiling. What he enjoyed most, though, was buying private lap dances for his buddies, and when a girl came up and led you by the hand to a more secluded part of the room, Gomez would give you a wink and cock his fingers as if they were pistols, to let you know who your benefactor was.

Once we were sufficiently drunk and emboldened, a smaller contingent ventured to one of the unnamed burlesques on an unlit alley off Bourbon Street. If the lack of a cover charge or even a bouncer wasn't warning enough, we very quickly realized that we had gotten what we paid for: There were no patrons at all and only a couple of dancers who could not have been less interested in their poles if they were covered with the complete writings of Andrea Dworkin. A third performer with missing front teeth and sagging bags like Ziplocs full of dead goldfish sat down, uninvited, at our table and ordered a round of beers—for herself—and started into some sob story about how she was saving up for the breast implants that would someday allow her to fulfill her dream of stripping at the classier joints. It was the reality of the life she had chosen for herself, or had had forced upon her, to have to shake what little she had for disapproving, disgusted guys like ourselves night after night, and it was sad and pathetic and pitiful, and we were gone before the guitar solo in "Sweet Child o' Mine" was over.

In shame we retreated to Parker's hotel room and crowded onto his tiny balcony. From just two stories off the ground, we could see the main thoroughfare in its entirety, storefront after storefront, sign after sign, advertising XXX REVUE and $1 HURRICANES and ATMS HERE!, stretching out into infinity, like a grown-up Disney World where even Snow White might whip 'em out for you. Amid the pedestrian traffic, the rabble and the roughhousers, and the parents rushing to get their children to bed before the real crazies came out, there was slight, silly Harold, propped up against a Gothic lamppost, strutting and preening like a gigolo for our amusement. As we waved down to him, two college-age girls caught sight of our frantic motions and came to stand beneath our parapet.

So we had a couple of nubile lasses who were ready to party, waving back at us and waiting for us to make the next move. But now what? Our limitless imaginations were too inundated with the unthinkably complex combinations presented by the *two totally random women who were actually paying attention to us,* and it was once again up to Gomez to take charge of the situation.

"Come on up!" he shouted to the curiosity seekers. "Come on, don't be shy!" The girls giggled and looked at each other, modestly pressed their fingers to their lips, and shook their heads no.

"How 'bout some beads?" he asked. When this elicited no response, Gomez darted back into the room, grabbed a bunch of necklaces from the collection of cheap plastic tchotchkes we had bought earlier in the day, and held them aloft. "You know what you've got to do to get them!"

Though one woman remained stationary, her friend fumbled underneath her own shirt for a bit, looked around nervously, then lifted up the garment to reveal her breasts poking out over her bra like two pink eyes peeking back at us with wonder and curiosity. While we cheered as though the Armistice had just been announced, she hurriedly pulled her shirt back down, and Gomez tossed her prize over the railing, where it landed in the gutter. And as quickly as these girls scooped up their beads and scurried away, another group would appear below our balcony, and another, and another. And Gomez would perform the same stunt again, and again. And again.

And again.

Incredible! Inconceivable! No matter how many times we saw him succeed, our hearts stopped with every instance that Gomez held out his worthless trinkets and challenged these women—*commanded* them—to show their tits. Would they do it? Of course they would, those fucking sluts! Because what's a tit or two among total strangers? Girls alone, girls in groups, girls with boyfriends, girls with girlfriends, the amply endowed and the flat chested alike—everyone was given a chance to stand beneath our window and be judged. We'd cry "Bitch!" or "Prude!" at the ones who ignored us, and we'd boo and curse at the unattractive ones who'd uncover themselves without any enticement, but it was Gomez who did the real work. Sometimes he'd give up easily on an uninterested passerby, and sometimes he'd spend precious minutes haggling with her, cajoling her while the street flooded with guys, crowding around her but keeping their distance, all hoping to catch a glimpse—not of the exposed skin, necessarily, but of Gomez, demonstrating his magic. He had no surefire system for winning over these women, but he understood this much: Once he had gotten their attention, those tits were as good as seen. Eventually, he was persuading women to disrobe with such regularity that it became boring, even to us, and the crowd dispersed; but when he had finished his exercise we knew we had witnessed a miracle—simply being in his presence and having seen it take place brought us no closer to being able to accomplish it ourselves.

Filing back into the hotel room, we discovered that Parker had fallen fast asleep, curled up among the remaining beads piled on his bed. "Aww, look at Baby Huey," someone said.

"Shouldn't we wake him up?"

"If he wants to sleep through his own bachelor party, then fuck him. Christ, there's more pussy in this bed than there is in all the clubs out there."

Having seen enough breasts for free, we returned to a club where we could once again pay to gaze upon them, one that graciously waived its after-hours cover charge when we presented them with our *Maxim* business cards. Among other things, this trip had taught us the value of getting out of New York once in a while; in our hometown we were vilified as enemies of journalism and scourges of literacy, but here, amid the people who read our magazine for the same reasons we patronized their businesses, we were not completely undesirable! We may have thought we were above them, regarding them as illiterate, inbred hicks, but they were our peers: They knew exactly how it felt to be perpetually surrounded by a party you can't participate in. They knew nothing of our mundane day-to-day struggles, of our interminable working hours and the fatigue that was calcifying in our bones—to them, *we* were the luckiest guys in America, the ones who got to meet the babes and write the jokes that kept them entertained for an hour or two on the can every day, and they couldn't have suspected that every single one of us would have traded places with any of them in a heartbeat.

It is a truth universally acknowledged that strippers should not want to show preference for any individual customer—that all things being equal, all men behaving equally crudely, and all billfolds being equally sized, they should want to thrust their mounds underneath the noses of as many patrons as possible to maximize their payout. So what could account for the pair of dancers, a curvilinear brunette in a matching baby blue bikini top and panties and a blonde, equally well proportioned, in a sheer white nightie, who had attached themselves to our table? Or, more accurately, who had attached themselves to our as yet unintroduced friend and cohort Ethan, or even more accurately, who had attached themselves to either of his legs, while he hadn't extracted so much as a dollar from his pockets in many, many minutes? These women were not simply stripper gorgeous, they were legitimately gorgeous, and with every measurable unit of time that they spent in his frugal company, they were *losing money.* So it can be safely said that Ethan was one desirable man.

I didn't know for sure if he was handsome; asking a man to understand what makes another man desirable is like asking a dog to differentiate between lanthanides and actinides on the periodic table. What I do know is that he had the bushy eyebrows of Elliott Gould, the pencil-thin beard of Trotsky, the soulful watery eyes of Adam Sandler, the husky voice of a young Neil Diamond—am I making myself clear here? The kid had kike appeal, and it brought the ladies to him. So what if, as was rumored, he had a girlfriend out of town somewhere? Anybody who got over this much deserved it.

Besides, sometimes it worked to our favor, like when Ethan used his time with the strippers to negotiate a private show for all of us. Someone, from somewhere within Dennis Publishing, had been gracious enough to give us an additional $500 for the trip, and this seemed the best time to dispose of it. Lucky for Parker that money was endowed to us with the specific instructions that it be spent on him, or else we would have let him sleep straight through until morning.

"Bitchkoff," Gomez told me, "go get Parker." And I ran all the way back to his room and slapped at his pudgy white thighs until he woke up, and we hurried back to the club. Rejoining our group in an upstairs room outfitted with Styrofoam soundproofing and opaque blackout curtains, we formed a semicircle around the two strippers as they danced for us and often on us. And the production was undeniably winning, in the way that a woman trying to make you come in your pants by grinding her knee into your crotch always is. Also, it was educational: I learned that in this scenario you can take incriminating photographs with a disposable camera, even when one of the strippers tells you to stop, and also that it is not frowned upon if you want to lick a girl's sternum, or suck on her nipple, or grab on to her ass. For the most part, our entertainers continued to focus on Ethan, but I was given a sufficient share of their attention, too. The blond one, in particular, was determined to make me drink some artificially colored alcoholic beverage from a test tube she had stuffed in her cleavage. Without explaining the process to me, she hoped to achieve this by placing the open end of the cylindrical glass shaft between my lips, then thrusting it into my mouth by squeezing her boobs together. Perhaps I was supposed to suck the shot down in a single gulp, but she jammed the pipe into my throat so forcefully that I couldn't take it all at once. I choked violently, and the liquid spilled out of my mouth, staining her nightie and my shirt.

"*Ucch*," she snorted. "Swallow it."

"Fuck you," I spat at her. "*You* swallow it."

The show effectively came to an end soon after that, but the ladies made it clear that for another $500 they would come back to our hotel for an even more private show, and for the sake of subtlety, let's just say that *blow jobs* would be involved. I thought we were being offered the best deal since the Louisiana Purchase, but no one was especially quick to respond, yes or no.

"Come on," I pleaded. "We've got to do this. I've got two hundred bucks right here in my wallet."

"Nah," Parker said. "I probably shouldn't."

"I've got an early flight tomorrow," Gomez concurred.

Not even Ethan could be swayed. "My girlfriend wouldn't like it," he said.

So we returned to our respective hotel rooms and went to bed for the night. If there was ever a more acceptable time in my life to jerk myself off to sleep, this was it, but for once I was too exhausted.

ON THE MORNING BEFORE my return flight, Harold and I found ourselves walking along the docks at the city's southeastern edge. In these earliest hours after dawn, he hadn't bothered to comb the remaining patches of hair on his head, leaving them to extend in every direction, because, as he joked, "I don't want anyone to know I'm going bald."

"How are you liking the job so far?" he asked. He was the first person in eight months who wanted to know.

"It's all right, I guess," I replied.

"From where I sit," Harold said, "you seem to be adjusting to it extremely well."

"I just wish I knew what people were thinking sometimes," I said. "It's impossible to tell if I'm accepted here or not."

"I was once the new guy, too, you know," he said. "And they were absolutely vicious to me. Every two words out of their mouths were 'Harold's mom.' 'Harold's mom is a slut,' 'I did Harold's mom' in this orifice, 'I did Harold's mom' in that orifice. It was the punch line to every single joke. They would send me e-mails, leave notes on my desk. I wouldn't let my mother call me at the office—I was so afraid of what they might say if they heard me talking to her. Honest to God, I used to go home from work each night and cry."

"But eventually you found your place, right? You got to know them better and they left you alone, right?"

"I didn't say that," Harold answered. He handed me his glasses, and with a running start, he jumped off a dock and dunked himself in the Mississippi River. Washed clean by the waters, he emerged with his clothes completely soaked through and the wisps of his wet hair clinging to his skull, looking like a vagabond, like a man who had no idea where he'd been or where he was going to next.

THE SCENE PLAYING OUT at every newsstand in every terminal of the New Orleans International Airport was surely being repeated at bookstores and magazine stores around the country: The first sight your eyes fell upon, whether you wanted to look at it or not, was row after row of *Maxim*, squealing out like a rat caught in a drainpipe, the gaudy primary colors of its cover helping it stand out easily against the sensible blues and mature grays of the competing men's titles that surrounded it. For all the effort we poured into the cover lines, it was always the photography that stopped you in your tracks, no matter how evolved you thought your brain might be: This month's cover featured not one but two women, clad in leather, one girl with her arm placed suggestively on the waist of the other, and if you tugged at it, the gatefold would open to reveal two more girls similarly arranged. Single men—men who were alone, whether or not they had girlfriends or wives—would approach the magazine cautiously, as if it were a steel bear trap, walk around it, past it a couple of times, then grab it in a flash before anyone else could see; then they would bend back the cover and comfortably comb through the interior pages. Teenage boys would peruse it unabashedly, then maybe buy the copy they had inspected or leave it in the wrong rack, next to *Thrasher* or *Guitar World* or *Electronic Gaming Monthly*. Women would buy *Maxim*, too, perhaps for someone else or perhaps for themselves, to help them better understand the men in their life, but who knows why women do anything? A black woman with a copy of *Ebony* under her arm, with her husband and adolescent son in tow, excitedly grabbed a *Maxim* and began hunting for the monthly feature in which our art assistant Hiroki reviewed microwavable cuisine. "I just love that little Oriental boy," she said. And through their plane rides and layovers, while waiting for loved ones or luggage to arrive, they were all engrossed in, or occupied by, the magazine, before they tossed it in a trash can or accidentally left it in the elastic compartment of the seat in front of them, stuffed between the flight safety card and the airsickness bag. These were our people.

FIVE DAYS LATER we were on our way to Ottawa for Parker's wedding, Harold and Ethan, Max and Alicia, and myself, sandwiched into a rented van for a seven-hundred-mile tour of the least scenic strip malls and corporate parks in these United States. But nothing makes one appreciate America more than arriving in Canada, the global equivalent of the dorkiest kid in class. Having long ago applied the metaphorical masking tape to the bridge of its national spectacles and accepted its loser status, Canada's capital city had set aside the same weekend in which the nuptials were scheduled for the commemoration of the one-hundredth birthday of Britain's Queen Mother; while we spent our Saturday morning schlepping in search of camera batteries, we were treated to a series of military processionals in the city's streets, intended to demonstrate that Canada still has a standing army, and it swears its allegiance to the figurehead monarch of an island nation three thousand miles away, whose mom was now old enough to have seen two world wars and four *Star Wars* in a single lifetime.

We'd had the whole day to prepare ourselves for the ceremony yet managed to miss it almost entirely. As we drove from our lodgings in the center of town to the church located on its outskirts, the views from our car windows devolved from civic centers to farming country so incrementally that we hardly noticed when we found ourselves ten miles deep in Canadian cow town. We turned around, located our destination, and tucked ourselves into a rear pew just in time to witness the happy couple saying their I-dos, standing before a priest who would come out of the closet a few months after presiding over the service. But Parker had done it—he had gone through with it as promised, and somewhere in America, Jim Kaminsky was out $200.

As everyone assembled on the church's front lawn, we kept to the back of the crowd, hoping to disguise our glaring lack of a gift for the newlyweds (it was—honestly—still on order from the registry); but Parker received us graciously, genuinely pleased to see the few of his colleagues who had bothered to give up a day of work and make the trip. His most ardent appreciation, however, was bestowed on our editor in chief, Keith, and his wife, Leslie, surprise arrivals who had flown in from New York that morning, and at times the whole observance felt like a tribute to our new boss and the uncomplicated domestic existence he maintained in suburban New Jersey, perhaps the only portrait of stability Parker had seen since coming to work for *Maxim*. Absent our group, the groom's party consisted of his immediate family, two Princeton roommates, a high school friend, and a cousin from Norway; it was a rogue's gallery of groomsmen who looked especially uncomfortable sitting at the elevated dais at the reception dinner, held in the ballroom of a former imperial palace that had since been converted into a luxury hotel. And if there wasn't a single piece of memorable oratory delivered by any of them during the meal, there was the spectacle of Parker's new wife stifling her sobs while admiring the stately affair he'd provided for her. "Every girl dreams of being a princess in her castle," she bawled, "and today you've made my dreams come true." It was the schmaltziest crap you'd ever heard in your life, and Alicia and Max were naturally reduced to tears by the sentiment.

We had made a commitment of our own to Parker, that we would stay and celebrate with him until the bitter end, but once we'd gotten over the novelty of the custom that dictates the bride and groom must kiss each other every time we rang our wineglasses with our spoons, and when we'd seen Keith and his wife toss pieces of bread at each other for about a half hour, we were bored. One by one, my four traveling companions got up from our table and migrated to a darkened corner of the ballroom, and I decided to follow.

"What's going on?" I asked.

Max reached into her purse and handed us each a single white pill, about the same size and consistency as generic aspirin. "This," she informed me, "is Ecstasy, and we're going to take it."

"We wanted to invite you," Ethan explained, "but we weren't sure how you would react." Understandably, I was shocked— shocked that my friends would assume I'd never done it before, even though I hadn't, and shocked that they'd conclude I'd be afraid to try it, even though I was. And while I probably could have come up with a dozen cogent reasons why someone with a family history of drug abuse should not consume a highly potent controlled substance at a close friend's wedding party, my curiosity and my outrage compelled me to pop that pill in my mouth and swallow it whole.

Max smiled at me. "Welcome to the summer of love," she said.

The next several minutes were spent staring at our watches and into one another's eyes, waiting for the drug's effects to kick in. Not knowing what to expect, I could feel my pulse fluctuating rapidly, partly from the amphetamines that the Ecstasy had been cut with and partly from my apprehension that I would be the one person in a million who had an unpredictable, adverse reaction to it, the one who dropped dead on the spot, the one whose senseless passing would prompt headlines like STUPID JEW DIES IN EXPERIMENTAL DRUG BINGE; BEREAVED PARENTS ASK, "HOW COULD HE DO THIS TO US?" And then I became utterly convinced that these were my last moments to live, and my heart was going like mad and *no* I thought to myself *no I mustn't no* and then—

Well.

The annals of recreational drug use are littered with forgotten pharmaceuticals that have tarnished the experience by failing to live up to their street names, but Ecstasy is not one of them. Once it takes effect, the high is so profound and all-encompassing that I can only describe it as religious—with just a single dose I wanted to rededicate my life to proselytizing its good deeds and converting the uninitiated. What if I told you that there existed a pill that would allow you to comprehend euphoria at the molecular level, that would let you feel every nerve ending in your body simultaneously and translate the slightest touch against your skin, by woman or by man, into the greatest, most relaxing sensation you had ever felt—would you take it? And if I said that this drug would take all the anxieties and social dysfunctions you've been harboring and melt them into ether, and let you enjoy loud Top 40 music and group sex and shiny, pulsating lights with equal gratification—would you want to try it? And if you knew there was a .01 percent probability of sustaining permanent spinal damage from ingesting it, would you still want to take it? Hell, even if there were a 78 percent chance of suffering a stroke and a 99 percent possibility that two of your limbs would fall off, would you still be interested? You're goddamn right you would.

"Wow," I said. "Wow. Wow." My partners in crime laughed approvingly, each of us experiencing the onset of the drug differently—Alicia and Max carelessly holding each other's hands for comfort, Harold and Ethan stumbling over themselves as they discarded their ties and loosened their collars. What I wanted to do most of all was make a phone call to my parents: I wanted to tell my mother and father that everything was going to be okay, that whatever had transpired between us was in the past, and that as human beings we could move forward, learn to help one another and love one another—that maybe one day, when they were ready for it, they could take the same trip I was currently on—we'd all do it together, and we'd all be able to see into one another's souls with the same degree of clarity I was now enjoying. Then I realized these were precisely the sorts of things my father used to say to us when he got high.

Before I could find a phone, however, I was gripped by another impulse—a rush of blood to my bowels that had me sprinting madly for the nearest bathroom. I was being reborn, and now I was going to waste the earliest minutes of my second infancy sitting on the toilet. After finishing, I charged out of the men's room and collided with Keith, who was on his way in. "Hey, sorry about that," he said, apologizing for doing nothing wrong.

"Hey, Keith," I gasped. I was gulping down air and trying to bite my front teeth with my lower jaw. "I gotta say, I think it's fantastic that you came out to Parker's wedding. It says a lot about you. You know, you've got a group of guys working for you who would do just about anything for you. You really saved us, you know that? I mean, we built this magazine with our hands—all of us did—with our blood and our sweat. It's in us, it's a part of us. We want it to succeed. And we want *you* to succeed. Sure, maybe we have some problems, but once we get them worked out, nobody's gonna be able to stop us. It's gonna be awesome. It's—it's just gonna be awesome."

Keith nodded at my every word as if it all meant something. "I know, man, I know," he said, placing his hands on my shoulders. "But I really have to take a piss."

Back inside the ballroom, I spotted Max standing at the perimeter of the dance floor and propped myself up against her spindly frame for support. "You're really enjoying this, aren't you?" she asked.

My fingers were making only a microscopic amount of contact with her waist, but with the sensation magnified by a factor of one million, it was at once more pleasurable than the most deviant sex act I had ever engaged in. "Could I ask you a question?" I said to her. "Would you make out with me? It wouldn't have to mean anything. I just want to see what it feels like."

"No!" she shrieked. "I am *not* going to make out with you. Why don't you go find Alicia?" I had been shot down, yet the rejection stung not even one tiny bit. It was comical—I actually felt better about myself for having asked and having been turned away. Boy, if only life were really like *this*!

Max was right, though—it *would* be fun to share this with Alicia. But the ballroom had become a demolition derby of sweaty guys, slam-dancing groomsmen colliding into one another, and aged husbands momentarily freed from their drunken wives making spastic, fist-shaking motions in an effort to keep up with the youngsters. Occasionally I'd see Alicia's head bob up, looking lost in her own universe, the makeup melting off her skin and a plastic glow-in-the-dark band wrapped around her head as if it were a crown of laurels. Surrounded as she was, I could not bring myself to approach her—I was living through every depressing bar mitzvah celebration, every miserable high school social, all over again, except that this time I was tripping my face off.

Finally, somebody invited me to take a whirl around the room, only it was my boss's wife. "You wanna dance?" Leslie demanded, one of her eyelids half-shut and the other fluttering wildly. She stood a good foot and a half shorter than Keith, but she was a compact powerhouse of a woman whose itty-bitty body had carried two children to term and cranked them out into the world. She had trained the well-behaved tots almost as perfectly as her husband, who had an uncanny sense for when Leslie was about to call him and would smother his phone as if it were a live grenade whenever he suspected she was on the line. If Keith couldn't fight her, what chance did I have?

"I don't really like to dance," I argued unconvincingly.

"C'mon," she persisted. "What're you, shy?" With the conviction of someone who knew shy when she saw it, she grabbed me by a floppy arm and pulled me onto the dance floor.

Now I realize that I am not arriving at a deep anthropological insight by stating that a dance shared between a man and a woman is not merely about arrhythmic gyrations poorly timed to some prefabricated pop song—it is a means of gauging a potential partner's attraction to you while communicating your own level of interest. If Leslie understood this as well, she expressed herself by gently placing a hand on each of my buttocks. Like a divining rod desperately pointing the way to sustenance, my body responded in the only way it knew how.

"Leslie," I whispered, "you're going to get me fired."

"Loosen up," she said. "Do you think Keith cares?" She pointed to her husband standing among the wallflowers. He was smiling pleasantly at us while I did my best not to grind my erection into his wife's pelvis. So I dropped my resistance and let my hands find her hips, let them work their way lower and lower along her body, waiting for a cry of "*Stop it!*" that never came. And somewhere in Parker's wedding album, there is probably a photograph of me dancing with Leslie, me with my tousled hair and my fogged-up glasses, she practically falling out of her dress, both of us looking like hell, with the devil in our eyes. But between the two of us, only I can legitimately claim that I was under the influence of a synthetic psychoactive neurotoxin.

My good name and my livelihood were rescued by Max's timely intervention, by her forcibly inserting herself between Leslie and me at the start of the next song. I was set free to explore the crowd in my state of cosmic awareness, to ricochet indiscriminately from Max and Leslie, who wanted to playfully assault me with their rear ends; to Ethan and Harold, who seemed not at all uncomfortable dancing with each other; to Parker, who in spite of everything was easily the most overjoyed person in the room, looking like a Chippendales dancer, stripped down to his tuxedo pants and shirt with the sleeves rolled up to his biceps; and, at last, to Alicia.

"Hey, baby," she said out of the corner of her mouth. "Having a good time?"

"I don't think I could possibly be any happier to see you," I said. I draped my weary, perspiring self around her, and she carried me around the room, slow-dancing to our own imaginary sound track, while she ran the tips of her fingers along my scalp to let me feel the electricity in her hands. "You wanna get out of here?" she asked me.

"You know it," I told her.

She put her hand in mine and hustled us out of the ballroom, past friends and relatives without so much as saying good-bye, past the hotel clerks and concierge, and out into the night, all the while our fingers tapping out coded messages to each other as we ran. It was not even ten o'clock, but the streets were empty, as if everyone in the entire country had gone to bed. Alicia sat at the edge of a fountain in the hotel courtyard, and though I could visualize myself tearing off all my clothes and diving in, I stopped short at peeling off my shoes and socks and dipping my toes in the coin-filled pond.

"I'm mad at you, you know," she said, watching the fountain jets shoot streams of water into the air.

"What? Why?"

"I don't understand why Max and I weren't allowed to come to the bachelor party."

"Alicia, may I point out that I am higher than I have ever been before? Is this really the best time to bring this up?"

"Well, I'm sorry, but we're both really pissed off about it."

"Who says I'm the one that makes the rules? It's a bachelor

party—that means no women allowed. If you don't like it, take it up with the other guys."

"I'm not taking it up with the other guys. I'm taking it up with *you*. I don't think of you like the other guys, all right? I thought you were better than that."

"Let me explain something to you: I am not better than anyone else. I am not sweet, and I am not caring, and I am not special. I'm just a guy, okay? And I'm just like every other guy you've ever known. Nothing more."

She was silent, except for the sound of her teeth grinding against themselves. "So that's it, then? So I guess I don't mean anything more to you than anyone else in that office? I'm just another coworker who goes in and out of your life?"

Under the cover of Ecstasy, it was tempting to admit that she meant so much to me that I would have been willing to give up my life for her—and that I almost did—and that at this moment I would have liked nothing more than to bury my face between her legs until the Québécois were given their own independent state. "This job is meaningless," I told her. "It has been a waste of time since the day I showed up, and every time I think it's going to get better, it gets worse. But if having met you is all I get out of it, then it was worthwhile, and I'm a better person for it."

"You really mean that?" she asked.

I thought I did, so I nodded yes.

"C'mere, babe." She reached out and lowered my head into her lap. "Do you like Leonard Cohen?" she asked.

"I don't know his music that well," I said, turning over to look up at her. "It's kind of a gap in my education."

"That's too bad." We had all of Canada to ourselves, and as she continued to tickle my scalp, Alicia started to sing:

> *Everybody knows that the dice are loaded*
> *Everybody rolls with their fingers crossed*
> *Everybody knows the war is over*
> *Everybody knows the good guys lost*

Everybody knows, everybody knows
That's how it goes
Everybody knows

I know that Leonard Cohen songs are supposed to sound ominous and frightening, but when you are high and someone you are deeply attracted to is massaging your temples and singing them to you, they're just sublime. Try it for yourself sometime and tell me if you disagree.

The passage of my life can be measured out in missed opportunities and misread signals, in women who, at a certain time, might have gone out with me or gone down on me, if only I had been a different person in those circumstances. Those circumstances made me the person I am, and they are the regrets I will carry, and occasionally masturbate to, for the rest of my life. Just this once, though, I was content to let the moment slip past me, knowing there was nothing to regret because there was no more intimacy to be gained. I didn't know how much further she would have been willing to go, and I didn't need to know. She was fully clothed, and she was showing me everything.

"We should probably go find everyone else," Alicia said, and we put our wet feet back into our socks and shoes and walked back to the hotel.

"Hey, do people have sex on this stuff?" I wondered.

"I can't see how," she said. "It's supposedly really difficult for guys to get it up while they're high."

"Oh, I wouldn't be too sure of that."

The festivities had since been relocated to Keith's hotel suite, and I couldn't even tell you how Alicia and I knew this or how we found ourselves there. Harold, Ethan, and Max were sitting cross-legged on the carpeted floor, while Leslie had tucked herself into bed and Keith had stripped down to just a T-shirt and boxer shorts. The air was thick with marijuana smoke, and Keith's eyes were squinty and pink with blood. I'd picked up hints from his behavior that he was a man who enjoyed a rich, satisfying toke—his proficiency with paper clips, his encyclopedic recall of the lyrics of Steely Dan—but I had never before seen him in action while he was stoned, and he was a markedly improved person. The closet comedian inside of him was unleashed, and everything he saw or touched became the subject of a comic riff. He was dynamic, alert, and clever—the complete opposite of what every other human being on earth becomes when they smoke pot—and the rest of us sat in rapturous amazement at the recital of his marijuanalogue.

On a thin hotel pen Keith found lying next to his telephone: "This pen is the perfect size and shape required for rolling joints. Do you think the people who designed this hotel were secretly stoners? I bet that all the lamps in this room are bongs in disguise."

On a tiny pair of high-heeled pumps that Max had crammed her feet into: "You can tell this shoe must have been designed by a man, because it's actually a portable torture device. If you want to see conclusive proof that men really hate women, just take a look at women's shoes."

On a basket of multicolored candies sitting on his minibar: "What if you were a superhero, but your only power was being able to tell what flavor a candy was before you tasted it? You have teammates who can fly, who have X-ray vision—you can look at a green candy and tell whether it's apple or watermelon. When is that ability going to be useful?"

I had to believe that Keith and Leslie were the coolest married couple in the world. Right now their children were safe in the hands of grandparents or a baby-sitter, safe in the belief that their mom and dad were loving caregivers and reliable providers, while their parents were getting drunk and smoking dope and partying in their pajamas with a bunch of E'd-up guests a decade their junior. They had it all, and I cursed myself for all the years I'd spent in fear of drugs, carrying a needless and prudish aversion to the tools we give ourselves to cope with our intermittently underwhelming and overwhelming lives, all because of one guy who couldn't find a middle ground between abstinence and excess.

As we left Keith's room, we were crashing pretty hard. Ecstasy is a tough drug to come down from, not just physically, but spiritually: One moment you are having the absolute best time of your entire life, and the next you're having only the second best, and the degree of difference between the two states is immeasurable, and it is crushing. When you know that you have it within you to experience that heightened state of bliss, how can you stand to look at the world as it is, without that enhanced perception, without that special shine, ever again? Harold did not even have the strength to get himself into bed—he paused to rest on the floor, and that was where his evening came to an end. For all the carnality that had been in the air and in our serotonin receptors that night, none of us had benefited from it. When I woke up around noon the next day, everyone was sound asleep in his or her respective bed, except for Harold, who was still on the floor.

There was a farewell breakfast scheduled for the new Mr. and Mrs., before they departed on their honeymoon hike across the Appalachian Trail, where Parker and his wife would consummate their marriage as jagged rocks poked her in the ass, but we had slept through it. There was nothing to do except pile back into the van and begin the return trip to New York, nursing the kind of hangover whose severity had not been seen since Sodom and Gomorrah were wiped off the map. In a manner known only to himself, Harold had somehow burst a blood vessel on his face and was sporting a black eye.

"How did that happen?" I asked him.

"I guess Ethan must have gotten rough with me when I tried to climb into bed with him," he joked.

"Boy, that was fun," I said, stating the obvious. "We should get together and do that more often."

"Eh," Harold said, shrugging. "I'm sure you figured out that wasn't my first time with it. And I know it seems hard to believe, but take my word for it, that stuff gets old." He reached into his pocket, thumbed through his wallet, and produced an obsolete student ID card that dated back to his abortive attempt at graduate school. He pointed to his faded picture, with his wide eyes and his long, hippie hair; I could practically smell the alternating layers of patchouli and body odor. "Now you can probably imagine the kind of trouble *that guy* got himself into," he said. "But you grow out of it."

Ethan drove the entire distance in a single eight-hour shift, without ever yielding the steering wheel, stopping for a bathroom break, or opening his mouth to speak. He allowed himself to violate this self-imposed vow of silence only once, at the Canadian border, as a customs officer conducted a routine inspection of our vehicle. Before letting us pass, she peered in through a window to see the five of us, depleted and baggy eyed, still wearing our soiled formal attire from the previous night.

"I bet you're all excited to be getting home," she said in her dopey Canuck accent.

"Lady," he told her, "we're fucking ecstatic."

9

SUCH, SUCH WERE THE JEWS

THERE ARE ONLY TWO THINGS IN THIS LIFE THAT FRIGHTEN me. One is the unfamiliar. The other is the familiar. Since I often don't trust myself enough to distinguish one from the other, it is my strategy in almost any situation to remain quiet until I can safely determine which of the two categories it falls into. But not everyone embraces this philosophy.

"Have you seen this shit?" Parker wanted to know. "I mean, have you *seen* it?" He had been away hardly a week, and he wasted no time in reasserting his presence. Toting an unpublished layout under his arm, he was making his way from one cubicle to the next as he proudly presented the pages to editor after editor, imperiously propping himself up on the front ends of his feet. Something we were about to print was evidently wrong, and he seemed both horrified and delighted to have discovered the flaw.

In a previous incarnation I had known, Parker was a man who could comfortably recount his liaisons with underclass coeds in painstaking, pornographic detail—it was he who had once taken me aside and explained to me the etymology and implementation of a sexual technique known as "the Jersey Meathook." With a wink and a smile, he could tolerate our jokes about his expanding girth, his sexual staying power, and the fidelity of his new wife. But what he could not stand to see in the pages of *Maxim* was a picture of a man in a skirt.

The image was part of a fashion spread scheduled to appear in our September 2000 edition; entitled "Rebellious Behavior," the feature had been photographed outside the dormitories of Princeton University (where else?), depicting a trio of models dressed in postmodern punk attire that would surely have sent old Scott Fitzgerald scrambling for his brandy snifter. Ordinarily, objecting to the impropriety of our fashion stories was as practical as protesting the clumsy mise-en-scène of the Zapruder film, but in this case, Parker felt he had a valid complaint with the sixth and final photo in the sequence: a young man with a distant look in his one eye not obscured by his tousled hair, with tattoos on both biceps, wearing a cutoff Smiths T-shirt, a sterling silver choker necklace, and a checkered kilt valued at $695. With its precarious mix of the sacred and profane, its delicate juxtaposition of Gothic architecture and Gothic rock stars, of androgyny and our alma mater, the picture had raised many issues that Parker was not prepared to confront. Or, as he summed up the circumstances, "It's a guy in a *fucking skirt.*" The honeymoon was over.

A few months into Keith's editorship, there were all kinds of evidence both numerical and empirical at our disposal to confirm that his first issues of *Maxim* were the most successful we'd ever produced. There were a dozen different ways of interpolating the data in the "pink sheets," the salmon-colored pages produced by the Audit Bureau of Circulations and distributed to our desks at regular intervals, to prove that we were connecting with the public. In every possible category, using every possible method of bringing in uninitiated readers—newsstand sales, Internet sales, direct-mail sales, sales from those goddamned subscription cards that we stuck in every sixth page of the magazine—we were seeing huge increases. We could look at our own pages and see layouts that looked brighter and more attention grabbing, articles that felt more relaxed and less oppressive, cover girls who seemed classier, who had absolutely nothing to gain by appearing in our publication, yet who wanted to get their clothes off as eagerly as we wanted to see them come off.

Our working hours were also on the rise. To combat this trend, Keith had introduced a new word to our vocabulary: *triage*. "I know you guys want to slave over every story, over every sentence, until you get it just right," he explained to us at an emergency planning session, "but you have to set that impulse aside if you ever want to get out of here at a reasonable hour. Just do the best you can—do what needs to be done—and then move it along." It was easy for him to say: He didn't have to read the raw copy that came in from our freelancers, from the aspiring screenwriters and failed stand-up comedians who'd never before been paid for their work, who now earned their livings supplying us with one-hundred-word assignments turned in at one thousand words, or incomplete, with postscripts that apologized, "Sorry I couldn't think of a way to end this," or so overrun with innuendo that it assaulted even our immodest sensibilities. He didn't have to witness the vision of *Maxim* reflected back to him in the rough language of its own contributors, at $1, $1.25, $1.50 a word—and cringe.

Still, we looked to Keith as a role model of efficiency and professional impartiality we could only hope to live up to. In these same short months, he'd already seen all his goals for the magazine fulfilled; he had realized his dreams of publishing the *Maxim* salary survey and the car feature and had been entertaining thoughts of creating a column, called "Turkey Talk," written from the perspective of guys who had undergone potentially life-changing experiences—the near death of a father, the unplanned pregnancy of a girlfriend—though this concept would ultimately never appear in print. Keith had achieved this while maintaining a strict regimen of arriving to his desk at ten a.m. each morning, taking a modest one-hour lunch at one p.m., and departing precisely at six p.m. every day, four days a week, except on Wednesdays, when he didn't come in at all. This last habit of his we could forgive: He had his wife, his kids, his novel, and an understandable aversion to the drudgery that essentially comes with producing two hundred pages of variations on the old "size matters" joke every single month. It was just a personality quirk of his, like the way he wore his sweaters tucked into his pants when the weather turned cold or the way he was too bashful to tell his barber not to cut his hair so short.

Besides, he had proven to be infinitely more approachable and obliging than his predecessor. He ran his editorial meetings more like open mike nights, where everyone was encouraged to chime in with spontaneous one-liners, if not actual story ideas, to layer joke upon joke in a towering, teetering pile until Keith toppled it with one last, grimace-inducing gag of his own. And how could the man not have an open-door policy? The space he worked from had no doors to close. When Parker delivered the offending photograph to his desk, we could not hear what the two were saying as they discussed it, but we could see, through their reciprocation of nods, chin scratches, and emphatic slaps against khaki-covered thighs, that an agreement was being hammered out. And when Parker returned from their conference, it was with all the pride of a fourth-grader who had just been elected hall monitor that he announced the ruling to us: "Keith said that he's going to get the picture taken out." And we believed it, until some weeks later, when we saw the photo of the model and his kilt in the September 2000 issue, intact and unaltered.

"I don't understand it," Parker said despondently, as if this potential outcome had not even crossed his mind. "Keith assured me this would never make it into the magazine."

"Maybe he tried to get it changed, but he wasn't allowed to," I said.

"Yeah," Parker said. "Or maybe he didn't try at all."

Or maybe he knew that the din of any conflict waged for too long within the company would eventually reach the ears of Felix Dennis.

Stately, plump Felix Dennis of London, England, the founder and chairman of Dennis Publishing, had lately taken up residence in *Maxim*'s New York office. At a little over a half century old, he was silver haired with wonderfully woolly whiskers, but he was seldom jolly. His appearance in the building could be interpreted as a sign that someone was in trouble, but more often it meant that we were all in trouble, because he wanted our attention, and he invariably received it. He would begin each morning by strutting into the editorial pen, his belly peeking out over the equator of his pin-striped pants and forever denying his lowest shirt button the pleasure of its corresponding buttonhole, to instigate a rhetorical assault that could not be—and was not meant to be—defended against:

"Does anyone have a copy of *The Elements of Style* I can consult? What? *No one* here has a copy of *The Elements of Style*? How do you put out a magazine without *The Elements of Style*? You people call yourselves *writers*? Do you understand how fortunate and privileged you are? In my day, we didn't have all this technology to make magazines for us—we did it with our minds, with our ingenuity. Sometimes I think I'd like to take away all your computers, just to prove to you that it really can be done. We don't need all these machines—and we don't need all these *editors*. You think all this time you spend rewriting people's stories makes them one bit better? You're just mucking about with *words*. Do you think anyone who reads this magazine notices? We could print these stories exactly as they're submitted to you and it wouldn't make a bit of difference. Not one bit."

Sated, he would return to the modest corner office he allowed himself on our floor. When Felix was not in town, this same grotto served as a makeshift war room where we gathered to draft the cover lines that Felix would eventually end up rewriting himself, where we racked our brains thinking up the names of women who might consider appearing in the magazine, where if you said the same woman's name enough times, no matter how famous or chaste or out of reach she might seem, she eventually began to sound like a viable candidate. Among the room's scattered decorations— a framed poster advertising a Josephine Baker performance; a wooden toy called Pandora's Box, designed to fall to pieces should anyone open its lid—my favorite was a photograph of a smiling, dapper Felix taken in 1971, at age twenty-four, before his hair took on its steely, pubic consistency, when his oversize noggin could barely be supported by his then tiny body and the tiny world it inhabited.

This was Felix Dennis, high school dropout and son of a broken family, when he was the business manager and coeditor of *Oz*, a journal of antiestablishment essays and pop art that was the essential periodical of the British counterculture. Published out of a London flat, *Oz* was a low-budget, high-energy affair, a venue in which a reader was as likely to find a review of the new Marshall McLuhan book or an exposé on Scientology as a feature entitled "The Disgusting British Breasts Competition" or "How to Drop Acid." The magazine's fuck-all sensibility took a full twenty-eight issues to reach its apotheosis in June 1970, when Felix and his partners, Richard Neville and Jim Anderson, turned the publication over to a group of high school students.

Wrapped in a cover bearing an erotic illustration ripped off from the artist Raymond Bertrand, the "School Kids Issue" of *Oz* was an incendiary document—to hold a tattered, yellowing copy of it in your hands today is to grasp a pop cultural artifact as radical as an original pressing of Elvis Presley's "That's All Right" or a reel of celluloid from *Deep Throat*. Its contents had been created almost entirely by a panel of adolescents between the ages of fifteen and eighteen, who began the issue with short, self-effacing biographies of themselves. (John, sixteen: "Circumcised but not Jewish. Finds atmosphere at school impersonal and oppressive. Thinks the headmaster is bullied by the rest of his staff." Anne, sixteen: "Says she is a bitch. Hates her parents, turns on regularly . . . will conform to anything as long as she gets something out of it.") Some poor taste was exercised in places (hand-drawn cartoons of school headmasters jerking off and molesting their pupils; a pull-out poster of a parochial girl labeled "Jailbait of the Month"), but it was vastly outweighed by articles written by the students themselves, in which they decried blind obedience to grown-up morality and contemplated the consequences of the few methods of stimulation available to them. One female contributor wrote, "I shall never forget the look of horror on people's faces when one girl lost her virginity at the age of 13, under a tree in the park." Another author, identified only as "G.B.," expanded on these themes in a piece called "Weekend Dropout":

> There's a certain satisfaction in having one's future nicely tied up and sealed off so that you can leave it and wallow in total abandon from Friday night to Monday morning and still have the deep-down security of knowing it's there . . . Blowing your mind on a sunny day, not knowing where or who you are, or caring anyhow, can be great fun . . . What happens when you come down with a blinding headache, throwing-up uncontrollably, and there's noone sufficiently tied to you to care what happens to you?

The rest of the issue was filled out by the usual advertisements for such products as "the first portable massager uniquely shaped to body contours" and a pill that promised "a sound and successful method of improving virility, and increasing the size of the male organ." But *Oz* #28 had made its mark. It had successfully captured the fragile voice of an uncertain generation in its own authentic language, with minimal pandering and an outright absence of condescension. It was perhaps the last genuinely cool thing Felix Dennis would produce.

It also got him thrown in jail. In 1971, he and his coeditors were arrested on charges of obscenity and corrupting the morals of British youth. Though Anderson and Neville were sentenced to prison terms of twelve and fifteen months, respectively, Felix got off with just nine, because he was deemed by the presiding judge to be "very much less intelligent than his fellow defendants." But by this time the lengthy trial had transformed the *Oz* three into icons of the revolutionary youth. They were swiftly bailed out by an army of supporters that included John Lennon and Yoko Ono, and their convictions were overturned on appeal.

While his two partners faded into psychedelic obscurity, Felix continued to work in the British media, publishing magazines about Bruce Lee (the "wonderful Chinaman who beat people up," as Felix called him in his obligatory *Vanity Fair* profile), and personal computers, and, finally, the lifestyles of young men. In doing so, he became one of England's hundred wealthiest citizens and amassed assets that included estates in New York, Connecticut, and Stratford-upon-Avon, as well as a house on the private Caribbean island of Mustique that once belonged to David Bowie. He'd also earned the right to command the attention of the *Maxim* staff whenever he wanted it and to have the last word on any aspect of the magazine's composition. It was he who had carved up Keith's "Turkey Talk" proposal before it ever had a chance to strut its stuff in the magazine. It was he who had lifted its very title from satirist Hilaire Belloc's couplet, written in honor of that great destructive implement of British colonial power: "Whatever happens we have got / The Maxim Gun, and they have not." The magazine, like the firearm, may have made for an awfully unsporting competitor, but Felix no doubt appreciated the name because it smacked of erudition while placing a giant letter X at the top of every cover.

In his later years, as he fought health problems brought on by crack cocaine abuse and other hedonistic pursuits, his money also bought him the freedom to cultivate some truly enviable eccentricities. He liked to sign his faxed communiqués as "the Bearded One" and bragged to us that he had engaged only in "nonpenetrative sex" for the past several years. He had claimed to one reporter that he was "the only survivor of Legionnaires' disease you will ever see" and to another that if he contracted lung cancer, he would "die by an overdose of crack cocaine with an eighteen-year-old perched on top of me." Occasionally, he would ask us to introduce features in *Maxim*—pheromone strips secretly applied to the pages, pictures of celebrities with their ethnicities digitally altered ("What if Gwyneth Paltrow were black? What if Jennifer Lopez were white?")—that we had to quietly ignore until he had forgotten about them.

Yet Felix was a master at getting you to listen to him, at getting you to buy whatever he was selling. For all his scrutiny of the magazine's interior pages, he worked us hardest of all on the cover lines and forced Keith to forsake all his other responsibilities until they were perfected, because he knew that each modification—a deliberately disingenuous double entendre, a judicious use of the word *exclusive*, a light sprinkling of exclamation points and three-digit numerals—could translate into another hundred thousand purchases. Felix was the quintessential maxim man, forever filling our heads with motivational slogans and nimbly reducing the complexities of the publishing industry to individual sentences. "We're not selling sex!" he had decreed. "We're selling attitude! We don't need to sell the magazine back to the subscribers! They've already bought it! Don't you understand? *It's all about the floating voters!*"

And because he genuinely knew the name of every person on his payroll, Felix Dennis happened to be the second-richest person with whom I have ever interacted. (I once met Bill Gates.) On this visit, Felix actually wanted to talk to me, as he spied me skulking past his door one late night. "David!" he roared with a voice that rattled the walls. "Come in here at once!" He had the lights off, so that the room was illuminated only by the slivers of the setting sun that slipped in through the drawn blinds and the burning end of a hand-rolled Silk Cut cigarette. It was his preference to read in almost total darkness, and he was intently studying the pages of a publication, one that was not his own, that he slid across his desk and into my lap.

He peered at me over the tops of his bifocals. "I want you to tell me," he said, "what you think of this." It was an early American issue of *FHM*, the magazine whose success in Britain had resulted in *Maxim*'s creation and which had, in turn, been given a launch in the States thanks to *Maxim*'s rapid expansion. Just because *Maxim* was, as Felix liked to say, "first into the desert with a beer truck," it didn't mean we'd be the last: In the months ahead, *FHM*'s parent company would sell off nearly all the other titles it published and had already brought over Mike Soutar's successor from

FHM's British edition to run its American counterpart. These people were girding for war, stealing our battle plans point by point. Of course, as I thumbed through that copy of *FHM*, with all its odd, unfunny British slang still intact, I began to see just how much we had stolen from them, too.

"Honestly?" I answered Felix. "Where do I begin? The paper stock smells weird. The photography is ugly, and the airbrushing is preposterous. I don't recognize any of these girls. The writing is terrible. The interviews are idiotic. The fonts are too small, the captions aren't funny, and the headlines don't even apply to what's going on in the articles. Anything I've overlooked?"

"Wrong," he said, yanking the issue back from my hands. "All wrong. I mean, *look* at it." He opened the cover and began turning the pages one at a time. "It's colorful. It's got lots of pictures. It's got lots of girls. There's a girl. There's a girl. *There's* a girl—she's quite a looker. There's a fellow with an alligator. Here's an adventure story, that's not a bad article. Here's some health advice, that's quite useful. It's got some laughs, it's got a joke page, it's got a bit of fun. Not a bad magazine. Not a bad magazine at all. Do not underestimate them." More easily than any other person on his staff, Felix could put himself in the place of his ideal reader—he understood what made his magazine unique, what it could do better than any of its competitors, and what it could offer readers to keep them loyal to its brand name: absolutely nothing.

JIM KAMINSKY'S thirty-nine-year-old back was a carefully calibrated piece of machinery, as deceptively simple as a Chinese finger trap and as unknowable as the tides, and like all the other works of man, it was on a set course toward an unrecoverable state of disrepair. He had thrown it out of alignment while playing with his baby boy—one moment he's giving the kid a horsey ride and the next he's on his ass—and had missed three days of work. It was a dispiriting sight to see his chair empty, even behind the stacks of cardboard boxes and piles of old magazines that kept it hidden; the time he spent recovering from the injury was more than he had taken off when his son was born. When Jim returned to the office, he returned as a reliable source of Vicodin, but also as a humbler, more circumspect man, whose dogged spirit had proven no match for the rickety vessel that contained it, whose future acts of charity would now be tempered with a sentiment of self-preservation. He would still offer to share cab rides home with me when we worked late, partly because he needed help getting in and out of the car and partly because he appreciated the company of someone whose sense of indignation was second only to his own.

"Do you realize that Keith has never spoken to me about this whole Wednesday thing?" he fumed on a drive up Sixth Avenue. "Not once. Never gave me an explanation, never told me, 'Hey, I don't come in on Wednesdays.' "

"He must know by now that you've figured this out for yourself," I said.

"Who knows what he knows?" he said. "He doesn't even tell me when he's going on vacation. I have to figure it out on my own. And I'm his executive editor. I'm his *second in command!*"

"Isn't that normal?"

"*Normal?*" The word exploded off Jim's tongue. "I've worked at a lot of magazines in my day. A *lot* of magazines. And you never totally get to choose the people you're surrounded with. You're always making do with the mistakes of all the other people who came before you. I didn't ask for this arrangement, and neither did Keith, but I'll tell you, I've never seen anything like this in my life." He sighed as he recalled that there were other magazines out there, beyond the one we worked for. "You heard from your old boss lately?" Jim asked.

"Mark, you mean? No," I said. "I think that line of communication is pretty much closed."

"Any idea what he's up to now?"

"Last I heard, he was the creative director for Moviefone."

"What is that? You mean the thing you call for movie listings?"

"I think they have a website, too."

"What do they need a creative director for?"

"I have absolutely no clue."

"Yeah, well, you'll see his name come up again, you can be sure of that. The next time somebody's looking to hire an editor in chief, I guarantee he'll be on the list. They always are. It doesn't matter how bad of a job you did. It's like being a placekicker in the NFL—there's only, like, thirty-five people in the world who can do the job. If you've been an editor in chief before, you can *always* be an editor in chief again. And if you've never done it, they'll never give you the chance."

"What about the guy at *Details*?" I said. The latest reworking of the men's magazine where my publishing career had begun was just now appearing on newsstands; with a cover bearing the likeness of a bare-chested Robert Downey Jr., an American flag tattooed above his left nipple, and the banner headline FIRST ISSUE, as if all previous versions before it had never existed, this *Details* was the creation of an editor who was only twenty-eight years old.

"Don't even talk to me about that," Jim said dismissively. "He's not younger than you, is he?"

"No, he's older. By about four years."

"Agh, why don't I just slit my wrists while I'm at it?" The taxi pulled up to the entrance of Jim's high-rise apartment building. "I've got to find something else to do," he grumbled, more to himself than to me. "I don't know how, but I've got to do it." As he carefully extracted himself from the car and slipped me some money for cab fare, Jim also offered me a free piece of advice: "Don't stay in this business forever."

THESE WERE SOME unusual talks, yet for futility and sheer awkwardness, they could not begin to match the phone conversations I was having with my father. He had been working again, reacquainting himself with a universe whose rules of operation he had completely forgotten in the time he'd been away from it, and was now calling me whenever he could not interpret them on his own.

"I had a nightmare about you last night," he says to me. I don't say anything in reply, but he goes on to describe it for me anyway. "You were yelling at me. You were saying that I had let you down, you know, that I had failed you as a father. When I woke up I realized it was just a dream, but it felt so real."

There is a long pause. "Do you expect me to apologize," I ask, "for something I did in a dream?"

"It's silly, I know. But like I said, it just felt so real." Another long pause. "You're still coming home for Thanksgiving, right?"

"Dad," I remind him, "when have I not made it home for Thanksgiving?"

"I know, I know," he says.

"When I was in college, didn't I come back every year?"

"You didn't come home for Rosh Hashanah."

"*What?* When have we *ever* celebrated Rosh Hashanah in this family?"

"We could if you wanted to."

"But I don't want to."

"I know, I know," he repeats. "It's just that the family hardly gets together anymore." This is true enough: With my sister away at medical school, it is now just my father and my mother and their ever expanding collection of pets, alone in that house. "Your brother is looking forward to seeing you," he jokes. (By this he is referring to the family dog.) "You can stay a few extra days in the house. Mommy can make up your bed, you can sleep there."

"What am I going to do all weekend? Watch you watch television?"

"Do whatever you like. It would be nice just to hear your feet shuffling around the house." There is such desperation in his voice that I am hoping he is high, because these words would be too sad to contemplate if he were sober.

"I don't know, Dad. I'll have to think about it."

Before I have answered in the affirmative, he adds: "And then you'll stay and live with me forever?"

"Hey, I just told you, I don't even know if I can stay the weekend. But I'm not moving back in with you. I have my own things I need to deal with."

"You think I don't know what you're going through?" he says. "I went through it, too. But we can be there for each other. We can help each other."

"I don't know what it is that you think I need help with. I don't think you remember who I am."

"I know who you are. I *am* you." He says it just like this and not the other way around. Then he waits for me to figure out what to say next.

"Well," I eventually say. "Good-bye."

YEARS AGO, MY MOTHER'S relatives had the good sense to move so far away from us that they were freed from further obligation to appear at family gatherings. Not so for my father's side, who had remained within kvetching distance of the Jewish enclave of Pelham Parkway, where they had grown up. In the past, our Thanksgivings had always been celebrated in the small Bronxville apartment of my father's parents; these were casual affairs, with decades of animus kept in check by the calming presence of two first-generation Americans who occasionally confused the names of their offspring, who had their own funny way of pronouncing words like *gorgeous* and *beautiful*, superlatives they denied their children but lavished upon their children's children. After my grandfather died, my grandmother died within the same year, and since then the rite had been in diaspora, with no permanent residence and nothing keeping it alive other than the unwavering belief of the family—of people who would not know the inside of a synagogue from the makeup counter at Bergdorf's—that the tradition, as sacred as any custom handed down to us by those nomadic sand people of five thousand years prior, must be preserved.

Now Thanksgiving was an annual observation of obstinacy, a battle of petrified wills in which the mere right to host the meal was first prize in this contest—not for social prestige or moral supremacy, but for the simple privilege of having something no one else could possess. The past ten rounds or so had gone to my father's older sister, and the reason had less to do with the spacious Park Avenue penthouse in which she resided than with her husband, the man who had bought it for her. When he was about my age, my uncle walked into the jungle of commercial real estate, and when he walked out, by God, he was rich—the kind of rich where you didn't have to worry about fluctuations in the price of raccoon skins to know where your next meal was coming from. He was also the only member of our clan to have facial hair, which he wore in a thick mustache that immediately marked him as the greatest traitor to the faith since the Rosenbergs. If these family assemblies made me anxious, they rendered my father apoplectic—imagine being so well-off that you possess more cars than children who are Ivy League graduates, and more refrigerators than cars, and you're *still* not the most successful man at the dinner table. But this year Uncle Mustache was at a disadvantage: He and his wife had been living out of a hotel room while they waited to move into a new apartment on Fifth Avenue, with an unobstructed view of the park, leaving them no choice but to hold Thanksgiving at our house. Now they were on *our* turf.

I was riding in the back of Uncle Mustache's Mercedes on the way to see my parents, taking the New York State Thruway like he wanted to and not the Palisades Parkway as I recommended, with his wife in the passenger seat and my cousin Mitchell sitting alongside me. Mitchell was nearly forty years old, with his own life and his own photography practice in Paris; when he and I are alone, we joke with each other about how lonely and celibate we are and how we expect that our circumstances will never change, but today we would hardly say anything to each other at all.

"Any new jobs this year?" Uncle Mustache asked me. It was sort of a running joke we shared—that every time I saw him, I was in the process of quitting one employer and joining another. I would be embarrassed that he brought this up, except that the joke was firmly rooted in the truth.

"Nope," I told him. "Still in the same place."

"That the magazine with all the girls in it?" he said. "Are you getting to do much writing?"

Boy, he sure knew how to ask the exact right questions to break my heart without anyone else in the car knowing it. "Not really," I said.

"Well, you're young yet. When you've got more life experience, you'll have more to say. You've got to write what you know." It was a funny lesson to learn from a man so wealthy that he could have—and had—paid humanities professors to lecture him on the lessons of their life experiences. "But you like working there, right?"

"Sure," I said, because the truth would have taken too long to recite.

"Then that's what counts. Do what you love and love what you do. That's what I always say."

"*When?*" asked his wife. "When have you ever said that?" I used to go to movies with her at the Angelika, until the rigors of sitting through art house lesbian sex scenes with my sixty-two-year-old aunt became too agonizing.

It had been so long since I last saw my parents that I feared they had lost the ability to clean up after themselves. Would we find ourselves wading in a sea of cat coughings and my father's discarded undergarments? Would my father be showered and shaven? Would he be wearing pants? To my surprise, the house was as tidy as it could be—floors swept, carpets vacuumed, the dining room table cleared of business invoices and credit card bills and properly set for a family meal. The piano, whose keys had not been struck since the day I moved out, had been optimistically dusted. The loose change and old newspaper delivery bags used to collect dog shit had been cleared off the coffee table and replaced with an array of *Maxim*s, furnished for the pleasure of our company with all the grace and dignity befitting the first folios of Shakespeare.

For the entire evening, my mother would exist only as a disembodied voice, constantly cooking, basting, carving, and cleaning in the next room over. But there, bounding down the stairs, was my father, all of him that I remembered and more, in his formal attire: a clean white undershirt and blue jeans rinsed free of the smell of fur. He offered me a jagged smile and a soft hello as he planted a kiss on my cheek, before going on to greet his other guests.

"How are you, Gerald?" Uncle Mustache asked him.

"Good to see you, Norm," my father answered.

If all you had to go by was the warmth with which these two men embraced each other, you'd never know that relations between them were once so badly strained that they could not be left in a room together—that the same hand now patting my father on the back had once been used to pen a letter to him, in which Uncle Mustache wrote that he never wanted to speak to him again. (Too bad for him my father lacked the attention span to read it all the way through before tossing it in the trash.) The same mouth my father had previously used to curse Uncle Mustache, his values, his summer home in Amagansett—that same opening from which two consecutive complete sentences could not emerge when I was speaking with him—would not remain shut for the rest of the evening, as he excitedly regaled my uncle with stories of his recovering fur business, and the two men traded aphorisms so simple and seductive, it would kill them to even contemplate the possibility that their empty proverbs were untrue.

"Anything that's easily done isn't worth doing," said Uncle Mustache.

"Live each day like it's your last," said my father, "because someday you'll be right."

Oy, Dad, why so grim? I wanted to ask him. But the easiest thing for me to do was sit and wait for dinner to be served, by which time a numbing, comfortable, ritualistic familiarity had set in. There was my inexhaustible seven-year-old cousin Alex, in a shirt I recognized as one of my old hand-me-downs. "I know that shirt!" I told him playfully. "It used to be mine."

Alex folded both arms across his chest to protect the garment. "It's *mine*," he said.

And there was his mother, my father's younger sister, known

during her teenage years as "Doobie," a nickname I could not fully comprehend until I went to college. "Alex just *adores* you," Aunt Doobie whispered to me. "You're all he ever talks about at home. He worships you. You're like the only man in his life." Her husband was seated within earshot as she said this.

Then we raised our glasses to the empty place setting for my absent sister, the family's own prophet Elijah, who would arrive at whatever hour she felt like, with whichever boyfriend she happened to be seeing at the time. And this, in turn, set up the special place I occupied in the liturgy.

"David, why don't you ever bring a girlfriend to Thanksgiving?" Aunt Doobie teased.

"He's just like you, Gerald," Aunt Mustache answered for me. "He's quiet."

Lady, if you would like to know what *he* is all about—he, who is sitting right here, by the way—why don't you just let him speak for himself? Why don't you let *him* explain that he has yet to meet a woman in all of New York City who does not intimidate the hell out of him—who is ready to believe him in the role of a mature individual—who does not make it abundantly clear, in her own way, that she could easily do better than him—who, come to think of it, does not inevitably remind him of *you*? Would you care to hear *him* tell you that he can't hold on to a woman long enough to invite her to one of your cockamamie get-togethers—that if his many insecurities couldn't drive her away, a few hours with you know-it-all *yentas* surely would? Or is it that you suspect *he* is a closet queer, and that while he is biting into his drumstick tonight he is secretly imagining it is his lover's tender ass, and that when he licks the gravy from his fingers, he is fantasizing that his tongue is wrapped around a nice thick cock?

How's that for quiet?

This formality has all been a prelude, however, to the evening's main event: a public hearing of the arguments in that landmark legal case *Gerald Itzkoff v. Everyone*. While the rest of us are worn out by the quantities of tryptophan and complex carbohydrates we have ingested, my parents are reenergized, my mother transformed into a dynamo of dish clearing and my father a dinnertime Clarence Darrow, ready to engage in a vigorous exchange of personal politics and revisionist family history. It is initiated harmlessly enough, when Aunt Doobie mentions the difficulty she is encountering in placing her son, Alex, into a private school.

"How d'ya like paying property taxes into a public school system, all just so you can send your kid to private school?" my father says, indifferent to his sister's plight. "*This* is what happens when you have an unelected board of education that's not accountable to *anybody*!"

"You know, Gerald," my cousin Mitchell gently attempts to interject, "it is possible the two problems aren't related to each other."

True to the debating style he taught me, my father offers a response that is amplified one hundred times out of proportion. "Ah, the great French Socialist speaks up! Have you *ever* heard of a system that rewards somebody for doing absolutely nothing—and that *worked*? Because don't tell me it works in France."

And now my father is on the verge of revealing what this argument—what every argument involving this family—is really about: "My father always said that Communism would fail, and he was right," he says.

"Not everything he said was right," sniffs Aunt Mustache, her voice just audible above the clinking of porcelain and stainless steel.

"He happened to be right about *this*," he says.

"Not about everything," she reiterates. "Was it right of him that he wouldn't let me go to college?"

"He never *stopped* you from going," my father counters.

"He didn't exactly encourage me. He never helped out financially."

My father can't wait to respond to this. Tell me, when were our people so patient that they could devote entire millennia to building the Pyramids? "If you wanted to go to college so badly," he says, "you would have found a way to pay for it yourself."

"If our father was so great," says Aunt Doobie, "then why was he so cruel to our mother?"

"How can you say that? If he didn't love her, then why didn't he just divorce her?"

"That's not the same thing. Just because he stayed with her, it doesn't mean he loved her."

"Did he ever leave her? Answer the question: *Did he ever leave her?*"

Again, Aunt Mustache: "I don't understand how you can stick up for a man who abused you the way he did."

"*Abused* me?" says my father in disbelief. "My father never abused me."

"Didn't he hit you?" she asks.

"Yes," he says, "but so did my mother. That's not abuse."

"Gerald," Uncle Mustache pipes up, "what else would you call it?"

Hey, not two minutes ago, weren't we just talking about *vouchers*? If these people want to see abuse, why don't they just look around the table? Why don't they get their heads out of their *goyische* delicacies, their candied yams and their cranberry sauce, to witness a man being flagellated before his entire family for the crime of loving his dead father? If he wants to remember the man as he might have been, instead of as he really was, why shouldn't he be allowed this one indulgence? And why doesn't he stick up for himself?

My father knows what this family is capable of—that the rest of us are as guilty of dissembling to one another and defrauding ourselves as he is. He knows our whole horrible history, of insults leveled and punches thrown, of money borrowed and loans left unpaid, of true loves lost and marriages of convenience, of relatives unacknowledged and uninvited, and still others left in hospitals and institutions on this very holiday. I know this, too, because he told it all to me, through night after night of those coked-up confessionals of my childhood, and you'd better believe I was too frightened to forget it. Was this appalling saga just one more product of his narcotic delusions? No—it was having to carry it around with him that drove him to drugs in the first place, that left him unable to express it to anyone but a tiny boy. That was how crazy it made him. Well, Dad, I'm here to tell you that you don't have to take it anymore. I know you've got it in you, old man—*now let them have it*! Because if you don't, sooner or later, *I will*!

But it's too late, the dinner is over. While my mother washes dishes, my aunts are trying to pump my sister for free medical advice, to learn if pharmaceutical science has discovered some new procedure that might prolong their lives for just five more years. My father is seeking counsel from Uncle Mustache for a lawsuit he will soon be facing. Outside the kitchen I am having my brains beaten in at chess by a seven-year-old prodigy. In the room the women come and go, talking of progesterone.

When everyone is crying—my aunts, my mother, my sister, my father—it is time to call it a night. Were I a human being capable of compassion, I would be crying, too—tears of pure delight, knowing that I am at the absolute furthest point in time before I will have to go through this again. My father finally notices that I did not arrive with any luggage.

"You're not staying?" he asks.

"No," I tell him. "I have to get home."

"But we hardly even got to talk."

"Whose fault is that?" I say, and the sheer, sadistic glee I derive from the look of disappointment on his face has made the whole visit worthwhile.

But there is a coda to this story that I will not learn about until several weeks later, when my father tells me that on his way out the door, the mercurial and easily offended Uncle Mustache stopped to castigate him about the proud and open display of *Maxims* around the house.

"How can you let your son work for this garbage?" he had complained.

"And what did you say to him?" I ask my father.

"What could I tell him?" he says. "I mean, we both know it's not a very good magazine."

"You could tell him anything," I say. "You could tell him it's just a phase. Tell him I'll grow out of it. Tell him someday I'm going to do something better."

"Yeah," he says, "I suppose I could have said that."

"Thank you," I say in resignation. "Thank you for coming to my defense."

Now imagine if these people weren't related to me.

10

BALLBUSTERS ON PARADE!

WHAT IS GOING TO GO WRONG THIS TIME? HOW COULD this night possibly be any different from all other nights? What single factor or set of combined factors will ensure that it ends like the previous ones? Will it be the pinched, twangy tenor of my voice? The beveled sheen of my surgically corrected nose or a single nostril hair suggestively dangling from it like a rope ladder? Those permanent, purple bags under my eyes, called eyelids, or the stray pimples I continue to get at the age of twenty-five? My tiny, underdeveloped body or the way I call attention to it with my slightly hunched posture? The creases in my pants, perhaps, or the way I sometimes wear white socks with brown shoes? The tattered condition of my wallet or the absence of money inside it? Am I more of a phony for having attended an Ivy League school or for preaching my present and continued aversion to it? Do I sound more pretentious for invoking the authors I only pretend to have read or for quoting from those I know by heart? Is it the job? Is it the particular magazine I work for that's so repugnant, or is the magazine industry repulsive enough on its own? My annoying laugh or my inability to pronounce the word *statistics* on the first try? Is it my radical politics? My unwillingness to give money to PBS, even for a tote bag, or my unwavering faith that Bernhard Goetz acted alone? My preference for staying at home or the faint panic I feel at the sight of a crowd? The excessive interest rates I charge for my moneylending services? Will I come off as so uncontrollably horny that the thought of physical intimacy with me seems grotesque or so sexually unthreatening that it seems ludicrous? Will I appear too self-involved or too silent? Too careerist or too shiftless? Will I be too passive? Too aggressive? Too passive-aggressive? Am I paying too much attention or not paying enough, and is it obvious that I'm paying attention to how much attention I'm paying? Is my lack of experience that transparent? Is it pheromones? Am I, unbeknownst to myself, emitting a chemical that preemptively radiates a message of failure to the opposite sex? And if not, why won't anyone just sit me down and explain to me what I keep doing to drive away the women?

Let us begin.

act one

THERE WERE, FOR REASONS that were never entirely clear to me, people whose fondest desire in life was to have an article published in *Maxim*. It was not an easy feat to see this fulfilled: It meant taking initiative, navigating past the magazine's unhelpful masthead page that provided no submission information, hoping your idea would end up in the hands of someone who would actually read it, and withstanding the disappointment of being told we'd already done it, were about to do it, or, most likely, none of the magazine's existing formats could accommodate it. I can't be sure if my colleagues replied to these queries, but I delighted in cutting them down by the dozens. When one prospective writer all the way from Oregon wanted to meet with me to have her ideas evaluated in person, I was happy to indulge—and happy to engage in a little professionally permissible cruelty.

This tiny girl had no business being in our break room, sitting opposite me at the same table where our receptionist ate her lunch, surrounded by bulletin boards decorated with year-old press clippings that commended *Maxim*'s sustained growth in circulation and advertising revenue. The light dusting of powder spread evenly across her face, her pursed lips, and her dainty features gave her the look of an antique porcelain baby doll, begging to be cradled and protected from the very real threat of falling to the ground and being smashed to pieces. What broke the illusion were her sizable breasts, even bigger in proportion to the rest of her compact body; stuffed into a black business dress and partially covered with her long blond hair, they were unavoidably the leading source of the attention—and embarrassment—she had garnered in her adult life. But those generous globes would not keep me from discharging my duty, which was to clarify for her why every one of her ideas was wrong, while she listened attentively. When the critique was over, she shook my hand and thanked me for my time, and I never expected to hear from her again.

Until the Baby Doll e-mailed me several months later to say that she had moved to New York to become a full-time writer, and would I like to meet up with her for a drink one evening? I had only the vaguest recollection of who she was, but I agreed anyway, directing her to the scummiest cantina I knew, located in the underground entryway of the grimiest subway station in the city, and making her wait for me to show up. I had been distracted from our appointment that night by the latest delivery of videos from a pornography studio that sent us care packages every month, gathered with my coworkers around a plain brown carton brimming with films called *Wall-to-Wall Balling* and *Black Dicks in White Chicks*, with cover art that featured their female stars smiling beatifically as their faces glowed with a commingling of bodily fluids. And we'd choke and cringe as each of the videotapes was passed around from one editor to the next, as each movie was rejected for being too disgusting to watch and relegated to a shelf for giveaway items—and within a week, all those videos would be gone.

The Baby Doll had since cut her hair short and dyed it a bright copper red, but she was unmistakable in a barroom full of men, still overdressed for the occasion and still stacked. Instead of scolding me for being late, she launched into an account of adversity as widespread in our industry as carpal tunnel syndrome. "Back in Oregon, I was publishing five articles a week in a major daily newspaper," she told me in a voice that was equal parts self-assurance and regret. "My editor begged me—*begged me*—to stay with him. But I had to find out for myself if I could survive here. If you're not getting published in New York, it doesn't count, right?" She had never considered a scenario in which you could be getting published in New York and it *still* didn't count; the thought had probably never crossed her singularly optimistic mind, spoiled as it was by parents who paid her for every pitch letter she composed, whether an editor accepted it or not, and a grandmother who was sponsoring her to quit smoking.

What she wanted from me were the details of my own perilous climb to the upper-lower-middle rung of the industry ladder, a story I was more than willing to relate. In this particular account, I was no longer the most self-loathing employee of a publication it was so easy to loathe. I didn't have to be the guy who once had blond highlights and an earring, who burned his bridges at the slightest provocation, who spent his college years frightening off any woman who expressed the most minute interest in him with his unrestrained, overzealous affection. She knew nothing about me other than what was immediately in front of her—in her eyes, I was the rising star to whom she could hitch her wagon, and if I could just project an air of complete confidence, *that's who I was.* Hell, I even got a hug from her at the end of the night, and I didn't buy her a single drink.

So I put an arm around her and pulled her next to me. When she didn't resist the move, I kissed her.

She remained silent for several seconds, the longest either of us had gone without talking since we met, her eyes frozen forward, not focusing on anything.

"Are you okay?" I asked her.

"Yes," she said through a smile. "Everything's fine."

We found a quiet corner to sit and hold hands, and when it was time for her to leave, I followed the Baby Doll onto the street and coaxed her into one final kiss before she departed. "You will call me, won't you?" I asked, and she nodded a rapid, spastic yes. As I stood and watched her walk away, my mind flashed forward to that hypothetical future date when she and I would look back on this evening and trade our romantic remembrances of the Night When It All Started. *Maybe*, I thought to myself, *it's just that easy.*

That was the last moment in which I held any power over her. Far from the helpless, dopey doe I took her for, the Baby Doll was surprisingly well connected, in possession of e-mail addresses, home phones, cell phones, work phones—an unending sequence of numerals and letters directing me to places where she never was. This became the operating dynamic of our relationship: she, checking in with me at irregular intervals of an undetermined but excruciatingly long duration, for irregular intervals of an undetermined but frustratingly short duration; me, hovering over my desk, frantically clicking icons labeled "Refresh" on my computer monitor and hastily talking my way out of work-related conversations for fear that I'd miss my chance to hear that honey-soaked rasp recite the legends of unrewarding bartending gigs that lasted all night and blind submissions to impossibly selective magazines that went unacknowledged, and of former accomplishments that all started with "Back in Oregon . . ."

"Hey, that's great!" I'd answer at every pause in her soliloquy. "But when can I see you again?"

Our social schedule was organized and executed with a clinical precision that would have made Mengele jealous: For every five e-mails I would get one phone call, for every five phone calls I would get a date, and for every three dates we'd set, two would be canceled and one would come to fruition. These encounters could be identified and categorized by a range of numerical data: minutes past the designated meeting time I spent waiting for her to arrive; times I swore to myself that if she didn't show in the next five minutes, I was walking away for good; times the state of Back in Oregon was invoked in our dinner discussion; times the discussion was interrupted so she could answer her cell phone; number of $25-and-up dinner plates ordered that went untouched; total dollars spent, expressed both as a whole number and as a percentage of my weekly salary. Now consider this little brainteaser: If you started with the number of requests that yielded real dates, when our schedules coordinated and she didn't blow me off, then divided by the instances in which she had to leave directly for work, had to go home to watch TV with her roommates, or just wasn't in the mood, then—wait for it—on how many nights did she end up in my bed? Exactly: I knew Catholic priests who were getting off more frequently than I was.

But on those rare and wonderful occasions when she could be tempted, good Christ, did this girl put out! The Jewish ones always do—it must have something to do with all those generations being fed a steady diet of Anne Frank's diary, intimidated into believing they'll be dead before they reach sixteen, cursed to come of age while locked up in an attic with only creepy little Peter Van Daan to appreciate their developing forms. There was nothing she would not do to me, no part of me that was not fair game for her to touch or stroke or lick or fondle. All she wanted in return was to be allowed to sit debloused at the end of my couch, to contemplate the small pockets of fat under her armpits that bothered only her, to unhook her own brassiere and let her pendulous, uncomfortable breasts breathe, indifferent to my clumsy attempts to derive more satisfaction from those drooping, veiny sacs than she ever could.

But that, sad to say, is as far as she would let me go. Any effort to assert myself below her waistline was vociferously forbidden. "I don't want you getting too attached to me," went her justification. It was like trying to fight the tide armed with only a Dixie cup: Wearing down her resistance to a point at which sex would seem less awkward—maybe even natural—called for a careful and consistent strategy waged over weeks and months, but there was no juncture at which her time line (first freelance clip in six months; editor for *Glamour* or *Cosmo* in one year; staff writer for *Vogue* or *Harper's Bazaar* in five) overlapped with mine (tongue kissing in two weeks; up her shirt in three; down her pants in four). We were an essentially fuckless couple.

I tried to fill in the emotional gaps with my unfettered devotion, with more unrequited phone calls and e-mails, debasing myself so far that I found myself offering to take her to a Sunday brunch followed by a showing of her favorite movie, *Breakfast at Tiffany's*. There was once a theater in New York where such a tradition had been going on for decades, and it was easily distinguished by the somnambulant men wandering outside it, searching forlornly for their girlfriends while trying not to make eye contact with one another. I threw myself in with these wretched souls one bitterly cold January morning, watching them pair off with one woman after another, until only I was left to blow into my freezing fists and wait for the Baby Doll while brunch started and finished without us. The winter sun was unkind to me, frying me inside my heavy fleece coat, and it was no kinder to her when she at last appeared, shining directly onto her face, lacquered with olive green eye shadow and bright orange lipstick. "Here I am!" she announced just minutes before the movie started, as if that were somehow supposed to make everything worthwhile.

I don't know what's more irritating about *Breakfast at Tiffany's*— the film itself or the way it has ingratiated itself into the hearts of millions of guileless, unsuspecting women. If you are fortunate enough to be totally unfamiliar with the movie or the Truman Capote novel from which it was adapted, all you need to know is that it stars that celebrated anorexic Audrey Hepburn as Holly Golightly, a fashionable, desirable Manhattan socialite who parties by night and window-shops by day. How she is able to afford her stylish togs or her apartment without a job is an absolute mystery, and the audience is invited to conclude that she prostitutes herself to her many wealthy suitors. None of this bothers her neighbor, the aspiring writer Paul (portrayed by George Peppard, later of TV's *The A-Team*), who falls in love with Holly despite the fact that she is a psychotic who suffers from panic attacks, despite the fact that she continually calls him by the wrong name, and despite the fact that she's really a runaway from Tulip, Texas, who never divorced her rube of a husband (played by *The Beverly Hillbillies*'s Buddy

Ebsen). Not only does the film prove that all the good female roles in Hollywood really are written by gay men, but it neatly demonstrates that even when a woman is taking refuge in the secure embrace of Jed Clampett, she is secretly yearning for the animal magnetism and chiseled jaw that only Lieutenant Colonel John "Hannibal" Smith can provide her.

As we watched Holly find her lost cat in the movie's climactic rainstorm, and "Moon River" played for the last time, and we were left to presume that Paul got his pussy, too, the Baby Doll was an emotional wreck, with olive green rivulets streaming down either cheek. The previous two hours of Audrey Hepburn's Method weeping and "mean reds" had failed to move me at all, but this—this was a real girl, crying real tears, and I didn't have any idea how to make her stop. As I had seen many a leading man do in his day, I tried to place a pacifying kiss on those quivering lips, but she just shoved me away—and I mean *shoved* me. If I'd ever touched her like that, I'd have been prosecuted.

But my greatest humiliation of the day was yet to come. The Baby Doll had to leave for work directly from the theater, so I hailed her a taxi and hugged her good-bye, and in the scant seconds it took us to complete this exchange, some Big Brown Bag–toting twat was trying to shove her way past us and into the car.

"Excuse me," I asked the intruder, "but what do you think you're doing?"

"If you're not going to use this cab," she sneered, "then get out of the way."

"Hey," I said, "can't I just say good-bye to my girlfriend?" The words seemed to hang in the air like a cartoon word-balloon, and they felt terribly wrong as soon as I had uttered them.

The Baby Doll pulled open the passenger door, positioning it between us. "Don't ever call me that," she seethed. "I'm *not* your girlfriend." She got in and slammed it shut. I had held back her hair while she vomited from alcohol poisoning, I had seen her on the toilet, and I had ejaculated in her mouth, and nothing had ever disgusted her as much as when I called her my girlfriend. At the next light, her cabdriver attempted to make an illegal turn and was pulled over by a traffic cop.

On our next date, sometime in the spring, the Baby Doll lowered the boom. From the scene of a restaurant opening, we had moved on to my couch; I was preparing to make my move, but she had an ulterior motive, too.

"I need you to understand," she said, slowly inching away from me, "I only came here to tell you: I can't see you anymore."

"It's because I called you my girlfriend, isn't it?" I asked.

"That's not it at all," she insisted. "I came here to have my own life. I don't want to be anyone's girlfriend right now."

"You know," I said, "it might have been a little more courteous to do this at the *beginning* of the night."

"This isn't the first time I've ever broken up with somebody," she said. "I was in a serious relationship the whole time I was in college. Did you even know that about me?"

Much as it pains me to use the following three words, she was right. I didn't know a single telling detail about her—didn't know the identity of her mystery ex, her home address, the color of her eyes, whether she preferred ultrathins to the kind with wings. I didn't give the girl enough credit to talk her way out of an on-the-street solicitation from a Greenpeace volunteer, and I had forced my way into her life. Now six months of our lives had gone by, and I still hadn't gotten what I came into the shop for.

I made one last plea: "But we never even—I mean, can't we just once, just so I can see what it's like? Just so I can say we did it?" My bed loomed large in our line of sight, the pillowcases fluffed and the sheets neatly pressed.

"*God*, no," she protested.

"Please don't leave," I said in my hoarse voice.

"I have to," she said. She pulled me close to her, let me nestle my head in that pacifying chest of hers one last time, for what felt like hours, even played along when I pretended to fall asleep in her arms. Then she gently got up, shut out the light, and closed the door behind her. She was gone, and it hurt, but it hurt in the same way that hurtful things have always hurt, no more and no less, and that, I suppose, was the problem.

entr'acte

I **DON'T MEAN** to brag, but I can masturbate to anything. There is simply no set of stimuli that my brain is not capable of construing as an image intended to induce arousal, no form that cannot be contorted and manipulated in my mind until it triggers that familiar message from my brain to my crotch, the one that creates the oppressive bulge in my pants that will not relent until I deal with it in the only way I know how. Pornography was most frequently the culprit when such material was still novel to me, but ever since they took the plotlines and the production values out of smut, who's to say I know it when I see it anymore? Those oversexed magazine advertisements and television commercials, populated with their luscious spokesbabes, intended to induce a sense of wanting—they only make me want myself more.

If I can't find a publication contrived for the specific purpose of giving me a hard-on, almost any other piece of printed matter will do; even the abstraction of sex—the sight of the undergarments as a substitute for the anatomy they hide; a flash of anything round, or smooth, or pink—can get me hot. But through an exhaustive, highly scientific study carried out over the last fifteen years—through cultivating an electronic archive of pornography so specific that it can only get me off and is now the only thing I can get off to—I have concluded that what works best is pictures of famous women, shown partially undressed. The suggestion of nudity is always more powerful than the real thing—that sense of capturing a woman in the act, of freezing time at the instant of revelation, on that border between a PG-13 rating and an R; the wonderment at what her parts will look like, and will they be different from all the parts I've seen before? All the better if it is a woman I recognize, whom I am not used to seeing in this way and who doesn't want me looking at her like that: It imbues me with a sense of power that I can then take out directly on my exhausted, overworked meat—a desire to pull on it till I just can't pull on it no more—and then pull on it some more. Because if you can, then why not? And if you're going to go there, then why not go all the way? As long as I haven't degenerated to a point where I'm gratifying myself in public, sitting in my office chair without realizing that my hand is halfway down my pants, then who am I hurting?

And yet—to see these pictures produced, to bear witness to the creation of the material, is so terminally boring and unsexy that I might as well be watching a high school health film on the horrors of chlamydia. If I am so unfortunate as to find myself at one of these torturous all-day sessions, at a downtown photo studio or penthouse hotel suite, it means that in exchange for a precious thirty or forty minutes of badinage with the hot body du jour, I will have to endure hours of lights being adjusted, of sets being built and broken down and rebuilt, of watching *Maxim*'s art director laconically smoke Marlboros and swig bottles of Heineken, of watching him watch the photographer shout his clichéd come-ons and bark his orgasmic instructions for the subject to perform all sorts of imaginary lewd behavior with his telephoto lens, while I leaf mindlessly through the same five or six other magazines that have been lying around until they all blur into a single, inaccessible collage of smug voices and traffic-jam layouts, and listen to a stereo blare the entire T. Rex catalog until it dawns on me that Marc Bolan spent his career writing the same goddamned song.

And maybe once or twice, I will see the subject stroll past me, stripped bare as she changes into a new bikini or a fresh piece of lingerie, parading herself around as if to make an unambiguous display of the one thing we are forbidden by convention to show in our pictures. And she is unconcerned that I am staring directly at it, already plucked and waxed of every hair before our photo retouchers could get to it, looking alien and unrecognizable, like the arid valleys of some dead, distant planet, left for earth's scientists to debate from afar if there might be any life stirring beneath its surface.

With the shoot over, it is my turn to interact with her at an appropriate, face-to-face level. Ushered into a hotel bedroom on the opposite side of the suite, we are guaranteed total privacy while the photographer and his assistants dismantle their equipment, and though there are chairs available, she insists on sitting on the floor, at my feet, while answering my questions; she has since donned a bathrobe that nevertheless reveals everything each time she crosses and uncrosses her legs. She is of an ethnic background that would give my parents simultaneous strokes if I ever brought her home and introduced her as anything other than my new housekeeper; she speaks in perfectly formed, easily digestible sound bites and, like myself, possesses a father who was instrumental in determining the course of her life—in her case, an army colonel who has only recently retired from the military.

"He's a lunatic when it comes to men," she tells me. "He's very open about the fact that he doesn't want any man to sleep with me, kiss me, or even touch me. But you know what they say about girls with strict upbringings: All hell breaks loose when they get out."

"How do you think your father would have reacted to seeing a stylist fussing over his baby girl's chest all day long?" I ask.

"That stylist was not as helpful as he could have been," she complains. "I had to tell him, 'It's your job to lather me up in baby oil. Now stop asking me if you can touch that. It's only a breast. It'll only bite you if you want it to.' "

"You're not living with your father anymore, are you?"

"I just moved into my own apartment in the city," she says. "You know, it's not too far from here. All I have is a bed, a couch, and all the kitchen supplies you could ever want. But they're just for show-and-tell. See, I get guys to come over by promising to cook them an amazing gourmet meal. Like that's what they're *really* interested in when they come to my place. Do you understand what I'm saying?"

"Oh, yeah," I agree.

She grins.

"Well," I say as I shake her hand, "it's been very nice to meet you," and I pack up my tape recorder and notepad and I leave.

A few days later, when Jim Kaminsky edits my interview from

behind the parapets of cardboard boxes that still surround his desk, he will ask me, "At what point in the conversation did you jump her bones?"

"What?" I will say.

"Come on, man," he will answer. "It's so obvious. She was warm for your form." This is the actual phrase he will use, because some people actually say such things.

"I don't think so," I will say, embarrassed by the very suggestion.

"She was flirting with you. Don't you know what flirting sounds like when you hear it?"

"She was just acting the part," I will counter. "She's been in this magazine before. She knows what we want to hear."

"Look, there's nothing wrong if one of these girls likes you, you know. You should have gone for it. If not for yourself, then for those of us who will never know what that's like again." So saying, Jim will hold up the hand with his wedding band on it.

When we finish speaking, I'll think he's nuts and he'll think the same of me, and we'll both wonder who's the bigger schmuck: he who has to go home and hump the same woman every night or he who goes home to no one and just yanks it?

act two

I HAVE THIS TERRIBLE habit of falling in love with my friends' girlfriends. I mean, how could I not? When I see these disconsolate, aimless oafs, who I am convinced have nothing more going for them than I do, with their good intentions and their half-finished novels, suddenly filled with passion and courage and a sense of purpose, all for the simple reason that they are now getting laid on a regular basis, it is my natural inclination to want what they've got. And it is not until I see their women brought to life, glowing with a continuous stream of positivity through a carefully doled-out regimen of affirmations, hand-holding, and back rubs, that I am able to appreciate what's good about them; but by then, of course, it is too late.

Except for the one time when it wasn't, when I found one such pair that was destined to fail, when I could use the damned minutes in their combined company making the observations that would be money in my purse. He was a big, boisterous fellow (and what is it, by the way, with all these gigantic guys I hang around?) and she was a gorgeously bone-thin girl with exotic eyes and the cutest little overbite, and there was a genuine connection between the two of them, as if the rest of the world could go fuck itself and it would have suited them just fine. But he was insecure and she was beautiful, and thus it could never last. Nine or ten months later—the amount of time is immaterial, you can do it standing on your head when you've got no one else to spend it with—they had broken up, through no intervention of mine.

She worked in the same neighborhood I did, as a fashion designer, and was as dedicated a student of superstition as I was, regarding each of our chance encounters on the street as a sign of a deeper connection between us. And though she had the same first name as the Baby Doll, an omen I should have imbued with greater significance, I will always think of her as my untamable, shit-kicking Cowgirl, who would absently light up a second cigarette before putting out her first, who called me to cry on the day that Waylon Jennings died, and who once confessed to me her unrealized desire to see two men fight.

"Like a heavyweight championship, 'and in this corner' boxing match?" I said.

"No," she cooed, "like just a plain old barroom brawl."

"You wouldn't fare very well in a fight like that," I told her. "You've got the heart, but what you need is a solid left hook."

"I didn't say I wanted to be *in* one—I just wanted to *see* one." A pause of anticipation. "Have *you* ever been in a fight?"

"Sure," I told her as casually as if she'd asked if I'd ever read *A Separate Peace.*

"Really?" she squealed.

"Of course. Don't ever let a man tell you he doesn't remember how a fight ended. He knows how they all turned out."

"Did you win yours?"

"All my fights happened in grade school—in locker rooms, on buses. None of them counted."

"So none of them were recent?" There was a tinge of disappointment.

"Nah, the last one was ten years ago."

"Omigod," she said, doing the subtraction in her head. "You're, like, so much younger than me. You're just a *kid*." This distinction seemed to excite her, and when I asked for her phone number at the end of this bit of banter, she surrendered it without delay. "I'm getting a really good vibe from you," she said, which sounded perfectly rational at the time.

I entered into our first date with the full understanding that it was not a first date at all, but a predate, a date to determine if I was deserving of a first date. She forbade us to engage in any activities that would cost money, so we were limited to seeing some movie for which I had free passes—some frivolous crap about rock stars or vampires, who can tell the difference?—where she hewed to her code so stubbornly that she wouldn't even let me pay for her box of Raisinets. Still, there were occasional moments of encouragement: the way she delicately held my hand open to pour some of her candy into it; the way she shared my fascination for any piece of film run through a projector, no matter how horrible—that sense of awe that if you played the images fast enough, you could *make the pictures move*; her nonchalant use of the word *vagina* in conversation, as in "A friend of mine just interviewed at that new Oprah Winfrey magazine. She said that entering the office was like stepping into Oprah's *vagina*." And when I asked to see her again that weekend, she happily agreed. "I'm available just about every weekend," she vowed. "I'm such a loser." *Maybe*, I thought to myself, *it's just that easy.*

"I want to come over and cook dinner for you," she volunteers over the phone the following Sunday, and I pause only to swallow the small glob of mucus and bile that my esophagus has nervously fired into my throat before I agree. And I am so enamored of my own latent charms, so certain that the circumstances can only lead to her sleeping with me on our first date, that half the day has gone by before I realize I don't possess a single cooking implement or even know if I have a working stove in my apartment. Then it is six, seven, eight o'clock, well past any reasonable hour when two people with no culinary skills between them could begin preparing a meal and have it ready before dawn, and she hasn't called me, and I cannot call her because it will only confirm how lonely and pathetic I really am, and I am passing the time by compulsively counting floor tiles, counting my CDs, washing my hands over and over until I have rubbed them raw, inspecting the ticket stubs I saved from our predate in case I decide to start a scrapbook, and I am facedown on my bed, sobbing with the certainty that somewhere in New York there is another girl laughing about how effortlessly she has been able to reduce me to a nauseous, blubbering wreck.

Finally, as always, I must be the one to phone her. "Were you still planning on coming over tonight?" I ask.

"Oh, yeah," she says, yawning. "I almost completely forgot. I suppose it's too late to cook anything now. Do you want to go out to eat?"

"Sure, fine, whatever," I answer. "Just get over here already." But when she steps through my door, all is forgiven—I am eagerly walking her around my apartment to point out all my favorite toys, the vintage action figures, the extensive video game collection, the feature on my television set that lets me view the security camera in my building's elevator.

"You weren't watching *me* on that, were you?" she asks.

"What? No. Of course not," I answer.

Wandering the sodium-lit streets of the Upper East Side at ten o'clock on a Sunday night with the Cowgirl at my side, I am made to confront my ignorance about the neighborhood I have lived in for nearly three years—my inability to find even one restaurant whose menu does not feature three different-size orders of French fries— and how ridiculous the two of us must look together, she in the intentionally mismatched apparel she swiped from her employer, and I dressed as though I just came from a yachting competition. I choose a family-style Italian establishment, cavernous in its emptiness, because it is the only place still open, but the Cowgirl doesn't eat, she just spends the whole meal plotting to help me shop for a new wardrobe; she wants to teach me how to eat sushi; she wants to collaborate with me on a book of vintage movie posters. Not wishing to contemplate the consequences of disagreeing with her, I swallow every one of her suggestions as eagerly as my veal piccata.

Retired to the opposite ends of my couch, we are back to interacting with the television set as mediator. From my video library I have selected a film called *The Gift*, an atmospheric and frightening supernatural thriller that should never be screened in any vaguely romantic setting, let alone while there are females in the room, because it is saturated with more exotic and perverse methods of torturing women than the Triangle Shirtwaist factory: By the end of the film, Cate Blanchett has been stalked and strangled, Hilary Swank has been beaten up, and Katie Holmes has been raped, murdered, and tossed in a lake. While this transparent misogyny is transpiring on-screen, I have the audacity to tell the Cowgirl, "You can come sit next to me if you'd like," to which she replies, "That's okay, I think I'm just fine where I am." And I am insulted that she has refused my invitation when really I should be relieved that she isn't on the phone with the police, telling them that she's being pursued by a maniac—and he's in the room with her *right now*.

When it is time for her to leave, I kiss the Cowgirl for the first time, and then a second and a third, and when I am finished my hands are shaking visibly. "I'm sorry," I say. "That's never happened before."

"See you around," she says, fully aware that I'll be watching her on the videocamera as she leaves.

"Maybe we could grab a drink sometime?" I ask.

"Not likely," she says. "Don't you know I'm an alcoholic?" From the look on my face, she can tell I don't believe her. "For real. I've been going to meetings for the last six months." From the look on hers, I can tell she's not kidding. *Alcoholism!* The great, secret shame of the Gentiles! I knew drug addiction was for real, but this—this malady seemed to me as impossible to believe in as Santa Claus or the Easter Bunny, as illusory as the Resurrection. Yet here was my first full-blown, flesh-and-blood alcoholic, in the tantalizing form of the Cowgirl, and, well . . . it kind of turns me on. This is a *real* problem, a *grown-up* problem, and it is a momentous occasion for me to have graduated from girls with imaginary disorders to a woman with an authentic affliction; I am so excited that I want to call my parents and tell them, "Mom, Dad—I'm dating a lush!"

It is also a challenge for me, to see if I possess as much temperance as she does—sufficient patience to overcome my tendency toward impetuous obedience. Though I lack her maturity, do I have enough restraint to keep my naïveté from getting in the way of her superior sophistication?

As it turned out, I didn't. Soon, the Cowgirl and I fell into the familiar routine of trading messages unreturned (mine) and undetected (hers). Somehow she always knew when I would be away from my desk, because these were the only times she would call me back, and when I would be out of town, because these were the only days she was available to get together. Somehow every friend she had was moving to a new apartment, because she was always making time to help them pack. Somehow I was surprised each time I asked her out and she answered, "Maybe," and from my seat at work I blurted out, "Maybe?" so loudly that everyone around me could overhear my humiliation and think, *Better him than me.* Somehow I let this go on for three months.

Then on some morbid and solitary Saturday night, in my loneliest loneliness, I was visited by a meanness and a rage such as I'd never known before. I wanted to find that malnourished, teetotaling prude—I wanted to break through all the barriers she'd put in my path, the lies and the alibis and the Caller ID, to grab her by her bony, padded shoulders and recite in painstaking detail her every unprovoked grievance that she visited on me, until that *shicker goy* was so racked with guilt that she crawled back into her bottle and never came out. But I got her voice mail, which I was content to menace in her absence.

"Listen," I muttered into the digital box, pacing my darkened apartment like some latter-day David Berkowitz, "I know what's going on, and I don't like it. I'm sick of how you treat me, and I'm not going to stand for it anymore. But what's the use? You're not even going to call me back anyway. In fact, don't bother."

The Cowgirl took the bait, and within minutes she had returned my call. "I got your message," was all she said, but there was fear in her voice. For the first time, she was aware of my capacity for violence.

"Well," I demanded, as I had done in my fantasies so many times before, "what is going on between us?"

"Yeah, about that . . ." I waited for the inevitable. "I don't think I want to pursue this relationship any further."

And it fazed me not at all—it freed me to say the things I'd always wanted to say to her, in the manner in which I'd always wanted to say them. "How could you do this to me?" I shouted. "How could you string me along like this—*for months?* If you didn't want to see me again, why couldn't you say so?"

"I'm sorry," she said. "I'm really bad at these sorts of things."

"One crappy date? That's all I'm allowed? I don't get a chance to redeem myself?"

"I just don't think you're ready for me yet. I think you need to do some growing up. We used to have great energy together, but I don't know what happened to it. I don't feel comfortable with you anymore."

"Hey, how do you think *I* feel? I'm fucking *mortified.*" Once again she had reduced me to tears, and I hated myself for it.

"Well," she said, trying to console me, "I hope that when this is all over, when you calm down, maybe a few months from now, that you and I can still be friends."

"I'm sorry, but that's never going to happen." I slammed down the phone so hard that I was shivering, and it was impossible for me to tell if what I had just done was right or wrong.

"Great energy"? How in the hell am I supposed to measure that? How am I supposed to provide you with what you want if you can't even ask for it in terms you can articulate? You want perfection? Go seek it out in your functionally illiterate self-help magazines, in your inspirational feel-good pablum masquerading as literature, in your vulgar cable TV soap operas and your reactionary, fearmongering talk shows, because it doesn't exist in the only medium that matters—the medium of reality! If you're going to dismiss every man who violates even one of your thousand and one unspoken standards, who isn't sufficiently assertive or deferential or says *stalagmite* when he means *stalactite*, then you *deserve* to be alone. You think you deserve better? Well, sweetheart of the rodeo, let me also remind you that you could do *worse*—that you could just as easily end up with some brooding, self-destructive type because he reminds you of your father or of yourself, who drinks ten times as hard as you ever did and beats the living shit out of you when his dinner isn't on the table or there isn't money in the bank or you so much as raise an eyebrow in his direction. Then see if a fidgety, infantilized Jew with a short temper and a Roth IRA is so bad after all!

I want to believe that I have grown as a person as a result of this, but I have gained nothing. All I have learned is that you should never court two women with the same name, at least not consecutively, because that name will be so deeply seared into your subconscious that you will speak it in your sleep, and wake up with it on your lips, and wear it like a millstone forever around your heart. Only that, and that I don't know.

I don't know. I don't fucking know.

11

TWELVE INCHES (12") OF PARADISE

S IT STILL A VACATION IF YOU SPEND IT SURROUNDED
by the very people you're trying to escape from? Can it properly be
called a getaway if all you're getting away from is the geographic
source of your suffering—if all you're leaving behind are the inani-
mate emblems of your servitude, while remaining in the exclusive
company of those naggingly familiar faces every bit as drooping
and defeated as your own? Can this same set of sad, sickly souls
find serenity simply by being broken apart and reconstituted at a
more temperate latitude? Or will such an investigation only prove
that they are the living, complaining embodiments of those benign-
looking household products that, when mixed in the correct
amounts, react to yield a noxious cloud of misanthropic poison?

Among the *Maxim* editors, the irrefutable belief that we deserved a corporate retreat had preceded the hushed rumors that we
were going to be granted one. We felt we were owed the reward, not
because the magazine was growing more insanely profitable by the
month, or because our morale could once again use the boost it
would provide, but because our advertising staff already got one.
The previous autumn, they had walked away from their expense accounts, their massage therapists, and their est workshops for a week
in the Bahamas, under the pretext that the balmy setting and the
trust-fall games would make them more effective salespeople. The

widening class distinction between our two departments, the two branches of power customarily referred to as "church and state," was nothing new; it was just becoming easier to tell which side was which. As editors, we merely provided the magazine's content—words that held influence only over those who gave their consent to be governed. It was advertising that brought in the money, and thus they ruled by divine right—their authority was granted from God on high.

By the following spring, after two seasons of our incensed rumblings, it was decided that we, too, should have an opportunity to travel hundreds of miles to sit in unfamiliar chairs and talk about "synergy." At first, the prophecies foretold of a weekend bus ride to Atlantic City, which we threatened to boycott; a second divination saw us traveling to the printing press in Memphis, Tennessee, where millions of copies of *Maxim* were produced every month, and a second time we denied it. So the omnipotent ones traded a few favors and conjured up a trip to Jamaica, and it was good. All we had to do was consent to visit a tropical nation at the onset of its blistering summer; to share our retreat with our ad sales team, even though we hadn't been allowed to attend theirs; and to keep the holiday a secret from Felix Dennis, who would never knowingly allow so many of his employees to enjoy even a fraction of the luxury he wallowed in every day. We readily agreed to all the conditions; for many of us, it was the first authentic act of generosity we'd witnessed in our careers.

Though the official itinerary did not begin until a Monday, those of us who could arrange to leave early—anyone blessed with tolerant spouses or unburdened by significant others, and Jim Kaminsky, who did not have to explain why he wanted an additional day away from his wife and kid—were flown into Jamaica on the previous Sunday. Everything about this first leg of the tour, from the airline safety instructions delivered in a soothing French Caribbean accent to the fried plantains that came with our in-flight meals, suggested extravagance, but as we stepped off the plane and into the resort town of Montego Bay, what we saw was blight. The airport was without terminals or even designated landing strips, one long stretch of primordial, undifferentiated tarmac, inhabited by dormant baggage carts and idle skycaps. Ours were the only white faces in an un-air-conditioned customs office, where the air was thick with moisture and Muzak arrangements of Bob Marley, Jimmy Cliff, and Desmond Dekker. Dozens of natives were already lined up ahead of us—how they had managed to leave was as mysterious as why they had chosen to return—yet we were ushered past them, almost certainly because someone had glad-handed the right civic official long before we crossed the Tropic of Cancer.

From there our party was moved into a van, for a lengthy drive along cracked mountain roads that begged like paupers for fresh asphalt, past innumerable shantytowns assembled from scraps of corrugated tin and cardboard; past gas stations each in possession of a single rusted pump; past goats, everywhere goats, active goats and goats in repose, chained-up goats and free-range goats, more goats in a single afternoon than I had seen in an entire lifetime; past billboard after faded billboard advertising a thing called "Ting," a beverage that purported to contain natural lemon and lime flavors but was probably milked from goats; past the facilities for Hedonism III, where otherwise sensible Americans migrated to fuck one another's wives; and to a compound bordered on all sides by concrete walls topped with barbed wire, whose massive metal gate was flanked on either side by a turret with an armed guard.

"Why are we stopping here?" someone wanted to know.

"Because," said our driver, "this is where you are staying."

Then the gate opened, and we were initiated into an opulence that was both completely expected and too awesome to comprehend. The four hundred acres of groomed landscapes and undefiled beaches would be ours entirely for the next three off-season days; in groups of five or six we were assigned private villas, each with its own white plaster facade out front, crystal blue pool in the backyard, and all-black crew in the kitchen. When the mercury crossed the ninety-degree mark, the corpulent mammies who cooked the meals and cleaned the rooms were still made to wear dark aprons, while the manservants who carried our luggage and performed the grunt work donned dress shirts and black slacks. To call the practice slavery would imply that these people had no other means of income available, but if they didn't like the hospitality industry, they could always become goatherds. Other familiar trades were open to them as well. "I can get you anything," our houseboy, Cassius, had assured us from the moment we left our bags with him. "*Anything.*" For someone with no concept of the Thirteenth Amendment, Cassius had a pretty good idea of what liberation was all about.

Their enticements to indulge ourselves came without judgment or expectation. They wanted to assist us as much as possible in this pursuit, and that spirit of permissiveness was everywhere to be seen, in their beaming faces, in the bountiful bowl of alcoholic fruit punch that awaited us in the registration office, in the boxes of matches and rolling papers that could be found underneath every cabana. All the circumstances were conspiring—with us, not against us—to ensure that the only R&R we would see during our stay was Reprobation and Regurgitation. *We were going to have fun on this island.*

I had brought about $200 with me for the week, but with the all-inclusive meals and booze, it was clear I wouldn't be needing the money, so I folded it up and handed it to Cassius. "Cocaine," I directed him. "Powdered." I even made a little sniffing noise to illustrate my point. He nodded in understanding, then grabbed my wad of bills and ran off.

"You realize you'll never see that money again," Jim predicted.

By sundown, however, the dependency weighing most heavily on our minds was the season finale of *The Sopranos* premiering that night. But as assuredly as our residences were outfitted with electricity and running water, they also featured cable television—pay cable television! broadcast on the same schedule as we were accustomed to in the States!—and our fears were allayed. As we congregated in a den to watch the program, only four men were in attendance—Jim, Harold, Gomez, and myself—and we were banished to the corners of the room. The rest of the audience was female, an assortment of our copy editors, fact-checkers, and photo assistants, the lower-level lubricants that kept the *Maxim* machine quietly humming, who never once showed any dissatisfaction with articles that promised to "turn any girl into your lust puppet" or the umpteenth pictorial in which a woman was depicted admiring herself in a mirror—and if they did, they kept it to themselves. Having reflexively seated themselves in two precise rows, as if they were posing for a class portrait, they forced us to observe complete silence as the show unfolded, shooting disapproving glares and hissing in unison if we asked for help with the plot points; and when it was over they bitched in consensus about this week's lack of violence and the fact that nobody got whacked. Then they switched channels to catch the concluding minutes of *The Natural*, to call attention to Glenn Close's angular facial features, and to again demand silence when Robert Redford stroked his pennant-clinching, lightbulb-shattering home run. The men could see we weren't needed here.

Several uncomfortable hours had passed since I'd sent Cassius on his errand, and as we rejects assembled in the foyer of our estate, our houseboy burst into the hall. Panting and wheezing as if he'd just completed a marathon, he approached me and pressed a small plastic bag into my hands. "It was the best I could do," he gasped.

"What the hell is this?" I asked as I inspected the contents, half a dozen tiny rocks the color of a junkie's rotten teeth. I passed the flimsy, transparent sack to Harold, who passed it to Jim, who passed it to Gomez, who passed it back to me. Despite the collective courage we had shown earlier in the day, we would each have to sheepishly admit that nobody knew what I had bought.

Gomez was the first to speak up. "Oh, my God," he cried. "I think that's crack."

"Can we get him to take it back?" I asked. Cassius stared at his shoes. This was an all-sales-final proposition—there could be no refund on this purchase, no store credit to be used on a future transaction. Either I humbly accepted that my first and only effort at scoring drugs in a nation whose entire economy was built on the stuff was a failure, that I had thrown away my savings on a pocketful of magic beans, or, well . . .

Within seconds we had scoured our lodging for every bit of debris that could be substituted for drug paraphernalia—empty beer bottles, soup spoons, the trap on the kitchen sink—and laid them out in front of us. Like savants of substance abuse, we rapidly sorted through the junk pile, connecting bits and pieces in never-before-seen combinations and then discarding our labors in frustration, until we seized upon a bit of tinfoil. We crumpled the foil into the shape of a bowl and placed one of the rocks in its center. In one hand Jim held out the makeshift device, and in the other, a straw. "Okay," he said. "Who wants to go first?"

There was a lull as we paused to admire our handiwork, and then it became obvious we were stalling. Jim himself wanted no part of the festivities—"I'm too old for this," he said in resignation—and neither Harold nor Gomez would touch the contraption. For the second time that day, it was up to me to pretend I knew what I was doing. "It was *my* money," I reasoned.

Gomez got down on one knee so he would be at my height, holding a lighter beneath the pipe, looking up at me with deranged, expectant eyes, as if he were about to see a man put to death in the electric chair. Harold and Jim both backed away, in case I accidentally exploded. Then Gomez lit a flame, and I cast aside my glasses and leaned into the thick white smoke rising up to meet my face, trying to suck as much of it into my straw as I could before it evaporated and its magical properties were lost forever. To my unrefined palate, it tasted like vanilla and bus exhaust fumes, like spoiled milk and camphor, burnt toast and rat feces, and not knowing whether to swallow it or let it seep out through my nostrils, I held it in my puffed-up cheeks and waited for something to happen.

Almost instantly I was high—high on my own audacity and fearlessness, the ease with which I shattered the social hierarchy by pumping my affluent, erudite blood full of street toxin, this artificial buffer people like me had designed for people like them, to keep people like them *away* from people like me. With this one act, I could feel myself being transformed before my weak-willed peers, bound to earth by their petty commitments to other fallible human beings, by their mistrust of the unknown and an unwillingness to risk the possibility of evolving into something greater. I, meanwhile, was free from worldly constraints, able to see myself from above as the most extraordinary specimen of manhood in the room. I was bigger than U.S. Steel, greater than any other man I had ever known in my lifetime, even greater than the man who had been responsible for my creation. For all the shit my father had ingested in his heyday—all that he had snorted, smoked, dropped, shot up, and rubbed into his belly—he'd never attempted anything quite like this. And fuck anybody who dared to dismiss this as youthful experimentation—there was no hypothesis I was seeking to confirm, other than my own intimations of immortality. In the race for worldly experience, it was not enough to be at the front of the pack; if everyone else was cruising at fifty-five miles an hour, I had to be hurtling at a hundred and ten. And with a single action, I had done something no one else could say he had done.

This feeling lasted for approximately fifteen to twenty seconds. Then my confidence melted away, along with what felt like a portion of my forehead.

"Look at him," said Gomez. "He must be halfway to the moon by now."

The other men leaned in, trying to gaze through my glassy eyes to see what I was seeing, but their approving smiles that I had nearly killed myself to earn looked unsatisfying and grotesque. What did their acceptance mean to me now? They had stood by and cheered me on while I defiled myself, for no reason other than it kept them amused. Didn't anyone feel an obligation to protect me? Didn't anyone understand that I needed to be defended—from myself? They playfully punched me in the arm and slapped me on the ass, but nobody had my back; we may have called one another "bro," but we were not brothers. We took from one another what we needed to get by, to get out from underneath one miserable day and on to the next one. It was every half-assed man for his own stultified self.

I had been up, and I had been down, and that was my high, all two minutes of it. I could not honestly say that it was so exquisite that I would abandon my children, steal car stereos, or turn to a life of prostitution just to get another taste, but there was plenty left where that came from. And as the women started to emerge from the TV room, we men must have presented a perplexing sight to their innocent eyes, as we huddled together for strength, barking and growling at one another like feral animals around some unseen kill. It was only our first night in Jamaica, but at least I ended it sleeping on a bed, I think, or a couch, or a surface that was intended for resting. When I woke up, I found Harold asleep on the beach, facedown in the sand, and a bag in my pocket with the same number of rocks that remained after I'd taken my first and only hit.

THE FOLLOWING MORNING our privacy was severely compromised, and with it, I assumed, my ability to consume highly addictive chemical derivatives in peace, as everyone else showed up at the resort. And I mean *everyone*: Ethan had grown himself a little Semitic beach-bum stubble around his chin to help him blend in, and Parker, in a pair of $5 sunglasses and a straw sunhat the size of a wagon wheel, might as well have had his American passport stapled to his ass. A trio of women from our Los Angeles office were in attendance, all naturally blond and golden brown in the appropriate places, as if they were born for the climate; as were the Brits from the art department, dressed in the same blue jeans they wore to work every day, as if they'd never encountered warm weather before in their lives. Alicia was with them, still doting on the English hunk who'd grabbed her by her hair and dragged her home all those months ago; and elsewhere stood our fashion editors, who couldn't have looked less thrilled if they had just arrived at a dogshit convention. The advertising women kept to themselves, speaking only to one another, and then only in whispers, lips pressed to hands cupped around ears, making no attempt to avoid looking at you even as they were talking about you; while the advertising men worked the crowd, shaking hands with their right hands while using their left to keep their hair plugs from blowing away in the occasional gust of wind. Finally there was Keith, our editor in chief, smiling wider than anyone else, greeting every coworker with the same hearty "Wazzup!" we'd all heard in that famous beer commercial from a year earlier.

In composing the invite list for this trip, no distinction had been drawn between *Maxim*'s full-timers and its freelancers. Somewhere between forty and fifty of us had been gathered together, each with his or her unique role in the process of producing the magazine, roles that almost never required us to interact with many of the people with whom we were obligated to spend the next seventy-two hours. With these jobs left behind in another time zone, what little we had in common was less obvious than all the ways in which our various demographics did not intersect: the men versus the women, the Americans versus the Brits, the six-figure-salaried executives versus the hand-to-mouth assistants, the libertines versus the puritans, the outwardly antagonistic versus the merely indifferent. With no agenda for the day and no one to tell us how we should be occupying our time, the freedom was almost as stifling as the heat. More than likely, most of us were thinking the same two thoughts: *What do we do now?* and *Where is the marijuana?*

I thought the previous evening had been sufficiently surprising for everyone involved, but there was one last surprise ambling his way toward the guests. In person, Drew Carey didn't quite resemble the blue-collar caricature he had perfected on his TV sitcom; he wore his hair a few millimeters thicker than the trademark buzz cut he sported on his show and had discarded his thick Buddy Holly specs in favor of contact lenses. You'd have hardly mistaken him for a wealthy Hollywood star if it weren't for the female accessory who came attached to his arm, a slightly homely woman with knockers the size of dodgeballs. "This is my girlfriend," he said as he excitedly introduced her to the group. "She's a stripper!" No shit, pal.

The seed for this surreal moment had been planted with *Maxim*'s very first issue, back when the magazine still shared *The Drew Carey Show*'s affection for the plight of the common man and its debut cover featured a modest, mostly clothed photograph of the program's female costar, Christa Miller. At a party in New York a week earlier, a few Dennis Publishing honchos had found themselves at the bar with the unlikely sex object and her rotund chum, and before anyone could say Monty Woolley, they had invited Drew Carey, all expenses paid, to the *Maxim* corporate retreat. I figured he had as much right to be there as any of us: By now, the television comedy that bore his name was less a continuation of his original vision than a loose confederation of hokey gimmicks and predictable jokes, and though the show was two seasons away from cancellation, he'd already made millions by selling the series into syndication. All he had to do here was sit back and bask in the awkward adulation of a few dozen casual admirers who'd probably never watched a single episode of his program. How could he say no?

His presence added to the general confusion of the day, his estimable mass further tipping the upset scales of order toward total chaos. So everyone did what came naturally: Those who wanted to go on hikes or sit poolside and complain about the soaring temperatures could do so, and the rest of us could return to whatever altered state of consciousness we were trying to attain. Side by side, the ladies sipped frothy daiquiris and the Brits tossed back bottle after bottle of Heineken, while I split my time between the office's pot scene and its cocaine crowd. Here in Jamaica, the pot scene felt totally at ease rolling its joints and smoking its blunts out in the open. The cocaine crowd, however, were self-imposed pariahs, who didn't tell you when or where the party was going down; you had to seek them, listening for the door with the muffled sounds of tapping and giggling coming from behind it. Even if the pot itself was not as transcendentally potent as smoking the ashes of Haile

Selassie himself, it made you want to recite Monty Python routines with Drew Carey and hang out with the girls from the Los Angeles office while they carved bongs out of tropical fruit. But the cocaine was like upgrading from vinyl records to compact discs—it made me want to try everything all over again to see if it still felt the same. Or better.

By evening, everyone had begun to feel dangerously at ease. A copy editor unpacked his acoustic guitar to serenade us with love ballads of his own composing. Parker and two young assistant editors leaped into the pool and began performing a spontaneous Busby Berkeley–style aqua ballet for any woman who walked by. ("What a bunch of fags," the Brits succinctly remarked.) A brawny art assistant and a frumpy, full-figured photo editor, approximately fifteen years apart in age, fell drunkenly into each other's arms, and their lovemaking did not cease even as people gathered around them to watch.

Ethan, bless his handsome heart, was simultaneously pursuing an adorable blondie from the Los Angeles office and being pursued by one of the fact-checkers, but judging by the way he and the blondie were already pawing and poking at each other, it was clear who'd won the tug-of-war. And by the distant looks on their faces and the way they were sweating even more profusely than the rest of us, it seemed to me that both of them were on Ecstasy. I was impressed: I'd always believed that convincing a woman to take hard drugs was one of the most difficult maneuvers in the book, more challenging than talking her into eating fast food or getting her to enjoy giving head. I would go so far as to say I could never have feelings for a woman who refused to use them on principle—a man could spend his whole life searching for a woman with enough bravery and impulsiveness that she'd be willing to do this for him, and Ethan had done it in a matter of hours. That, to me, was romantic. That was true love.

"Are you guys . . . ?" I asked Ethan, to confirm my hypothesis.

"Yeah," he answered with a guilty smile. "You want to join us?"

"What do you need me for?" I said. "I'd only get in your way."

That seemed to be the gentlemanly thing to do—there was no need to come between another man, his woman, and their endorphin overload.

"Come on," he persisted. "We don't mind. It'll be fun."

"What happens when you two decide it's time to go off by yourselves? How much fun is that going to be for me?"

"If you're that worried about us abandoning you," he said, "why don't you get Alicia to take it with you?"

At a table, Alicia sat fully disengaged from whatever drunken discourse the Brits were conducting. She had stripped down to a bikini top and a pair of cutoff jeans, showing more of her skin than I had ever seen before or likely would again. I made a stealthy gesture for her to come over, and she glanced in either direction before slinking over to us.

"We were thinking about taking some Ecstasy," I told her.

"Actually, some of us already have," Ethan corrected.

"Anyway," I continued, "we wanted to extend you an invitation."

She thought over the proposition. "Wait here. I need to go ask *him* for permission," she said, nodding her head in the direction of her boisterous Brit. I turned my back on her as she walked away. I didn't want to know anything about how the two of them interacted, didn't want to accidentally overhear the baby-talk nicknames they had created for each other, didn't want to see whether he sent her off with a kiss on the cheek or a playful slap on the ass. A few seconds later, she reappeared.

"Okay," she said. "I'm in."

Alicia sat next to me as Ethan opened a plastic prescription bottle and extracted a single pill. It looked different from the only other one I'd seen, smaller, with a bluish tint. "It's the last one I have," he explained, "so you'll have to split it." The brittle tablet broke apart easily in his hands, and he gave half to each of us. I swallowed my portion quickly, before my fidgety fingers could do something stupid like drop it in the dirt. Alicia preferred to take her time, sticking out the end of her tongue so we could see the pill on it, then sucking it back in and gulping it down.

His dispensary responsibilities completed, Ethan took the blondie by the arm and ran off with her, as I knew he would. "I guess they had other things on their minds," I said.

Alicia placed her hand in mine, in anticipation of what was about to happen. "Let's go somewhere," she said.

We wandered out to the beach, past the tall reeds that wavered capriciously in the wind, until we reached the shore, where we sat in the sand to let our toes touch the incoming tide and our ankles be devoured by bugs.

"I'm two for two," I told her eagerly. "This is only the second time I've done this, and both times it was with you." But as fastidiously as I had tried to duplicate the formula that had resulted in that one glorious, random night in Canada—the girl, the drugs, the water—the elements refused to coalesce. The uplifting effects of the Ecstasy hadn't kicked in, and Alicia seemed anxious and distracted, looking constantly over her shoulder as if she were expecting someone to come up behind her. The ocean was seeping into our shorts, and the uneven shale embedded in the sand was poking and pinching our skin.

"Aggh, I'm sorry," she said in aggravation, yanking at the wedge of denim that had accumulated in the crack of her ass. "We can't stay here."

We retraced our steps back to the villa, past the merry pranksters we both wanted to get away from, and around to the front of the house. Her grasp around my hand tightened when she spied a row of unattended golf carts.

"I want to drive one," she declared, inspecting them one by one until she found a cart whose keys had been left in the ignition. I searched in vain for a seat belt, then reluctantly plopped down in the passenger's seat. How much trouble could we get into driving a vehicle whose top speed was five miles an hour? I figured. She revved the machine's feeble electric engine, and we began our puttering, plodding escape.

Under the spell of the machine, Alicia forgot about me, gripping its padded steering wheel with all her might as we drifted past empty manor houses identical to our own, dilapidated laundry facilities set aside for the resort staff, and sprawling tennis courts that had been locked up for the summer. Once she felt comfortable with the cart's jittery handling, she allowed herself to let go of the wheel and hold her hands in the air. She shouted a soft "Woo-hoo!"—a cheer that was unexpectedly drowned out by the honking of another golf cart trying to pass us on the dirt road. "Go around us!" Alicia screamed, annoyed that this tentative celebration of her independence had been interrupted. I, meanwhile, was contemplating some liberties of my own: So what if she belonged to someone else, someone who'd lent her out for the evening—pawned her off on the one guy he believed was too chickenshit to violate the terms of the loan? Let's see how trusting he is when my tongue is halfway down his girlfriend's throat! Already, I had my arm around her shoulder and she hadn't objected; did this mean I'd be allowed to cop a feel—tastefully, over the shirt—when we reached our destination? And if it all went wrong somehow, could I blame it on the drugs?

I never found out. With a mighty and sudden wham, our miniature conveyance was rear-ended by the cart behind us. In the spirit of coupling that had overtaken our entire organization that night, another pair of freelance employees had hooked up in a love buggy of their own and plowed into us from behind. The two cars had themselves become conjoined in the act, and after throwing ourselves to safety, we watched the profane union writhe and topple over itself before it collided into a palm tree. Covered in each other's vital fluids, the two carts then split apart, each rolling onto its back as its motor croaked a final, postcoital sigh.

"That's it," Alicia said. "I'm going to sleep." Her frustrated intonation implied that this was not a request to join her.

"Shouldn't we do something about this?" I shouted after her, but she was already too far gone. Our amorous pursuers were lying in the grass, chuckling at the damage they had wrought, and if I'd still had a working golf cart, I'd have run them over myself—not because they had ruined my night, but because their chances of getting laid were now one hundred percent more likely than my own. As I started the long walk back to the compound, I was finally starting to feel high, but it was an obstructed high—the kind that feels as though it's about to set in at any moment but never does, always just out of reach no matter how desperately you chase after it—and it wore off as soon as I returned to the party.

The orgiastic spirit had since been sucked out of the room. People were now clustered together in the corners of the house, whispering—*always whispering*—to one another, and it was obvious that something had happened in my absence. The dead giveaway was the trail of blood spattered across the white tile floors of the lobby, leading halfway up the stairs to a pile of glass shards that had once been a beer bottle, where the blood was most abundant. The shattered remnants, still on display, were screaming to be stepped on by somebody's bare feet and, as it turned out, already had, by—*oy!* who else?—Jim, who, with his recurring back spasms and the weight of the world on his shoulders, did not need another injury to complain about. I could not bear to think of the damage being inflicted—the skin splitting open, the tendons tearing—but I could visualize its aftermath, as Jim staggered outside, his bleeding foot wrapped in someone's scummy, sweaty T-shirt, waiting to be transported to the resort infirmary, only to find that all the golf carts were missing! And then, in some back alley emergency room that doubled as the Montego Bay post office, with wooden walls and a floor made of straw, he would be—*gevalt!*—forced to sniff ether or bite down on a block of wood while he worked on, because the local witch doctor had no anesthetic, because he had never before seen a patient that didn't walk on four legs.

But eventually, those who had been present for Jim's butchering resumed drinking their drinks and smoking their joints, through their stupefaction—*Omertà! Sealed lips*, ladies and gentlemen!—not out of callousness, but out of conviction, out of faith that no member of the household staff would at some future time put his insolent black head in the doorway to proclaim, "Mistah Kaminsky—he dead." We knew Jim would survive, because he was better equipped to handle it than anyone else. Tomorrow he would recount his war story to us through gritted teeth, and then the high jinks would resume. Hopefully his sacrifice would ensure that the rest of us would not suffer similarly; the spilling of his blood had lent an air of legitimacy to the whole sordid affair. Now we had our first casualty. Now it was a party.

THE FOLLOWING DAY began with a reunion of the very first evening. Gomez and Harold were off in the distance, dashing headlong into the water with their snorkeling gear, while Jim and I sat by the beach. His mutilated foot was propped up on a chair, gracefully prepared in a thin layer of gauze, like a gift waiting to be unwrapped.

"They made us take off our shoes before we went into the quote-unquote doctor's office, if you can believe that," Jim said. "I don't know if it was for sanitary reasons, or a religious thing, or what. Not that I had to worry about it." He indicated the mummified limb at the end of his leg. "The only patient ahead of me was a woman waiting for a penicillin shot. I think she was a prostitute."

"Can I see it?" I asked. Jim removed the fastener that held together his bandages and unwound them with care, in case there were no more to be found anywhere on the island. The gash, though cleaned off, was gruesome, running the length of his foot and held together by no more than nine or ten stitches. It looked as if a centipede had burrowed underneath his skin. "It's horrible!" I said. "Get it away from me!"

"Is it that bad?"

"Actually, I'm jealous," I told him. "Now you've got a story even I can't beat. You've got a souvenir no one can match."

"Terrific," he muttered. "A vacation I never wanted to take in the first place, and now I'll never be able to forget it. I'm still trying to figure out how I'm going to explain this to my wife."

"Do you have any idea how this happened?"

Jim's already grim expression grew somehow grimmer. "Yeah, I think I know who did it," he said, placing the blame for the broken bottle that had sliced him open on a female copy editor, one with a history of inserting unwanted corrections into our text—it wasn't until you opened the magazine and saw that the phrase *after-hours slam session* had been transformed into the words *late-night nookie* that you realized she had worked her magic. The gears already turning in his mind, Jim offered a forthright solution to the problems she presented. "I'm going to kill that fucking bitch," he said.

Harold and Gomez had returned from their undersea exploration and were toweling off in front of us. "You want to give it a try?" Harold asked, offering me his mask.

"Eh," I said decisively.

"What's your freakin' problem?" Gomez demanded.

"I'm not a big fan of swimming," I said. "I didn't even bring a bathing suit."

"So?" he replied. "Go get one."

I didn't want to explain that my hangup had nothing to do with what I had to put on, but what I had to take off: Displaying my bare chest was a custom I hadn't participated in since sleepaway camp (coincidentally the same time I stopped attending *Shabbat* dinner services). In my adult life, I'd taken for granted my sickly, almost anemic thinness, which was unsightly enough—then one day I peeked underneath my collar to discover this was no longer the case. My abdomen, which once maintained its washboard shape without any effort on my behalf, had been replaced with a genuine belly, an asymmetric alpine slope of flabby deposits and creases, an abandoned garden of chest hair that had given up growing beyond my navel, and a sternum that was now a fertile crescent of acne. I preferred to keep it all concealed beneath a T-shirt that unfortunately bore the sole, polarizing word PRINCETON.

"Why do you always have to throw it in our faces like that?" Jim asked.

"It's just a shirt, okay?" I said. "I wear it because it covers my chest." But it was more than that. In a lifetime of guilt, it was one more goddamned thing to feel guilty about.

From halfway across the beach, I could see someone coming for me with a single-minded sense of purpose. This was Lauren, an assistant in our marketing department and another import from our London office, a wobbly girl with a generous nose and a slight lull in her voice. Prior to the trip, it had been her unenviable responsibility to book the travel arrangements for every last one of us, and here she had been cast in the equally regrettable role of authority figure, playing caretaker for a resort that could barely take care of itself and chiding us when we did something naughty, which was often.

"I wanted to talk to ewe about the golf *cahhhts*," she informed me sternly. "There's two that's been damaged, vewy badly, and I know ewe was dwiving one of 'em last night."

"No," I said, "that's not true. I was riding in one of them, yes, but I wasn't driving it."

"That's not what I heard," she said.

"Well, what else can I tell you? Ask Alicia if you don't believe me." We locked gazes briefly, and then Lauren turned around and walked away in a huff. I hadn't been particularly helpful, but I was confident the resident detective of 221B Bitch Street would solve the case. A word with Alicia would clear this misunderstanding right up. Women listened to one another. Women *believed* one another.

My atonement was coming soon enough: For the next three hours, the whole company was gathered in a dining hall for a strategy meeting that would, at least, justify the future writing-off of the retreat as a legitimate business expense. No one was excused from the obligation, not the ad girls, though they sat together at the back of the room and whispered comments and passed notes the whole time, and not Drew Carey, though he soon wondered what the hell he was doing there and excused himself while Keith's eyes longingly followed him out the door.

The first to address us was our circulation director, a likable, gregarious man who seemed to be one of the few people determined not to embarrass himself during our stay. He narrated a slide show history of *Maxim*, starting with its American launch in April 1997, and didn't whitewash over the tumultuous early editorships of Clare McHugh and Mark Golin. The presentation was merciless in its sense of manifest destiny, as the magazine's rate base grew from 175,000 copies a month to its present tally of 2.5 million, and it ridiculed long-ago-surpassed competitors *GQ* and *Esquire* at every possible juncture. But it had a sense of humor as well: A slide announcing the birth of *Maxim*'s Polish edition was run upside down, and a portrait of Mike Soutar had devil horns and a Lucifer-like beard drawn onto it. We learned that *Maxim*'s biggest markets were not flyover states with more bug zappers per capita than flush toilets, but bona fide metropolises like New York, Los Angeles, Chicago, and San Francisco; and that the single biggest aggregate seller of *Maxim*, somewhat paradoxically, were Canadian 7-Elevens. At the end of the display, we clapped and cheered in appreciation, to congratulate ourselves for playing for the winning team, even if it was a bit like rooting for the tanks in Tiananmen Square.

Next to speak was Lance Ford, formerly *Maxim*'s publisher and now its general manager, a title that meant he oversaw both its editorial and its advertising—he was now our boss's boss. He was yet another grinning Brit, with graying hair he combed back from the top of his scalp, and when he approached the front of the room, the ad girls sat up in their chairs and turned to face him.

Lance then expounded on a topic he dubbed "objectionable content"—objectionable not in the eyes of the readers (there was no such thing) but in the eyes of our sponsors. He had prepared slides that cited specific examples from stories we had already published: A service feature on buying engagement rings, in which the diamond market was described as "a racket," was objectionable to jewelry advertisers. An article about throwing the ultimate Super Bowl bash that said serving liquor at a Super Bowl party is "like having apple pie at a wedding" was objectionable to liquor advertisers. A throwaway item about a Hitler-themed bar in South Korea was objectionable to anyone who didn't want his $150,000 ad running opposite a piece about a Hitler-themed bar in South Korea.

"But wait," Parker interrupted in the thunderous, emphatic voice he reserved for meetings at which executives were present. "Our readers depend on this magazine to say whatever's on our minds—they know we're going to give it to them straight, because we don't care who we offend. How can they have any confidence in us if you're censoring us the whole time?"

"No one's *censoring* you, Parker. We just want you to be"— Lance fumbled for the precise word—"*sensitive* to these issues as you plan your stories."

And why was this important? Lance had slides to explain that, too. The first was a simple pyramid that listed, in descending order of priority:

$MONEY$
To pay the bills
More editorial pages
Afford brand extensions
To build the Dennis empire

Had anyone stopped to contemplate it, it would have been clear that the pyramid was unsound, built with its foundation at the top and its proper apex at the bottom, but by then Lance was on to the next slide, a set of three equations:

More Ads = More Editorial
Big Fat Magazine = More Chance of Newsstand Purchase
More Ads = More Editorial = More Circulation = Less Felix

The last of these syllogisms was punctuated with a microscopic photo of our beloved chairman's frowning face.

Gomez gave Ethan a nudge. "Look," he said softly. "A little head. Just like you were getting last night."

"Shhhhhhh," an ad girl chided from the rear. "Pay attention!"

"If I wasn't going to listen to Lance," Gomez told her, "why would I listen to you?" Her further scolding was drowned out by our proud laughter.

Having endured the last of these indoctrinations, we expected to be released to frolic among the various powders available to us, but Lance had one last item on his agenda. "Since we are all here and will not have the chance to do this again for several months," he said, "I wanted to use this time to discuss the magazine, its future and where it's headed. If anyone has any questions about what was said here, any concerns about what they've been seeing in *Maxim* recently—or if anyone has any ideas for what they would like to see—please feel free to voice them, now, in this forum." He waited to see whose hands would go up.

As surely as there are magnitudes of presence, there must also be corresponding degrees of absence, because I had been in silent rooms before, but none so silent as this. For almost a full minute, no one said anything. Certainly, many of us had questions, if not outright apprehensions: Where *is* this magazine headed? Doesn't it seem that the language is getting coarser, that the pictorials are getting sleazier, that we're just doing the same crap month after month? Why do we have a boss who regards Wednesdays as national holidays? And, hey, these free vacations are swell, but how about some *raises* around here?

Parker was right: If we were worthy of being called *Maxim* men, we should be able to speak our minds without fear of reprisal. If what we said here and now bothered the wrong people, what could they do? Put us on a boat to Cuba? It is one thing, though, to make these comments confidentially, over lunch in the employee break room or a bong hit on the fire escape, to sublimate your protest in a snide headline or photo caption that a reader will laugh at but won't fully understand; it is another thing altogether to voice your dissent in full view of every last person with whom you share a health plan. For guys who could always invoke a comically convenient amnesia when it came to social convention, we had been suddenly rendered speechless by a concern for what others might say.

Lance did his best to stoke the flames of debate. "Hasn't anyone got something to say?" he pleaded. "Anyone at all?" Then he gave up. "Don't say you weren't allowed to express yourself," he grumbled. We hurriedly filed to the exits.

For our final night at the resort, we were treated to an outdoor dinner at a picnic area on the beach—one that had been decorated to look like a Hawaiian luau, complete with tiki torches, servers dressed in leis, grass skirts, and grass hats, and a roast pig, rotating in blissful ignorance on a spit. In peak months, the same cultural misappropriation was probably staged here three or four times a night; it was an institution guests simply expected, like the reefer and the subservient blacks. The seating arrangements for this last supper, ostensibly free and open, broke down along the same boundaries we had been made keenly aware of throughout the trip, and there was one location where we were not permitted to sit at all: at the table closest to the water, occupied by Drew Carey and his girlfriend and Keith, who could be seen gesticulating wildly with his silverware or the bones of his jerk chicken or whatever other impromptu props were within his reach. Though we were given no explicit instructions to stay away from them, the disapproving glare Keith shot at anyone who dared approach was all the warning we needed.

This was the first public appearance of our editor in chief in some time. Whenever he had been sighted outside the structure of our organized retreat functions, it had always been at the side of Drew Carey, poking our conspicuous guest in the ribs to emphasize another joke he had just told him. Perhaps the best way to understand Keith's behavior was to assume that he imagined himself the star of his own sitcom—it explained why he peppered every third sentence of a conversation with an automatic one-liner and why he embellished the delivery of each quip with canned, coerced laughter. This was a man incapable of taking anything seriously except his nonstop efforts to prove just how funny he could be. Now that he had met someone who really *did* have his own show, he was not going to let the opportunity pass him by. As he was

editor in chief, this was Keith's right—to court the celebrity contacts who would be useful to him in some future career after leaving the magazine; it was just unusual to see someone do this in
front of his staff. But the strategy seemed to be working: Through
continued exposure to each other, he and Drew were blending into
identical doughy guys in identical relaxed-fit shorts. We creatures
seated outside looked from husky man to man, and from man to
husky man, and from husky man to man again; but already it was
impossible to say which was which.

This was also the first time in three days that I had been completely frustrated in my efforts to find drugs—if you operate long
enough under the assumption that someone else is going to come
through for you, you're eventually going to be disappointed—so I
had to settle for the second-best available vice, which was the pork.
Stepping up to the serving line for a third helping, I was stopped by
Lauren, who had been stalking me from a distance through the
whole dinner, waiting for me to wander off alone so she could
pounce.

"I know it was ewe who crashed the golf *cahhht*," she said, pick-
ing up where she had left off. "I spoke to people. Evewyone says it
was ewe."

"Well," I snapped back, "was Alicia one of those people?" The
sudden rise in tension—and, perhaps, my pheromones—had attracted the interest of a few of Lauren's female sidekicks from our
advertising team. "No?" I continued. "Then you don't know what
you're talking about, do you?" I could feel my first rush of adrena-
line in nearly twenty-four hours. I was starting to enjoy this.

"Why won't ewe just take wesponsibility for what ewe've done?
Look at me—I organized this entire twip. *That* took wesponsibility."

"So *what*?" I cried. The women were encircling me now, and I
had to speak loudly enough for all of them to hear me. "Does that
give you the right to needlessly harass people?" Lauren's face froze
up—too shocked, I figured, by my swift and strenuous rebuttal to
fight back. I had to hit her with everything I had left. "There is ob-

viously nothing I can say to you that's going to change your mind. But you're wrong. So do me a favor, okay? Just *leave* me *alone*, so I can enjoy what's left of my vacation—"

I was being accused of a crime I did not commit, and in my all-out desperation to defend myself, I should have been allowed to say whatever I wanted.

"—you stupid cunt."

Except that.

I have heard the word *cunt* used many times, both before and since then, heard men use it to describe women, heard women use it to describe other women, even heard the Brits use it to describe one another as a term of affection—"You great big cunt!" But before that day, I had never called anyone a cunt to her face, and I doubt Lauren had ever heard the term applied to herself. It had been an eerily, infinitely quiet evening, and for all I knew, everyone at the dinner had just heard what I said. The women flanking her did not respond, but Lauren completely shut down. In that moment, I saw her robbed of all her dignity—saw the color drain from those chubby cheeks and the air escape her lungs. I saw a woman die before my eyes. There was no feeling of victory, only the understanding that it was possible to brutalize a person without even laying a finger on her.

I heard Lauren, in a choked-up voice that was a shade away from sobbing, tell her friends, "I've never had anyone speak to me like that before in my entire life." Then I fled—a rapid jog that broke out into a full sprint. I ran straight to the table where Alicia sat side by side with her British boyfriend, our roadside escapades from the night before already forgotten. "Alicia," I begged, "you've got to get Lauren off my back. She thinks I'm the one who crashed that golf cart last night, and you *know* that's not true, but she won't leave me alone about it." I turned to the Brit: "Come on, man, you speak her language, can't you get me out of this?" I was oozing sweat and talking a mile a minute.

"I'll try to talk to her," Alicia said.

"That's not good enough," I said, pounding the table with my fist.

"It's all I can do," she said, returning her attention to her man.

I fled further, racing to Jim's side. In his crippled condition, he couldn't have run from me even if he'd wanted to. "Jim," I said, "I think I made a terrible mistake."

"I know," he said. "I heard what happened."

I could feel my face getting hot—the news of the incident was spreading faster than I could keep up with it, the shame so immense that it was crushing Jim along with me.

"What should I do?"

"Look," he answered angrily, "you can't go around talking to these people"—by whom he meant only our advertising women—"however you feel like. You need to find a way to work with them. Even if you don't think you do, trust me, they can make your life a living hell if they want to."

"But I didn't do anything wrong. She came after me for absolutely no reason."

Jim threw up his hands in exasperation. "Fine. If you don't want my advice, don't take it. I can't make you do anything. I can only offer you what I know—the things that maybe—just *maybe*—I know better than you, from the few years I've been on this planet longer than you have. Or do you not want my help? Do you think you know everything better than everyone else?"

"Okay, okay, I'm sorry," I said, the first of many times I expected to utter the line.

"Just let it go for now," Jim recommended. "Give her some time to cool off. But tomorrow, I suggest you apologize as quickly and as profusely as possible."

I agreed without hesitation. The mere intent to set things right, however, did not make them so. An uneasy stillness had fallen over the banquet; now no one was talking to anyone else, much less to me, and it made every oblivious burst of laughter originating from Keith's table that much more irritating. For three days I had been awaiting a catastrophe that would ruin the experience for all in-volved, one that would make it impossible for anyone to return home without at least a sour taste of disgust irritating his palate, a half-chewed morsel of doubt stuck between his teeth, a shred of suspicion that the people involved with making this magazine were fundamentally incompatible. I just never thought I'd be the one to instigate it.

IT WAS EASY enough to find Lauren at breakfast, sitting alone at a table, cloth napkin neatly unfolded and refolded in her lap, pick-ing absently at her sliced fruit and yogurt. She turned her head away from me as she saw me approach and made no effort to look at me as I crouched beside her and nervously recited the lines I had spent the entire night composing in my head:

"Lauren, I, uh, I wanted to apologize for what I said to you last night. Those words—I don't know where they came from, but I swear to you that's not what I think about you at all. *At all.* I . . . I have tremendous respect for you. You put together this whole re-treat. That's amazing. Anyway, ah, again, I'm just really sorry for blowing up at you like that. I hope—I hope you can forgive me."

I had imagined any number of reactions this statement might elicit, from flame-throated retribution to teary-eyed absolution, but what I did not expect was total indifference. Without a word, a ges-ture, or even a glance, Lauren kept right on chewing her bits of ba-nana, letting my speech float over her like the tropical breeze. That was fine by me. I had made a sincere gesture toward reconciliation, and if she wanted to use the episode as an excuse to hold a grudge against me, to make it a symbol for everything this big bad world owed to her and her gender, that was her decision. My conscience was clear. *Stupid cunt.*

Then it was one final inspection of our bags to make sure we had not accidentally stashed any contraband in the various pouches and compartments before we were escorted back onto our buses and driven to the airport. Drew Carey and his girlfriend were provided their own private carriage, perhaps to a stealth hydrofoil that would carry them back to Hollywood, California, at twice the speed of light. No one but Keith said good-bye to Drew as he departed—not one of us had been able to interact with him in any meaningful way, and we knew no more about him by the end of the trip than we did at the beginning.

While we drank our last bottles of Ting and waited for our buses, Harold laid himself on the ground, resting his head on his backpack. He had just gotten comfortable when Ethan started screaming: "Harold! Look at yourself!" We all looked—was his torso turning black? Was his impressive chest hair growing thicker before our eyes? No—his body was being engulfed with ants, so overrun with the insects that they were crawling out of every hole on his ragged T-shirt. Alerted to the infestation, Harold let out a yelp of surprise and sped into the ocean, leaving a trail of discarded, torn-apart clothing along the way. We knew how he felt—at that moment there was nothing any of us wanted more than to rush into the water and get as far away from this island paradise as we could, to immerse ourselves in a baptismal font that could rinse the grime of this vacation off us.

Four hours later, as Jim and I shared a town car to our respective homes, the symmetry was undeniable: he, toting crutches and a mangled, maybe gangrenous foot; and I, newly outed as a misogynist with anger management issues. We had each done something in Jamaica that we could never completely take back and were returning to New York as smaller, more defective people than when we departed—and that was just in our car. Who knew what life-altering incidents had occurred among the other members of our delegation—who else had permanently injured a vital body part, jeopardized a marriage, been photographed asleep with someone's dick in their mouth—and who wanted to know? The retreat had succeeded as a bonding exercise after all: Now we were bound together by our offenses, united in the hope that we could keep one another's secrets—in the belief that, along with whatever brain cells we had destroyed, we could wipe our memories clean of the entire vacation before returning to the office the very next day.

Somewhere on the Van Wyck Expressway, Jim turned philosophic. "The magazine can't get any bigger or any more successful, if you think about it," he mused. "Once Felix figures out why nobody's answering his phone calls, you can forget about any more perks like this. Not that I'd want to do this again. We're probably working for this company at the best possible time. Sad as that is to say. What if we were living in a golden age, and we didn't realize it?"

"Jesus Christ," I said. "You mean it could get worse?"

12

FREE PORK

IT WAS AUGUST, AND I HAD JUST STEPPED OUT OF A SCREEN-ing of Woody Allen's latest piece of shit when I noticed there were two messages waiting for me on my cell phone. I had begrudgingly bought the device only a few weeks earlier and hadn't given the number to many people, so it seemed impossible that I could be this desirable, this much in demand. I wasn't, of course—both messages were from my mother, left within minutes of each other. There was a sense of urgency in her recorded voice, a repeated plea to "call me as soon as you get this," but no details about what was causing her concern. This was a woman who loved to talk about nothing, and now that something was clearly at stake, she could not bring herself to say anything at all. When I tried to call her back, the three thousand various phone numbers attributed to her were all going unanswered.

So I dialed my sister, who picked up on the first ring. "It's Daddy," she said. "He's in the hospital."

"What happened?" I asked.

"Do you really want to know?"

"Yes," I said emphatically.

"Are you sure?"

"Yes, *goddamnit*," I shouted. "Now, just *tell me already*." I was starting to have flashbacks to any number of conversations from my adolescence, when I would ask what was wrong with my father and I would be told, by my mother or my sister, that he had "gone crazy," he was "out of his mind," which was their euphemistic way of saying that he was so high on cocaine that he barely recognized his own name, a bit of doublespeak we had retained long after his drug abuse was common knowledge. And before my sister uttered her next word, I knew what was about to happen: This was the moment I had been waiting for my entire life—the phone call that, as the child of an addict, you anticipate the way a Super Bowl MVP waits for that congratulatory message from the president, the way a spunky understudy waits to hear that the star diva has come down with laryngitis. The fact that my father was now at such an advanced age and in such poor physical shape that even a relatively minor binge would likely be his last—the fact that he had kept himself straight for so long now—these indicators meant nothing. His fate had been as predetermined and unpreventable as an intifada bombing or prostate cancer.

"He had an overdose," she said. "But they think he's going to be okay."

A conversation with my mother later that night confirmed as much. "I don't know where he got it from," she said wearily, as if enunciating the word *cocaine* would make her complicit in his crime. "I don't know where in the house he could keep it."

"And are you sure he doesn't have any more?"

"I looked," she said. "I couldn't find any."

"And how is he now?"

"They had to pump his stomach with charcoal, and he aspirated some of it, but he's stable. They just want to keep him overnight for observation, then they'll release him tomorrow. He's going to have pneumonia for a couple of weeks, but he'll live." She sounded simultaneously pleased and disappointed with the prognosis.

"Well," I said, "let's be glad *that's* over with."

I was barely settled in at my desk the next morning when my sister called. "His blood pressure dropped tremendously during the night," she said in the dispassionate tones of a nascent doctor. "It's been dropping all morning. David, we have to get up to the hospital. This is it."

Now it was my turn to be indifferent. "I'm not going," I told her.

"What do you *mean* you're not going? You *have* to go."

"No," I said. "I don't."

For the record, I place no value in the practice of the deathbed vigil. I don't see how, for the afflicted, the presence of a few comforting faces can outweigh the magnitude of the infinite, and as with bad shellfish or Emily Dickinson poems, I don't believe that the suffering of one must become the burden of the many. It's a sort of family tradition that began with my grandfather, who did not attend his mother's funeral because—in a story my father would proudly relate to you within five minutes of meeting you, in words more sacred than the Shema itself—he was "too busy with his business at the time." Was I not busy with my own work? Would my father have expected any less of me?

But I soon changed my mind, and I cannot claim it was entirely an act of good conscience. There was the hope that in his last lucid moments, my father might finally reveal the secret location of the buried Itzkoff family treasure. If nothing else, I figured the experience might give me something to write about. I called my sister back to tell her I would meet her in fifteen minutes.

The route my sister and I were driving this day was the reverse of one I had become familiar with in my teenage years, one I could follow from memory before I even had a license. In my father's borrowed car, it would take me from the stillness of the suburbs to the seediest part of the city, where I would find him, his nostrils clogged up with dried blood, skin peeling from his lips, his eyelids stuck shut with *schmutz*, standing helpless in a rented flophouse room littered with dollar bills too bloodied and crumpled up to be useful and perhaps the occasional porno mag. (The heart wants what it wants.) Too disgusted to touch him, I would lead him back to his car with the sound of my voice, watching vigilantly as he shuffled and shambled and stank up the street, to make sure he did not wander off or fall down on his face. If people wanted to stare at us, I couldn't stop them; I couldn't pause to explain to each and every one of them that this quivering, sniffing, belching vagrant following behind me was not just some bum — *this was my father.*

But what my sister and I found waiting for us in the intensive care unit of an upstate New York hospital was not my father. It was a pile of meat hooked up to machines, with tubes running out of its arms and legs, up its nose and down its throat, and a roomful of electronic sensors to remind us that it was in fact alive. As soon as he recognized his children, his eyes crinkled up — he looked as if he wanted to cry, but he could not produce tears, could not even make a sound. He clutched for his blanket, and when that eluded his grasp, he tried to block his face with his own arms. His instinctive reaction on seeing us had been not gratitude or comfort, but shame.

Alerted to my father's sudden cognizance, a nurse rushed in and ordered us out of the room. She was there to stabilize him, but no more — that was how hospitals dealt with a suicide attempt. And really, what else could you call it? At the age of sixty-one, after almost seven years of sobriety, a single self-inflicted act of passion had finally done what more than twenty sustained years of drug use could not: It had brought him *down.* Beyond the doors of the ICU, I fell into my mother's arms. "How could he do this to himself?" I sobbed.

In private, my sister was indignant. "Can you believe that Mommy was home the whole time while this was going on?" she fumed as we waited for news of any change in our father's condition. It was our mother who had contacted her earlier the previous morning, after noticing that my father was breathing with the unevenly applied force of a steam locomotive struggling to get out of its station, but it had taken the expertise of my sister to deduce what had happened. "I mean, I'm sitting there as she's describing the symptoms to me and I'm telling her that she has to call 911 or he's going to die, and she *still won't do it.* Why did they send me to medical school if they won't even listen to me?"

"Why wouldn't she call an ambulance?"

"Because she was embarrassed that the neighbors would see." We both had to laugh at the futility of her statement. "I had to threaten her that if she didn't call the hospital right then, I was going to do it myself. I'm telling you, David, they're *both* crazy. She could *see* his lungs were slowing down. Any longer and they would have stopped altogether."

"Slowing down?" I asked. "That doesn't sound like cocaine."

"It wasn't just the coke," she said. "He was mixing it with Dalmane."

"Dalmane? What the hell is that?"

"It's a depressant—they prescribe it to people who have trouble sleeping. He was probably using one to counteract the other."

"Excuse me," I said, "but how long has he been taking this?"

Didn't these people understand that by permitting him to take drugs, they were placing a daredevil at the edge of a cliff and then daring him *not* to jump? Arguing that these were *only* prescription drugs was like noting that Ivan Ilyich screamed for *only* three days—the injustice was already done. What instructions were printed on the bottle? What directions did the doctors give him with the pills? Did they tell him to take them every time he felt stressed? Or did they tell him to take them until he didn't feel stressed anymore? Didn't they understand that that condition was never going to come to pass?

I would never know, because my role in this family was to have things kept from me. His death, burial, and first *shiva* call could all have taken place in the time it took the two women of our family to inform me that anything was even amiss. Now he was as good as dead anyway—it was a matter not of *if* but *when,* and not of *when* but *how soon so we can get this over with.*

And once he died, then what? After we got over the initial sense of relief that the inevitable had finally transpired, my mother would be too much of a wreck to attend to all the loose ends his death had left. My sister was headed back to school in the fall, to resume learning how to preserve the life of our remaining parent—

I was the one with the frivolous magazine job and the dispensable existence, so it would be my fate to move back in with my mother and get his affairs straightened out. And because I was allegedly the creative spirit of the family, the would-be writer, the one who supposedly knew how to string a sentence together, it would fall to me, at the somber minyan of whatever synagogue would still take our money at this point, or our living room, smelling of cat piss covered in Lemon Pledge, before a gathering of people who had been notified only that he died of lung failure, to give my father's eulogy. Only how do you eulogize someone whose obituary everyone has been compiling in their heads for nearly a decade?

"LADIES AND GENTLEMEN, my father, Gerald Itzkoff, was a frightened man. He was a furrier, yes, but more important he was a worrier. He was a brilliant man, an ingenious and creative man, and it was that imagination of his that protected and provided for him and the family he loved so dearly—'They can't get you if you're always looking over your shoulder,' as he would say—but it was that same imagination, that limitless capacity to consider all the ways in which things might turn out for the worse, that did him in. Since his childhood, when he forgot his textbooks at home and threw up on his walk to school every morning, he was a human stock market of fear, sensitive to every adverse indicator that could bring the whole scheme crashing down upon him—and in his eyes, *every* indicator was adverse. Every opportunity for self-improvement was just the potential for downfall in disguise—every new, unpredictable day brought with it a situation he could not control. He feared nothing so much as failure, and he died the way he lived: worrying about how he was going to die.

"Please, don't tell me it was the drugs. My father's chemical dependencies were an integral part of his being, and I probably owe my own existence to them. Here's a memory I'm sure he'd share with you himself if he could: In his teens, my father had been busted for smoking marijuana, an arrest that remained on his permanent record when he appeared before the draft board a couple of years later. For all the U.S. Army knew, the emaciated Jew standing in front of them was an incorrigible dope fiend; they told him the American military employed the finest doctors money could buy, and they could help him kick the habit—if he wanted to. 'I'm sorry,' he answered, 'but I just don't think I could give it up.' Thus he was pronounced 4F and ineligible for combat, a sleight of hand that might have saved his life, and my unborn one as well. And he didn't even have to pretend to be queer!

"He made up for this, though, by acquiring his cocaine addiction—so the family lore has it—right around the time of my birth; it is a legend I have investigated no further, because, really, am I any better off knowing which one precipitated the other? So maybe he was too caught up in his habit during my formative years to teach me how to hit a ball, how to communicate my interest in a woman without scaring her away, or how to cheat on my taxes, but just look at the many other things he gave me: He gave me my habit of wetting the bed until the age of ten. He bestowed upon me the inability to digest my favorite foods, that persistent queasiness I wake up with in my stomach each weekday morning, that urge to vomit that stirs as soon as I apply the toothbrush to my teeth, that special knack for nudging at every scrape and sore inside my mouth until it explodes into a full-blown canker. He imbued me with his antithetical system of beliefs by which I cannot feel completely at ease unless I am at least in a partial state of anxiety. But then he also gave me my sense of humor. He showed me that self-deprecation was far more entertaining than self-loathing. He taught me that the definition of a Jewish dilemma was free pork.

"I'm sorry, people, but he chickened out. He chose the coward's exit, leaving his long-suffering family to close his account, when all along I thought his stubborn survival proved that to be alive was to be tormented through every miserable second—but that suffering had value as long as you endured it. That was the lesson encrypted within his favorite Yiddishism: *Gornisht helfen*—Nothing helps. Why are we now asked to celebrate his life when the principles supposedly guiding it have been proven counterfeit? Are we expected to be sympathetic to his plight because he worked in the one field with a less dependable retirement program than the Mafia? Does he deserve a special exemption for the years he toiled at a job he never wanted, the miles he journeyed along a path he never chose? Spare me the altruistic bullshit—that's what a man is *supposed* to do. That was implicit in the agreement you made when you were born with testicles. You say you are tired, but true of heart? Well, I've got news for you: *Fuck you and get back to work.*

"Now I have a dilemma of my own. For as long as he was alive, *he* was the man of the house, and I could still be his boy. I would always have that big, fat, acquiescent safety net, that freedom to try anything without the obligation of succeeding—or not to try anything at all. How is my selfish debauchery any different from his? It's different because *it's mine*, because *it's me*—because I could get away with it and he couldn't. Now that world of responsibility and perpetual uncertainty that I always associated with him is mine to inherit, and let me tell you something: *I am not ready for it.* At minimum, I thought I was good for another two or three years of smoking and snorting and dropping and shooting and chasing, of behavior that wasn't really self-destructive as long as my annihilation had no effect on anyone else—as long as no one else was depending on me. Okay, let's be honest, I would probably have kept at it until someone else told me to stop, but I was fairly confident I could give it up by age thirty—maybe thirty-five, tops. He had no right to take that freedom away from me. He can't be dead now— I need him alive until he's no longer of any utility to me, and then he can die in a manner of my choosing—*then I'll kill him with my own two hands.*

"Thank you, and enjoy the Manischewitz."

I NEVER DID get to deliver that speech. One night my father woke up in his hospital cot to find that he was attached to a ventilator, and the grizzled old bastard reached into his mouth and pulled the tubes out of his throat himself.

His safe recuperation was not yet assured. He still had an infection in both lungs and had to be kept heavily sedated, to lessen the pain of the damage he had done to his body and to keep him out of the hospital staff's hair, to suppress his frequent accusations that they were all a bunch of parasites living in a welfare state created by a chief executive who had murdered Vince Foster and married a lesbian. He was able to speak again, but only incoherently: He wanted to know why my sister and I had followed him here to the airport and why we were making him late for his flight; he vowed that once he got out of the hospital, he was going to write two books. "One," he said, "is a mystery novel, and the other is going to be about my voyages to China." (Not bad for a man who rarely traveled farther east than Montauk.) In the days he had been incapacitated, the lucky son of a bitch had grown an imposingly scruffy beard, one I could not cultivate if I went years without shaving, and when his arms and legs were freed from their restraints, he made repeated attempts to rip off his bedsheets and expose his nakedness to us. It was traumatic, especially for me: There was his once magnificent cock, a dick I was fully accustomed to seeing as a child—a *schlong* such as I could hope to possess only when I reached adulthood—shriveled away to nothing, as if it had gone into hibernation and would not come out until the following spring. I was the first to understand this was his way of telling us he wanted his catheter removed.

After following my mother's cautiously elated reports on my father's improving health for the next several days, I returned to the hospital to see him for myself. He had been moved to a wing of the building set aside for patients who weren't likely to die within the week, into a double bedroom he shared with a local drunk whose worst malady was the rosacea around his nose. My father had given up his delusional literary aspirations, but he was extremely weak and could not feed or clean himself without assistance. Fortunately he had a ready and willing aide in the form of my mother, who had spent a portion of every day by his side for the past two weeks. When I found them, she was in the middle of giving him a sponge bath; his beard had been shorn off, and the discarded tray from the lunch she had fed him was balanced precariously on top of a machine that provided a continuous display of my father's vital signs. I wanted to be furious at them, for the ease with which they had forgiven each other after they had both nearly been responsible for his death, for the carelessness with which they had immodestly put him on display without bothering to shut the curtain meant to shield him from inquisitive eyes, but the sight of them smiling instead of screaming at each other was too irresistible, and too unfamiliar.

"You look better," I said to my father.

"I *am* better," he declared. "And I'll be even better as soon as your mother goes down to the cafeteria and gets me some ice cream."

She gave him a good *zetz* over the head with a wet washcloth at the suggestion. "He's been talking about ice cream all afternoon," she explained to me. "But it's not going to happen, d'you hear, so stop asking for it."

"It's okay, Dad," I said. "I'll go get some for you."

"No," he replied with a mischievous grin. "I want *her* to do it." This was greeted with another blow from the washcloth, this time to his bare back. "Owww," he whined. "Maddy—*Mindel*—please, are you trying to kill me?"

"*Kill* you?" I said, the hostility welling up inside me again. "This woman is the only reason you're still alive. She was watching over you every single day you've been in here, whether you knew it or not—she was the only one who didn't give up on you when the rest of us did."

"That's right," she whispered to herself, an accidental tear slipping from a corner of her eye.

"Now, tell her thank you and that you love her," I commanded. He obeyed, calling upon all the strength he had to sit up in his plastic bathtub and kiss her softly, but squarely, on the lips.

"*Bllleeeeeeeaaaarrrghhhh,*" babbled the wino in the next bed over.

"I think he feels left out," my father joked. "You want a kiss, too, old-timer?" he shouted. "Maddy, go give him a kiss, wouldja?"

"Absolutely not!" she said.

"Then get me my ice cream. One or the other."

"You got it," she answered, sufficiently charmed, and left me alone with my father.

"Shouldn't you be at work today?" he asked, still dazed and depleted.

"Dad," I answered, "it's Saturday." I might have been concerned that he had sustained some mild brain damage, except that this was the standard inquiry with which he opened all of our conversations. *Are you at work? Did you work today? Why aren't you at work?*

"Oh, right," he said, more amused than embarrassed. "Anything happen while I was out?"

"I got a raise," I announced quietly.

"Really?" he said. "How much?" I told him the dollar amount, and he frowned. Even in his current condition, he could recall my previous salary, compare it with the new one, and calculate the rate of increase in his head. "That's hardly five percent," he fretted. "That's terrible."

"They said that's the most they're giving anyone for the time being," I explained to him.

"But you've been there for so long now. Can't they do better than that for you?"

"Look, a few days from now you won't even remember that we had this discussion. Pretend it was a ten percent raise instead. The next time you think of it, maybe you'll actually believe it."

"You're probably right," he said, chuckling.

"You know you can't keep living like this," I blurted out.

"Living like *what*?" he said, perplexed.

"You're sixty-one years old. You were supposed to be getting clean. You were supposed to *be* clean. How many more overdoses do you think you can survive?"

"David," he asked, "do you think this happened because I was using cocaine?"

"Well, didn't it?"

"No," he said. "I haven't touched that shit in years. This was because of the Dalmane. It fucks with your head, you know? I couldn't keep track of how many I had in me. Every time I popped a couple, I didn't realize I'd already taken four, or six, or ten before."

"So you're saying this was all an accident? Because that's not what Amanda told me. That's not what Mommy told me."

"*I'm* telling you that's not what happened," said the man who should have known best. Without the benefit of his glasses to focus his gaze, my father's eyes looked swollen with solemnity. The fiery zeal had gone out of them, replaced with a jaundiced desperation—the need, above all, to have his words accepted as the truth. A surgical incision beneath one eyelid, still unrepaired from when a cyst had been removed a few weeks ago, flapped open, shining with the crimson intensity of fresh blood. "Now, who are you going to believe?" he asked. "Them or me?"

Had the version of events put forth by the women of the family come to pass, I would have gone to my own grave resenting my father, believing that he had killed himself with cocaine, and quite deliberately. My father's account was not much more attractive; it placed his brush with death on the level of slapstick comedy, a cosmic pratfall that ended with him exiting the stage by means of a pharmaceutically prescribed banana peel. I knew my father's capacity for honesty, both when high and when straight; but I also knew where my loyalties resided: with myself.

"I'm not sure that I believe *any* of you," I said. "But be grateful that you now have the opportunity to convince me otherwise."

My father eventually got his ice cream, and he and I spent the afternoon watching the Little League World Series on television, in silence, as we did all our baseball games, bewildered by routine feats of physical prowess whose greatness we could neither articulate nor duplicate. The significance of the day seemed confirmed when the winning team's pitcher successfully completed a perfect game—the pastime's Holy Grail made routinely transcendental, achieved right before our eyes. The paternal bond was resolidified through the accomplishment of the young athlete; he was the child my father would have loved to have, and I would have loved to be for him, if only I'd had the talent, if only my father had taken more time to nurture it in me. Two days later, it was revealed that the pitcher was much older than the players he was competing against, a fourteen-year-old buck dominating a game meant for twelve-year-old fawns—in other words, a total fraud.

THERE IS ONLY so much stress the human body can sustain. There is only so much tension you can keep bottled up inside before it begins to overflow, only so much time you can spend oscillating between the twin calamities of your father's brush with death and your own undesired celibacy before the usual means of manual release are powerless to prevent your rage from reaching critical overload. I was muttering racial slurs to myself, yelling at strangers in elevators, trying to run over traffic cops with my car, and I knew of only one way to calm down. It was nature's antidote to my intrinsic narcissism—the failsafe to prevent me from completely neglecting the value of human contact. And that is what makes prostitution the great equalizer: It says you don't have to work at earning anyone's intimacy—you can be as repellent and antisocial as your heart desires, knowing that you—*yes, you!*—can still get laid whenever you want.

In my continued exploration of the Internet, I had discovered that the current crop of premier escort services now advertised themselves through websites—only the *classy* ones, you understand. You were free to pick out your ideal mate from dozens of listings, from the comfort of your own home, while your pants dangled affably from your ankles. In order to set a date, however, you had to contact the service the old-fashioned way, by telephone, where an operator would quiz you on personal details: full name, full address, credit card number, Social Security number—the sort of information that can get you a bank loan or bring down your marriage, corporation, or political administration. I gave it all to my inquisitor without hesitation, because she spoke so pleasantly and so gently, alternately calling me "sweetie" or "honey" at the end of each perfume-soaked sentence—as long as I was throwing money around, I wondered, could I just fuck her instead?

These phone operators could make you feel attractive, could convince you that there was a universe in which your particular perversity was fully acceptable, but what they could not do, apparently, was keep appointments. At the designated hour, after having selected a thin, youthful-looking brunette named Chloe, having withdrawn the money from my bank account and tidied up my apartment and taken my Princeton diploma down from the wall and hidden it in a closet, no one rang my buzzer. Even when I paid for them, they stood me up.

"Hang tight, honey," I was told apologetically. "I can have Chloe there in forty-five minutes."

But Chloe—the Chloe I saw on the website—did not arrive. Instead, the woman who appeared in my doorway, looking as surprised to see me as I was to see her, was short and blond, and zaftig, and thirty-five if she was a day. She was dressed appropriately for the warm weather but not sluttish, in a white blouse and blue jeans, exhibiting no obvious outward signs of her profession. I was disappointed, but I could not think of a way to dismiss her without hurting her feelings, so I invited her in.

"You're just like a little baby," she said. From her accent and her directness, I guessed she was Eastern European. Perhaps we even had common ancestors back in the old country, and by screwing her, I would be screwing my own bloodline, screwing myself back in touch with my roots, realigning myself with the shared generations of family who died in the pogroms and the camps and the showers, at the point where our two paths diverged, where a great-granddaughter grew up to be a woman who solicited sex for a living, while a great-great-grandnephew grew up to be a man who solicited prostitutes for fun. "Do you have my . . . arrangement?" she asked.

I reached into a drawer and produced an envelope containing five hundred-dollar bills. "Would you like to turn on the television?" she wanted to know. "Some guys feel more comfortable that way. Or some music, maybe?"

"No, that's okay," I said. "Shall we?"

We made polite small talk as we undressed ourselves; she had a three-year-old son at home and the cesarean scar to prove it, and a man's name, Alexey, tattooed in Gothic lettering across her back.

"It's very nice work," I said, tracing the characters with my index finger.

"Please," she sneered. "It's the biggest mistake I ever made in my life."

She had the smoothest, most fragrant skin of any woman I had ever been with, flesh that was plasticine and pliable, the way you'd expect a giant Barbie doll to feel. Only she didn't see it as her purpose to provide me with any pleasure whatsoever. My $500 had bought me the access, but it did not buy me control. Anything I wanted to do or have done to me could not be done for more than three minutes at a time, and then only with a coating of emulsified rubber sandwiched between our respective surfaces. Anytime I placed a hand anywhere on her body, she complained that those areas were "sensitive" and reaffixed my palms to her ass. All I could seem to say was "sorry": "Sorry I put my knee on your belly." "Sorry I tweaked your nipple too hard." "Sorry for the lint that keeps turning up in unexpected places." As we cycled through every position in her repertoire, more in a single session than I had experienced in my sporadic but occasionally daring sexual history, as her sighs and moans of "my little man" gave way to grunts and then nothing at all, it was clear she wanted nothing more than to get me off and get out. Like the uncomfortable prophylactic I wore, choking every bit of gratification out of the increasingly mechanical process, her scam was supposed to be airtight.

What she hadn't counted on, however—my ace in her hole—was my incapacity to get off in any circumstance that does not fully simulate my own hand on my own dick. And when one-quarter of the time I paid for had elapsed and she could not cause me to reach orgasm, she turned abusive, tearing off my condom and attacking my member with a palmful of K-Y jelly in her fist, tugging and rubbing on it as though she expected a genie to appear. She had pinned down my arms beneath her hefty thighs, and every time I tried to sit up and swat her away or cried out in pain, she thought it meant I wanted more. We were both buck naked and drenched in sweat, and it was the least erotic thing I had ever experienced.

"You're holding back," she insisted.

No, I'm not, I thought to myself. *You're just not good at your job.* She was shaven clean, and I was one continuous mangle of hair. How could she stand it?

When I finally, mercifully, finished, the woman sitting atop me was visibly disgusted by the act, as though she hadn't seen it coming, so to speak, as if all her previous clients spouted fountains of pure gold. She handed me a tissue and left me to clean myself up. When she came back from her shower, I was wrapped in a black-and-white floral bathrobe I had swiped from the Jamaican resort, savoring the draft blowing up my skirt.

"Could I just have twenty bucks for a cab ride?" she asked.

I actually had another three hundred set aside. I had fantasized that if things had gone especially well between us, I would give her the entire wad as a bonus, tell her there was plenty more where that came from and I had no idea how to spend it. I wouldn't even have expected to be serviced in return—just if she ever needed money to buy nice things for herself, or for her kid, or for no reason at all. Just to prove that I could do it. *Her little man.* But if twenty bucks was all it would take to get her out of here, it was hers.

"Take care of that son of yours," I said as she left.

"That spoiled brat?" she scoffed. "If I take care of him any better, he's going to think he's my husband."

—

"THIS IS DAVE" is how I answer my office telephone.

"This is your mommy" is how my mother replies when she calls me at work. "Hold on, I've got someone here who wants to talk to you."

I had been back at my desk for several weeks. My father had been discharged from his hospital bed and returned to her care a few days earlier. It had been their custom to talk on the phone to me one at a time, so that I could have the same conversation twice and they could be spared the ordeal of having to share information with each other. But today was a special occasion—they wanted me to understand that not only was he getting better, *they* were getting better, and listening to them banter like the stars of some forgotten Depression-era radio show made me nostalgic for a side of them I'd never seen.

"You should see how nice he's been eating," my mother related happily.

"I've gained back all the weight I lost while I was in the hospital," my father confirmed.

"And then some," she added.

"And how is the infection?" I asked, his last obstacle to a completely clean bill of health.

"It's still got a hold of me pretty good," he answered, letting loose with a long cough to demonstrate his point. "But they've given me all sorts of antibiotics to treat it, and I've got your mother to make sure that I take them all when I'm supposed to."

"And when he does," she said, "I get him ice cream."

"I've even started getting out of the house," he continued excitedly. "I've been walking in the neighborhood, around the block, to the park. Sometimes your brother comes with me." Again, by this, he meant the family dog.

There was no talk of rehab or therapy meetings, because there wouldn't be any. This was as close to cured as my father got. My parents didn't want to be healed any further, didn't need to have some practitioner of medicine fold his arms like a mystic and proclaim my father sober in order to achieve closure. Their stake was only in the status quo, and now they had it back. They were each in a state of perfect, personal joy: He was having his every need attended to, and she had someone who needed to be doted upon. I had another screening that night, a new Robert Altman movie I wasn't especially looking forward to seeing. It was September 10, 2001, and everything was back to normal.

13

FIGHTING THE TRAFFIC
IN YOUNG GIRLS, or WAR ON
THE WHITE SLAVE TRADE

THERE IS PROBABLY NO SUCH THING AS A TOTALLY FALSE perception. I didn't write that line, somebody else did, but I imbue myself with the right to plagiarize it because I appreciate it better now than I ever did before. I came to understand this as I sat at my desk, peering past a tiny partition and beyond an empty cubicle, watching Gomez as he sat in his chair, performing his impersonations of every single *Maxim* editor for an audience of one. We were the only two people on our floor, possibly the only two people in our building, and we had nothing better to do. How we ended up in this situation is a very funny story.

Gomez's impressions were devastating because they distilled people to their unsympathetic essences, which was far more difficult than simply saying what they might have said in the voices they might have used; his power of mimicry came not from possessing a true mastery of his subject, but from assimilating the bare minimum number of traits to make it seem as if he did. He portrayed Jim as a brusque bully who barged his way into the office each morning without acknowledging another soul; in the guise of Alicia, he bit down on his lip and rocked silently beneath a pair of imaginary headphones that drowned out everything but a beat only he could hear. He played Keith as a grinning idiot with mouth dimly agape and arms that flailed violently from their shoulder joints, nodding obsequiously as he greeted you over and over with the same saccharine, nasal "Hi!" He played Parker the same as he played Keith, only with his chest puffed out.

I had sampled from the appetizers, and now it was time for the main course. "Do your impression of me," I said to Gomez.

Excuse me, did I say this was a funny story? Because what I meant to say is this is the absolute least funny story I know.

ON SEPTEMBER 12, Gomez and I were the only staff members who did not receive phone calls informing us that we did not have to be at work that day. It was a minor inconvenience, no more annoying than having to walk the lengthy distance home the day before, when the subways were shut down. Yesterday I had seen people lunging for taxicabs as if they were the chariots of the gods, coming to blows over $2 bottles of water at twenty-four-hour grocery stores that were closing their doors for the first time ever. Today Gomez and I were trading our most vivid remembrances of the previous morning. His day began on the roof of his apartment, with his new fiancée, watching the towers collapse, and ended with him applying grout to the tile in their bathroom. I'd had a phone conversation with my father that began with my telling him, "I'm safe," and his replying, "Yeah, I know," and ended with his arguing that the blacks were going to use the day's events as an excuse to demand reparations for slavery.

Today's companionship was decidedly better than yesterday's, when I could choose between the security guard in our lobby, who was able to identify every female tenant by the dimensions of her ass but still asked me from time to time if I worked here, and Marshall. Marshall was the worst-dressed member of our team; eschewing Gomez's predilection for slippers and a T-shirt bearing the silkscreened likeness of James Joyce, Parker's collection of hockey jerseys, and my own wardrobe of secondhand *schmattes* that hadn't been overhauled since college, Marshall preferred checkered flannel shirts, like the kind my father wore, except Marshall's were always ironed to a pristine perfection and did not stink of red fox musk, and jeans, usually white, with black boots. He worked in the magazine's fashion department, which meant it was his responsibility to look at clothing and produce photography of men wearing this clothing, to keep his mouth shut if he should overhear us discussing how faggy the fag models looked in our fag fashion features, to overlook the countless wisecracks we made in our copy at the expense of Richard Simmons, Paul Lynde, Michael Flatley, and the Village People, the jokes that depended on things being inserted into or removed from orifices, and to ignore, if possible, the sound of Peter Allen's "I Go to Rio" blaring triumphantly from the speakers of Parker's computer a few feet away from his own office door. When I was set free into the editorial bullpen, after I'd ditched my earring and grown my once frosted hair back to its roots, Marshall was moved into the closet, because he had an abrasive speaking voice and a laugh like a helium duck call. He rarely talked to anyone else at work anyway, because when he opened his mouth to speak, all we heard was *gaygaygaygaygaygaygay*.

On the day of the attacks, he had been in a state of panic since the first rumors reached us that a portion of one of the towers had fallen off, when you could look out the window yourself and see the rising clouds of dust and debris, of steel and glass and paper, rumbling their way up Fifth Avenue like time-lapsed jackrabbits. He maintained that there was still a third plane in the sky, looping around Manhattan, looking for a target, much the same way he was pacing in continuous circles around the perimeter of our abandoned quarters, around vacated desks and empty chairs that hoped someone would return to them and resume writing pithy headlines and clever captions. "You shouldn't stay here," Marshall told me. "I'm going to call my mother and then I'm going home, and I suggest you do the same." It was the only sensible remark I heard all day.

236 | Dave Itzkoff

Today, however, I would have gladly traded places with Marshall, in all his mincing, lilting ignominy—to be him instead of myself as seen through Gomez's eyes. In Gomez's depiction I was less a human being than an aggregate of tics and irregularities; I was constantly touching my hair; I shielded my face with one or sometimes both hands while I spoke; every sentence I uttered, in that shrill whine I can hear with my own ears, concluded with the word *right*, three or four times in succession, *right, right-right, right.* It was easy to dislike Marshall, because there was one obvious quality to fixate upon, but it was even easier, apparently, to dislike me, because there were just so many things I did wrong. *Right?* If this was Gomez's affectionately mocking conception of me, could the rest of my colleagues love me any better? I thought I must have been the most detested man in the office. *Right-right, right?*

That was before Keith Blanchard took the helm of the conference room on the morning of September 13, to sit at the head of the everlastingly sticky meeting table, before a cast of characters largely identical to those who had been shamed into silence at a similar assembly in Jamaica. We had not seen Keith in command of a situation in several months: His regular Wednesday sabbaticals, now accepted as routine, had since been expanded to include the occasional Thursday and even Friday, and always for a different reason. He was revising his novel; his wife wanted him to stay home with the children; he had risen one morning and seen his shadow. Working directly with subordinate editors to get a story into a publishable state had never been his strategy anyway—he preferred to take articles home with him, to rewrite all the gags to reflect his choice of punch lines. And calling mass meetings had never been his style—he preferred to confer with people one-on-one, to delegate responsibility away, piece by piece, until he had none left to call his own. This strategy kept *Maxim* formulaic and a little bit stale, but it kept the circulation steady. It gained him a well-rounded life in which his editor in chief's duties occupied his mind for only a few hours a week, and all it had cost him was the loyalty of everyone in his employ.

None of that mattered now, not when the parking lots of the train station in the New Jersey suburb where Keith resided were still jammed with the same Land Rovers, Lincolns, and Mercedes-Benzes that had sat empty since they were left waiting there on Tuesday morning, the same hollow husks he would have seen Wednesday morning—had he gone to work on Wednesdays—and the same vacant shells that watched him on his way into the office today. None of us had been killed, though a few of us knew of people who had, and so we all knew people who knew people. As we'd been told repeatedly over the last two days, it was an experience no words could describe, and when Keith attempted to convey its meaning to us, we expected nothing, which is exactly what we received.

"*Mumble mumble,*" he began softly, his hands clasped over his mouth as if to prevent all remaining sound from escaping. "*Mumble mumble* an experience no words can describe. *Mumble mumble* tragedy. *Mumble mumble* loss. *Mumble mumble* try to go on. If anyone needs *mumble mumble, mumble mumble* will provide *mumble mumble.*" Then, by providence, someone came into the conference room and told us we would have to leave right away. A bomb threat had been called in to the Condé Nast building, by wily militants who knew that the most effective way to instill fear in the hearts of Americans was to strike at our nation's largest privately owned publisher of general-interest periodicals. No direct danger had been posed to Dennis Publishing, but our Condé Nast envy knew no bounds: We wished we had their silver metallic headquarters, we wished we had their advertising revenue, and we wished we had their bomb scare.

We were still living in that Golden Age of Terrorism, before the anthrax panics rendered us catatonic, and with an entire day to waste, we did what we did best: We partied. We found a midtown bar in the looming shadow of the Empire State Building that opened at noon, and we drank, none of us more so than the Brits, who happily informed us, "We don't give a shit about this city." Some of us, myself included, stepped out onto the streets and

238 | Dave Itzkoff

smoked joints in full view of the police officers swarming everywhere, who we knew had more pressing issues on their minds.
When Harold and Ethan made their pilgrimage to the site now
known as Ground Zero, to participate in the bucket brigades that
were spontaneously converging on the scene to help rescue workers sift through the rubble, the two were so overwhelmed by the
sight of an overnight graveyard, of the ruins that had jarringly replaced a pair of stolid and seemingly permanent monuments, that
they dropped the pails full of detritus and human remains being
passed to them and had to go home.

It was Friday, September 14, before we were able to resume
work on the magazine. The Close was already upon us, and it
would have to start all over again, while each page of the issue
was redistributed to editors to inspect every unprinted square inch
for material that, in the new national climate of pants-shitting anxiety, could be construed as insensitive. It was too late to amend
the issue currently being delivered to newsstands, with cover lines
that advertised PAIN STREET U.S.A.: "Horrible tales of human an-
guish . . . you'll laugh your damn head off!" and THE COMING
PLAGUE: "It's fast, it's fatal, and it's already here." Such inadvertent
offenses reminded us why it might be worth scrutinizing the unfin-
ished proofs we had in front of us, to consider if, say, an article about
American cities too polluted to live in, or a sidebar comparing
the height of basketball titan Shaquille O'Neal to other enormous
structures—such as the World Trade Center—might be upsetting
to our readers.

Not even the most trivial by-product of contemporary American culture was beyond the impact of the single most significant
historical event of the twenty-first century: Any reference to fire-
fighters or law enforcement officials in our text now had to be preceded by the word *heroic*; the picture of a United States flag, with
the caption "Home of the Brave," was affixed to the *Maxim* logo on
our cover, where it would remain for exactly one more issue. And
then there was Keith's editor's letter: Normally, his introductory remarks were just another page of amiable chauvinism that preceded

the magazine proper, perhaps a disingenuous argument that guys deserved their own holiday ("Friendly Skies Day, on which every man's treated to a world-class hoovering by the stewardess of his choice"), or a bogus rant that actresses should be allowed plastic surgery only after the approval of their loyal male fans ("If a starlet of sufficient prominence wants a boob reduction, that should be our decision, not hers. Am I crazy?"), and always concluding with the traditional imperative that is no imperative at all: "Enjoy the issue!"

But this month's missive was different, as attested to by the reverent, serious portrait of Keith that appeared beneath a sunset photograph of the reconstituted World Trade Center towers, beside the title "New York forever." His essay opened with an uncharacteristically calm and genuine sentiment, praising his two-year-old son's innocently professed wish to become a fireman. He went on to offer his gratitude to those who sacrificed their lives in the efforts to save workers trapped in the collapsed buildings and his blessings to the dead and their families. And to the "dirtbags" who engineered the terrorist attacks, he fumed that they had "no freaking idea the beast [they] just awakened." He confessed that even he had difficulty summoning the energy to put out a "sexy humor magazine," that it was normal for anyone to believe that the work he did for a living was insignificant if it wasn't directly contributing to the safety and well-being of the country. But this feeling of inadequacy was one we'd have to get accustomed to, because, as he informed our readers, "this is war, baby."

Baby. On that one curious word his entire composition turned, shifting its focus, its tone, and even its assumed audience. Unleashing the full extent of his vitriol, he continued as if he were addressing Osama bin Laden directly:

> Oh, Osama. Did your desert-sun-addled mind actually think this would weaken our resolve? The country that destroyed the Nazis . . . contained Communism . . . squashed Iraq like a hippo sitting on a gingerbread house. Wow. Somebody was

cornholing a camel when they should have been doing their homework.

This is America — 11–1, the international champion of the world. . . .

Maybe there will be more casualties; we'll survive. But you won't. Until now we have allowed you to live as a parasite; now that you've mutated into a virulent strain you've left us no choice but to wipe you out. You single-handedly united the states of America in one goal: to root out all your little grubs and pinch them between our fingernails once and for all.

Congratulations. When you hear that final incoming whistling sound over your tent, we hope it sounds a little like a Bronx cheer.

Perhaps better than any of the two and a half million potential listeners whom he was lecturing, Keith understood what it was to be both collectively notorious and individually anonymous — to feel impotent within a vessel of considerable power. He wanted his words to be as powerful as the retributive actions they were intended to incite, but when he opened his mouth, all that came out were platitudes and schoolyard taunts. And though he may have lacked the might to affect the course of international politics, he wanted the publication to resonate with his language and inflection, so that when he spoke, he spoke with the institutional weight of *Maxim* behind him — because when he did, he truly believed he spoke with the vulgar voice of every straight American male between the ages of eighteen and thirty-four.

The new national preoccupation with war, one that was about to be waged everywhere and for all time, was a mentality we were already prepared for, as it bore a certain resemblance to our ceaseless and insurmountable struggle to compel women to appear in our magazine. Even at the rate that our popular culture unfurls, the speed with which buses are dispatched from all over the United States to deliver fresh meat upon the doorstep of Hollywood, there had always been a very finite talent pool we could draw from to populate our magazine, and the pool was evaporating with each passing month. To alleviate some of the pressure, we had created backup plans to fill the vacuum of celebrity skin: There was a pet project we'd been saving up, called "The Girls of Iraq," in which we would run stock photos of oppressed Muslim women costumed in their head-to-toe burkas, accompanied by the same breathlessly masturbatory prose we generally reserved for their undraped, irreligious counterparts, and for obvious reasons that now had to be shelved. We had also been toying with the idea of an annual "Models of the Year" issue, the rationale being that when we could not give our readers authentic famous people, who choose their magazine opportunities based on the publicity it will provide them, we would give them good-looking models, who just want money. It was a foolproof plan, unless the models we wanted did not want our money.

The models did not want our money.

But we weren't licked yet. Along with all the other tricks we had for pumping up our sales—using proven sell words on our cover like EXCLUSIVE! or READERS' CHOICE; sealing the issue within a polyvinyl bag or bundling it with an inexpensive gift or supplement— we knew that people liked to buy magazines with cover lines celebrating the cities in which they lived. What if, in the hilarious spirit of capitalism, we published a special edition for each of the twelve major markets in which *Maxim* was distributed (and a token Canadian edition, so the Canucks didn't feel left out), declaring every one of these metropolises the best city on earth? We could sell thousands of additional copies of the joke issue long before readers realized the joke was on them.

That we were even thinking this way—about what we, as editors, could do in a single issue to yield instantaneous results at the newsstand—indicated that more had changed at the magazine than our view of the skyline. *Maxim* had moved the game twice before in its history: While the rest of the industry was contending that a magazine was only as good as its content, we were making the case that a better indicator of success was circulation growth. And when our circulation topped out a year ago, we argued that a magazine should be judged on how closely it reflected what its readers wanted to see. Now, it is a fine and noble thing for a magazine to be a servant to its readership; it is another thing altogether for it to be a slave to its circulation.

When those towers went down, we all thought of our loved ones, but there were others within our organization—let's just call them . . . *people*—who were also thinking of their fives, and their twenties, and their hundreds. These people could anticipate the economic hardships that lay ahead for the magazine and the company. They appreciated the precarious situation we were in, that of the two and a half million copies of *Maxim* we moved every month—the number we promised—the number we *guaranteed*—to our benefactors in return for the $150,000 they paid for their full-page advertisements, one and a half million of those issues went out to subscribers whose names would remain on our mailing lists until the Rapture cometh. The other million had to be purchased by capricious, unpredictable human beings willing to risk shame and degradation when they furtively snapped their copies off a magazine rack and handed them to cashiers, sandwiched between the latest editions of *Social Revulsion* and *American Transvestite*. Otherwise, we failed to fulfill our end of the bargain we made with our advertisers. If we sold a mere seven hundred thousand copies—numbers for which any self-respecting editor this side of *Modern Maturity* would go down on Helen Gurley Brown—it wasn't enough. The people who knew this also understood that missed sales targets meant lost revenue, in the form of complimentary ads, or actual money, we would have to return to our sponsors. Even if they could not fully appreciate the devastation that September 11 had brought, these people understood that enough of these refunds, coupled with the advertising we already stood to lose in the new era of uncertainty, would be ruinous.

For all their dismal auguries, these people could not actually tell us what to do in our half of the magazine. They could suggest that we make the atmosphere of *Maxim* a more comfortable one in which to advertise. They were free to say, "Hey, wouldn't it be cool for our cover girl to wear a tattoo of the logo for that new energy drink, as a reward to the beverage company that just committed to six issues?" Or, "Wouldn't it be awesome if we photographed that pinup babe holding a long-stemmed rose, as an enticement to the floral delivery service that's thinking of buying a page opposite her pictorial?" And, "Wouldn't it be super if one of you editors would hop on a plane and come down to Virginia with us, to convince the major tobacco companies *not* to cancel all the ads they've already agreed to purchase?" (Not you, Keith.) And, "While you guys are having your esoteric debates about which emerging stars will look hot on our cover while advancing the cause of *Maxim*'s cultural relevance, could you do us a favor and just pick a piece of ass who *sells magazines*?" These were just recommendations that we were free to embrace or ignore. These people had no real power to tell us what we could or could not write, right? *Right-right?*

As it turned out, it would have been possible to produce the "Greatest City on Earth" issue, but the timing for such a stunt was all wrong now. We couldn't leave New York off our list, and we couldn't dare declare any other American city superior to it, nor could we, for all our carefully cultivated callousness, make it the victim of a hoax like this. Also, it would have cost money.

HERE'S AN OLD industry joke for you: A writer walks into the office of a risqué young men's magazine and asks to speak to someone about his many outstanding invoices, totaling $3,865 for articles published months ago, for which he has yet to be paid. When he is told that no one is available to speak with him, the writer builds a tent in the magazine's reception area and confines himself to it for several hours until an editor delivers him a check. While encamped, the disgruntled writer contacts several major media

244 | Dave Itzkoff

outlets, and once they report his story in the days following the incident, no self-respecting freelancer will contribute to this magazine again. Within a couple of years, it folds.

Good one, right? Only it ain't no joke. This scene had played out at a rival publication a few months earlier, back when things were so bad that it would take the senseless and brutal murder of three thousand innocents to remind us that, yes, they could be considerably worse. And as was often the case, all that separated *Maxim* from its competitors was a sheer layer of luck. We, too, had been weathering an economic drought, one that seemed to have affected only our freelance contributors, the writers whose stories we rewrote and the photographers whose pictures we retouched, for whom a single check could mean the difference between the carefree lifestyle of the *nouveau riche* and total insolvency. None of us knew how far the financial famine had spread, but nearly every editor had someone in his or her Rolodex who hadn't seen a check since the era when the greatest threat to our national security was shark attacks. There was no one we could turn to with the authority to see the impasse broken; the makeup of our accounting department seemed to be changing on a daily basis, and Keith, when we could find him, was always on the run from one meeting or another with his own superiors. "They just told me I have to fire three people from the magazine," he'd inform us meekly, his chin pressed as far into his chest as it would go. Perhaps now was not the best time to approach him.

It was no small measure of my desperation that, in the midst of this, I turned to my father, still relaxing at home, comfortably running his business from his couch.

"How much longer will it be before *we* stop getting paychecks, too?" I fearfully asked him from my desk.

"But that's not happening now, is it?" he answered.

"No, but it *could*," I said.

"So what do you intend to do about it?" he wanted to know.

"I don't know," I said. "Go work somewhere else, maybe." I wanted to hear him tell me again that I was absolved, that I could chuck it all and start over and he would bear the load for me. *Come on, old man. One last time, get me off the hook, for old times' sake.*

"I don't see any way out of this one," he finally said, sighing. "Where can you go? You don't have anything else lined up. Looks like you'll just have to ride this out."

There was another solution I had once proposed to Harold, on an occasion when I had answered my phone to the sound of hot and heavy breathing and realized it was his voice. "Maybe we should all get second jobs," I suggested.

"This *is* my second job," he answered. "My first job is being apathetic."

Harold used to be the kind of guy who'd bet you $50 he could get the phrase *clams casino* into the magazine before you could. Now he was the kind of guy who had two places in the office from which he preferred to conduct business: One was his desk; the other was a secret spot located underneath it. When he was above-ground, he was miserable. Unlike my job, which consisted of selling heterosexual men on the idea of attractive women, convincing them that they were plentiful and readily available, Harold's main responsibility was selling them products. He composed and edited the pages of flat-screen TVs, mobile DVD audio/video receivers, and robotic vacuum cleaners we published each month at no cost to their manufacturers. The gadgets were presented as sensually and appetizingly as the equally unobtainable people I wrote about, but after his thirty-seventh portable cable/satellite/DVD/VHS projector or his eighty-eighth all-in-one digital camcorder/MP3 player/voice recorder hybrid, Harold was losing his grip. "I'm writing frickin' catalog copy here," he would complain to no one in particular.

In his subterranean state, Harold's disposition was harder to determine—all we had to go by was the top of his head, reflecting light as it poked out from beneath his workstation and a curlicued telephone wire extending into the void like an umbilical cord. His daily work routine had changed so drastically of late that it was as if he had gone sweetly retarded: He conducted the majority of his phone conversations from that pit, in the company of a garbage pail, computer cables, and dust bunnies; he had given up his Buddy Holly glasses for a set of contact lenses, washed his surviving strands of hair each night with salon-bought shampoo, and in the earliest hours of the morning sat upright at his desk, applying moisturizer to his face and hands; he smelled faintly of aftershave.

I thought we would need to rely upon each other now more than ever. With each issue, with each Close after Close after Close, the world outside our office had been increasingly difficult for us to negotiate. Those who could go directly home at night to their wives, or fiancées, or the coworkers they were dating, had it a little easier; they had their Tuesday night soccer matches, played in a local gym, and their Wednesday morning recaps, arguing over which players were most directly responsible for their unending tide of losses. The last bachelors standing on the *Maxim* masthead were Harold, Ethan, and myself, and by coincidence we were seated at the office in a single, isolated row. So we did what Jews always do when we are confined to close quarters: We plotted. We spent our lunch hours eating only with one another, swapping complaints about our jobs and the people in power, how we could conspire to get rid of them and whom we would replace them with. We had names for one another that no one else could use; to one another we were Abraham, beadle, beanie, Berkowitz, dick-nose, eagle-beak, heeb, Hebrowitz, Itzik, Jewbag, Jewstein, kike, Kikestein, Moishe, the Mossad, Porknoy, sheeny, Sheeny McSheen, Shylock, Steinmetz, yid, yiddle-diddle. We were the Three Meeskite-eers, the Three Hebrews, which somehow got shortened to the Three 'Brews. But one of us was trying to break up the act, and I couldn't figure out why.

On an unseasonably warm night in the fall, when the city air was still swirling with microscopic bits of animate matter, we had chosen to gather the crew from our Canadian adventure for the first of what was supposed to be many reunions. At a dimly lit table in a basement-level Italian restaurant, Ethan and I were seated opposite Max and Alicia, an arrangement that yielded an awkward chiasmus: There was Ethan, who could have just about any woman he wanted, across from the one woman he hadn't yet landed; and there was the latest in a long series of women I'd convinced myself were the only women I'd ever want, across from me, and I had not a single idea how to go after her. In their tank-top T-shirts, the two women pawed playfully at each other, adjusting each other's shoulder straps and excitedly swapping tales of Max's latest failure of a first date—he had stopped off at Burger King before taking her out to dinner, can you believe it?—and the news that Alicia had recently moved in with her British boyfriend. While Ethan and I wordlessly wondered if men were allowed to share their food, they picked from each other's dinner plates, unaware that they were the two most alluring creatures in the room, coursing with the kind of energy that makes men unable to decide whether they want to write novels, wage war, sire offspring, or slit their wrists. Or maybe they were aware. Either way.

"Where's Heshie?" Max asked. It was a pet name for Harold that only she used, and for some reason it always reminded me a little too much of the name of our family dog, Alfie.

No sooner was the question posed than Harold entered, followed by his new girlfriend, the one he had kept secret from us until this very moment, who trailed behind him by a few feet, quiet as a geisha, and took the seat next to his. She had short, captivatingly tousled hair with lightly freckled skin and the black, inquisitive eyes of a child, and though she was too polite or too intimidated by our group dynamic to say much to anyone, she was the only person to whom Harold paid any attention. As we chewed our salads and slurped up our pasta, they were addressing each other as "love" and sitting in each other's laps and generally carrying on as if it were the year 1966 and they were Michael Caine and Britt Ekland. Two women seated at the same table may be gorgeous, but three are dangerous. A few minutes ago we had no idea this girl existed, and now we couldn't even remember what other women looked like. The two remaining females in our company had entirely lost their luster.

What's it all about, Heshie? Are we meant to take more than we can give, or are we meant to be kind? And where did you find the time to find her? Because I know you spend as many unfruitful hours at work as I do, if not more, and I know, from eavesdropping on the conversations you try so hard to keep private, that your social calendar is equally as barren as my own. Who introduced you? And when? And where? And why wasn't I invited? Does she comprehend just how desperate, perverse, and fucked-up a person your colleagues know you are—how you, like all the rest of us, are racked with self-doubt? Did you vow to acquit yourself of your many deviances and defects before she finds out about them, or did you already confess them to her and she told you she didn't care? I believe in true love, Heshie, but I don't believe that you are somehow more deserving of it than I am, and I know with every fiber of my wounded soul that this romance of yours can't possibly last. She'll see through your deceit and dump your sorry ass—send you right back to sitting next to me, cradling your balding head in your hands, wondering where it all went wrong. It's just got to be wrong, right?

Right-right, right?

14

THE GENTLEMAN'S AGREEMENT

I COULD TELL THAT THINGS WOULD SOON BE COMING TO AN end because continuity was breaking down. Events were occurring in the present irrespective of the past, and with no relationship to one another. I just hoped that for once it would be a good end, one that would let me depart peacefully and with dignity—that I could leave well enough, even if I couldn't leave well enough alone.

The *Maxim* editors were gathered as a group around a single computer monitor, hard at work on another of our mock cover designs. This one began with a scanned photograph of a baseball batter in midswing, that ultimate expression of playful, pantomimed virility at its full tumescence, to which we took turns approaching a keyboard and affixing cover lines that read SWING FOR BALLS!, CHOKE UP ON THE BAT!, PLAYING PITCHER AND CATCHER!, AND, OH YEAH, HOW TO SUCK AT BASEBALL! (Nothing delighted us more than expressions that suggested the idea of a penis without actually using the word *penis*.) After hours of careful composition, this dummy cover would enjoy a print run of exactly one pressing, at which time it would be hand-delivered to our counterparts at another magazine office three blocks away from our own, whereupon it would be read and deposited in the trash.

At the turn of the twenty-first century, at a point in time that followed the publication of *Pale Fire* but preceded the theatrical release of *Star Wars: Episode II—Attack of the Clones*, a national periodical dedicated to the art of gentlemanly refinement had expanded the focus of its content to include an article on the subject of "smoothies," being the colloquial term for gay and straight males who desired to be castrated for their own sexual gratification, and another essay, entitled "My Mentor, My Rapist," which offered the true first-person account of an aspiring male writer seduced into a lifestyle of aggravated buggery by his successful gay editor. (The author first suspects foul play when, after having been slipped a sleeping pill in his drink, he awakes to find a dildo lodged in his rectum.)

For months it had been impressed upon us that this magazine and the people who produced it were our enemy, that they were our sole adversary in the zero-sum competitions for readership, for advertising dollars, for respect and credibility. In private, we mocked their fashion photography, flush with expensive cuff links, cummerbunds, and other luxuries we had no use for, even as we advocated $2,000 suits and $15,000 television sets in our own pages. We never missed an opportunity to ridicule them for printing the names of their contributors *on their cover*—as if that would ever help them sell more magazines!—as if selling more magazines were the highest virtue to which a man could aspire! And we derided them for their conflicted sexuality, for their willingness to explore the basest, most repugnant extremes of a lifestyle we knew was foul through and through, even as we fought with our advertising department over whether we could or could not publish a health story about the leakage risks posed by having anal sex with a woman. ("Just push it through," Keith would advise us each time the rejected copy was returned to us. "Just push it through.")

With the arrival of spring came the opportunity to best our foes in a pickup softball showdown. These staid, beer-fueled intramural contests were, by now, an industry ritual as old and stale as Cracker Jack, staged more for the publicity value than for the thrill of competition; but to us and our angried-up blood, the match meant the opportunity to look our nemeses square in their Oakley sunglasses and stomp them into pieces. We spent days strategizing when we should have been putting out a magazine, assigning positions, and sending our top prospects to batting practice; we made plans to hire a dominatrix to sit on our bench, and if that wasn't enough, we sent our opponents that declaration of war we had composed, the one about swinging and choking and sucking. And when the game was ultimately rained out, our archrivals did not have the gentlemanly courtesy to reschedule.

A few weeks later, on an upper floor of our building where we were not normally allowed, in a conference room we had never seen before, outfitted with space age chairs that provided posture-correcting spine support and a metal table clean of unidentifiable stains, an elite subset of the *Maxim* staff was being presented a crudely edited videotape on an elaborate projection system. There was a time-code countdown, a few seconds of black, and then a fade-in on a woman, the sort of gorgeous yet vacuous young thing who exists only in advertisements and pornography. We were reasonably confident that we were watching the former.

"What makes a man a *Maxim* man?" the woman asked. Good question. Fortunately, she also happened to have the answers.

"A *Maxim* man is a natural leader and the best at what he does," she told us. "He works hard and he plays harder." Cut to scenes of our handsome, dashing, Buster Crabbe–like *Maxim* man, bounding purposefully through his office and goofing around with his boys at the bar. It occurred to me: Did everyone in this video look *blonder* than usual? Not Aryan—just . . . blonder.

Cut back to our spokesmodel. "A *Maxim* man," she said, "is smart and sophisticated, and *definitely* good in bed." She flashed a suggestive smile. "A *Maxim* man is bold and outgoing," she continued, "and unafraid to try new things." Cut once again to our exemplary *Maxim* man, being bold and outgoing in his bathroom, having just emerged from his shower. He faced himself in the mirror as he dried himself off, and when he pulled the towel away from his head, we saw that his hair, once brown, was now streaked with pillow white highlights. As our avatar smiled confidently at his reflection, having successfully tried a New Thing, the camera zoomed in on a red box propped up on his sink, one bearing a *Maxim* logo we instantly recognized, and beneath the brand name, some text, which a voice-over artist was kind enough to read for us:

"Introducing Maxim for Men hair color, the first hair color product from the makers of *Maxim* magazine. In the men's section of finer pharmacies and salons everywhere."

Fade to black. The show was over and the houselights came up. Sounds of groaning were audible, as were those of open palms being smacked against foreheads.

While we were watching the video presentation, we ourselves were being watched. A mustachioed, avuncular Jew sat off to the side with a pad and pen and an expression that hovered between anticipation and dismay. He was Dennis Publishing's director of brand extensions, and for all the proud, priapic glory that the title might confer, this was not a happy day for him. He was not the first person in our company to have served in this capacity, and from his cringing posture to his drooping countenance, there was considerable empirical evidence that what we had just witnessed was probably not his idea, though it was now his responsibility.

"Well," he asked with one eye toward the door, "what did everybody think of this one?"

Parker, as always, was the first to speak up. "Why are we doing this?" he said. "Why, of all the products we could be selling our names to, is this going to be the first one on the market? Why aren't we doing *Maxim* condoms? Or *Maxim* beer? That's what I'd rather see."

His pronunciation of the word *rather* was oddly affected, to rhyme with *father*. It reminded me of another meeting he'd presided over a few days earlier, one of several planning sessions he'd tried to organize in defiance of Keith's prolonged absences, when Parker had contended that what he'd *rather* see in the magazine was a story about the Big Dig, a decadelong effort to rebuild Boston's infrastructure. To illustrate his point, he'd passed around an oversize book of photographs depicting the heavy-duty equipment being used in the project, the shiny man-made instruments of mass construction that rose into the sky. "Parker," someone had eventually asked him, "isn't this a children's book?" It was.

The exasperated Jew in the room—for once not me!—let out a sigh. "We don't have a choice in the matter," he said. "We've just got to make the best of the situation. Come on, now, there are two more commercials we've still got to watch."

This magazine publishing business—when it actually confines itself to the business of publishing magazines—operates by some funny rules. You can, for example, spend years cultivating the value of your brand name—the only thing you've got to distinguish you from the rising tide of look-alike, read-alike, tits-alike competitors who lacked your head start—and then as soon as that asset accumulates any equity whatsoever, you can sell it out and slap it on a hair care product your readership wouldn't be caught gay with. (Gay, to them, being a fate far worse than death.) You can work exhausting, torturous hours with no hope of remuneration, for the sake of a common goal, and be deemed a team player and a fine addition to the organization, but as soon as you express dissent—the moment you begin to suspect that the magazine's values and your own are not in perfect synchronicity—you are branded difficult, an agitator; your reputation graduates from passive-aggressive to *aggressive*-aggressive.

Only what if your hair trigger has been shaven so short and so close to the skin that everything offends you immediately and to your fullest degree? What if every battle is worth fighting? What if everything you see is worth complaining about—or so you think?

I NEVER REALLY knew what validation meant until I came to Los Angeles. That's where I learned it was a method of stamping tickets so that the bearer may park his car free of charge. Los Angeles is a town with automobile culture so deeply embedded in its DNA that within a single visit, you will become convinced that every action movie chase sequence and television car commercial was filmed on its highways or its empty downtown streets, on an asphalt-hot

254 | Dave Itzkoff

day in December or just after a rainstorm in May. And if you drive long enough on Wilshire Boulevard, you'll eventually pass the glistening corporate edifice that is the headquarters of Flynt Publications, the house built by *Hustler* magazine, full penetration pictorials and a cover that once bore the image of a woman's body being run through a meat grinder. Magazines must surely be the city's second most precious commodity after cars, because you can see them displayed at the breathtaking outdoor newsstands found on nearly every corner of nearly every block. You want to talk about the Promised Land? You keep your Bethlehem, Jerusalem, and Tel Aviv—I'll exercise my right to return to terrain where every color glossy gets equal treatment and equal eye-level placement, where it's as flattering and as useful to be featured in a Chanel dress on the cover of *Vogue* as it is to be shown in a pair of gynecological stirrups on the cover of *Leg Parade*.

A select few of us were sent here to enjoy a *Maxim*-sponsored party called the Hot 100, a celebration intended to create publicity for a supplement we included with newsstand copies of the May 2002 issue—a promotion to promote a promotion to sell magazines, one that cataloged and ranked emerging female talent. I had earned my spot on the trip by editing the supplement, by fighting for days with my superiors over whether the actress Jaime Pressly should occupy the thirtieth- or fifty-fourth-ranked slot—and by the way, who is she?—and also by begging a bit and demonstrating that I could behave myself. I had my round-trip flight paid for and was furnished the same rented Mustang convertible each of my colleagues had no doubt treated himself to, and as the first to check in at our West Hollywood hotel, I sat at the pool and waited for my fellow rock stars to arrive.

There were a few more of our Brits on hand than usual, who had won their passage by virtue of their accents, and that was because of Andy, our new general manager and everyone's new boss, an Englishman whose pronunciations of the words *girls* and *gulls* were indistinguishable. Much of our former advertising department had been dismantled and dispersed to different jobs elsewhere in the company, women replaced with men—British men wherever possible—in a revamped power structure that put Andy at the top of both the editorial and advertising chains of command. With a single wave of his hand he could kill entire articles, cancel an awards show we'd been planning for months, or order us to drop our plans for whatever apathetic cover prospect we were futilely pursuing and just give the bloody thing to Pam Anderson again.

Next to appear was Jim, the man we turned to when our editor in chief riddled our copy full of jokes about "purple helmets" and "meat curtains" and we needed someone to restore it to its former decency; the man our executives relied upon when yet another advertising trade journal had named *Maxim* its "Magazine of the Year" and they needed someone to receive the award because our editor in chief had blown off the acceptance ceremony; the guy who remembered to take his staff for celebratory steak lunches at Christmas; the man who, as defeated and discouraged as he often appeared, always prodded and provoked us to make *Maxim* the magazine we wanted it to be, encouraged us to pursue stories with Paul Newman and Eminem and Johnny Cash, even though they'd all ultimately turn us down—who did everything he could short of begging us to exert our influence over the publication's pages before Keith returned to the office and changed everything back to the way it used to be.

Ah, Keith! Ah, humanity! Like everyone else in life, he had his own peculiar set of aversions, a personal list of things he would prefer not to do; he also happened to have mastered a system that allowed him to avoid all of them. His most recent extracurricular project had been a script he was working on for *The Drew Carey Show*, one he said required him to be out of the office for several days at a time and which also necessitated a weeklong sabbatical to visit with the show's writers. And when Keith's episode finally aired, and his new female assistant, the one with the smooth skin and the hills like white elephants, had sent around an e-mail encouraging us to watch the program that our boss had "taken time out of his busy schedule" to author, we spitefully ignored the suggestion.

We would prefer not to have him around, anyway, because when he was in attendance the only diversion that could hold his interest was saturating the magazine's copy with off-color political commentary (hidden among the questions in a post-9/11 trivia quiz: "True or false: all terrorists end up sucking Satan's greasy cock in hell") and still more references to deviant sex (advising readers that it was perfectly acceptable to tell a hesitant lover that "anal sex helps to prevent colon cancer in women. Wink, wink"). Any piece of text that landed at his feet became the target of his overflowing ballpoint pen, until every column inch of it was soaked in his pith. We had long ago forfeited control of the magazine's name, its finances, and its destiny, properties that never really belonged to us anyway, but now we were losing our only stake in it, the only thing that ever kept us committed to its continued prosperity: our voice.

Then there was the "Greatest City on Earth" stunt. Once a concept we thought would stay confined to the dustbin of history, where it belonged, the nominal prank had been resurrected last month, in our April 2002 issue, when another routine shortage of enticing cover girls coincided with *Maxim's* fifth anniversary issue. With only a couple of weeks to go in our monthlong production cycle, the elaborate hustle was set into motion: Thirteen different versions of the magazine were produced, one for Boston, Chicago, Dallas, Denver, Detroit, Los Angeles, Miami, New York, Philadelphia, Phoenix, San Francisco, Toronto, and Washington, D.C., each with its own feature story praising the particular town and a brightly colored cover burst announcing the distinction. By late March, the delivery trucks had been dispatched, carrying each variant issue to its respective city, while we sat back and waited for the weeks' worth of free publicity to start rolling in.

The whole endeavor fell apart in about two days. When the *Detroit Free Press* became the first local publication to take the bait and printed its own story announcing the "honor" (they should have been suspicious that anyone would have something com-

plimentary to say about Detroit), the miracle of the World Wide
Web ensured that every journalist or consumer in possession of a
modem would know about our ruse. By the time newsstands in
Philadelphia began accidentally receiving copies of the New York
issue (in which we declared the City of Brotherly Love "a glorified
piss break" between Manhattan and D.C.), the jig was up. Periodicals that had never acknowledged *Maxim*'s existence before were
now mocking the crass commercialism of the idea; the *Philadelphia Daily News* described it as "an inside joke at our expense" and
"a desperate scheme to boost circulation"; the stoic folks at NPR,
not normally prone to outbursts of anything resembling emotion,
declared to our editors that "we've caught you in your own tangled
web of deceit." And in an unsigned editorial, the *Los Angeles Times*
noted:

> Things must be really tough in the men's magazine circula-
> tion business these days . . . [if] the circulation-boosting
> ability of partially dressed starlets who profess a passion for
> snorkeling, for watching football while eating snack foods
> and for strong men who'll never relinquish the TV remote
> is no guarantee anymore of moving expensive glossy men's
> mags off the rack. There are only so many clothes one per-
> son can remove, no matter how desperately she seeks fame.

They declared the sham "a finalist on any list of Shamelessly Cyni-
cal Journalism Ploys" and the "Greatest City" issue "the Worst Single Magazine of the Week," all while steadfastly refusing to mention
Maxim by name. Even the Internet, our last connection to a universe of uncensored information and viewpoints, expressed cogently
and without exclamation points at the end of every sentence, had
turned against us; if we were ever uncertain about how the rest of
the world felt about *Maxim*, we could read about it from our desks
in the scathing rebukes of every other publication on the globe. No
number of partially dressed starlets, no matter how shiny their bod-

258 | Dave Itzkoff

ies had been airbrushed to appear, no matter how close their nipples came to poking out of their petite garments, could revive our collective self-esteem.

There had been a day, not long into the tenure of our new general manager, that Keith had spent confined to Andy's office, while the two of them furiously debated some unknown subject and the rest of us took turns skulking past the office door, peering hurriedly through a windowpane, looking for clues—a bulging vein on Andy's forehead? tears in Keith's eyes?—to what it all might mean. We knew what we wanted it to symbolize: Keith was being fired, and the editor in chief's position was, finally, being given to Jim. But when Keith walked out of that room several hours later, weary but still smiling, we realized we had been wrong—about everything. His contract was not being terminated; it was being extended, and the meeting was just a formality, a renewal of his vows. Hadn't Keith been delivering the circulation numbers they wanted, by whatever means necessary? As long as the sausage was landing on their breakfast plates, who needed to know how it was being made?

But just because his continued employment had been assured, it didn't mean anyone else had to like it. And when he at last came ambling up to our poolside caravan in Los Angeles, one big doughy grin in a polo shirt and khaki slacks, the rest of us suddenly had more pressing engagements to attend to.

"I have to go survey the party space," said Andy. "I have to go over the list of gulls who are coming tonight."

"I have to go do an interview," I said.

"I have to go . . . ," said Jim. He stood up and left Keith alone.

OUR AFFAIR THAT EVENING was held at a fortresslike restaurant high in the Hollywood Hills, a vantage point where Californians stood sixty years earlier and kept watch for waves of invading Japs. Tonight, with all the floodlights shining upon it, the venue was an impossible target to miss, but for all the *Maxim* logos on display, on banners, cocktail napkins, matchbooks, and toilet paper, the celebration was not really for us. For almost an hour we were denied entrance into our own event while we worked the red carpet, helping paparazzi crews identify who the celebrities were and restraining Keith from pouncing upon every famous person he saw. Drew Carey did not attend, but there was a surprise appearance by Hugh Hefner, the skeletal founder of *Playboy*, the man to whom we owed our livelihoods, who entered with a retinue of pocket-size blondes, each of whom he was allegedly fucking, and politely introduced himself to the *Maxim* staff. "Like shaking hands with a corpse," someone said.

The interior of the restaurant, once we reached it, was a playground stocked with an open bar, one where we were welcome to insinuate ourselves among the intertwining strands of male stars, in their dark sunglasses and hooded sweatshirts, hitting on female stars, who went braless in their belly T-shirts and hip-hugger jeans. We were free to fulfill any dream we'd ever had involving a celebrity in which we kept our clothes on.

"I want to get high with Woody Harrelson," said Keith.

"I want to try to have a conversation with Benicio Del Toro," I said.

"I want to ogle Christina Aguilera," said Jim.

When we reconvened minutes later, we had each achieved our individual objectives. We then spent an ungodly amount of time on a receiving line, waiting to be introduced to Cameron Diaz, at which point we were each allowed to say one thing to the actress. "I'm sorry," I told her, "but I thought I was going to be meeting Camryn Manheim," and she laughed. It was a minor accomplishment I would have recounted back to me for days by everyone who witnessed it.

The remainder of the night was occupied by my fleeing repeatedly from a member of our ad sales team who knew that I had cocaine, cocaine that we had been doing off restaurant tables, our business cards, the keys to our rental cars; cocaine that I set aside for a special occasion, which was any time I was out of town, in any

260 | Dave Itzkoff

free moment when I wasn't being watched, and even when I was.
My stalker looked like any number of the beer-guzzling football
killers from my graduating class who, on the day the recruiters
came to fraternity row, traded a backward baseball cap for a Brooks
Brothers suit and never looked back. How he knew I had the drug
was unclear, although he certainly had a nose for such things—an
uncanny instinct for sniffing me out in the moment I was about to
cut myself a couple of lines. But it was completely understandable
why our publication was so successful if my associate went after his
clients with half the tenacity he was exhibiting in chasing after my
stash tonight, and even more obvious why *Maxim* was so popular
with ad sellers and ad buyers alike: They were the only people in
America who actually matched our demographic—the only ones
young, wealthy, and reckless enough to lead the life our magazine
was endorsing.

By the single-digit hours of the morning, I found myself in Jim's
hotel suite, my drug supply depleted and our discarded dress
clothes forming a trail that led to us standing over a pair of $13
sandwiches we had ordered from room service, which ceased to be
appetizing the moment they were delivered to our door. In the
background, two cable TV sports announcers continued their pre-
recorded prattle about the previous day's events, unaware or unconcerned that their abrasive banter was completely inappropriate
for this time of night and the condition we were in.

"Well," said Jim, "that was really . . . something."

"That it was," I said.

"I still can't believe you got Cameron Diaz to laugh." Jim was
down to just his undershirt and suit pants. Setting aside the experience of the Jamaican retreat—and I am still trying with all my might
to do so—it was the most denuded I had ever seen a coworker.

"*Herm,*" I snorted.

"Huh?"

"Sorry," I said as I swallowed my own mucus. "Just enjoying the
last of my nasal drip."

"So," he said indelicately, "two more years of this."

"Two more years? Is that what they gave him?"

"That's my guess. Usually you get one year gratis, just for renewing—just if they want to keep you around long enough to find somebody else. Two if they really like you. So, probably, two."

"I'm not going to make it," I said.

"Sure you are," Jim told me.

"No," I said, "I'm *not*. I can't make it another two weeks, let alone two years. What the hell am I supposed to do? Pretend like I love it while we turn into a jerk-off version of *Highlights for Children?*"

"Look," he said, "you're forgetting that I had to spend years working in trade publications, climbing my way up mastheads, before I ever got to touch a consumer magazine. Here I am, all this time later, and look at me—what have I got?"

"I know, I know."

"No, I'm asking you—*what have I got?* For once, I just want to hear someone say it out loud."

I thought about this for a moment. "You've got our support. Ethan likes you. Harold adores you. I'm sort of indifferent, but I'm leaning towards a favorable opinion."

"That's just great."

"Come on, man. You know you're the only thing that keeps the rest of us sane. We need you around."

"Hey," he said, channeling his remaining energy into an index finger he applied directly to my sternum, "we *all* need each other. And we're going to get through this together."

"Easy for you to say. What's a year to you? Nothing. What's a year to me? Everything."

"Don't you get it?" he said incredulously. "Anything that you want to do with your life, you're going to get to do it. Eventually. Just not right this second."

"And until then, what?"

"Just promise me that you won't quit before I do. That when we go, we *all* go, as a group. And then we torch the place."

"What?"

"Promise me."

It was the last thing I heard him say before I conked out completely. When I woke up on his couch, Jim was gone, but his sport coat was draped gently over my body. On TV the sports anchors were still screaming and squawking at each other in mock seriousness, in a perfectly preserved simulation of argument that played every hour on the quarter hour, one that was just as disingenuous at eleven-fifteen a.m. Pacific standard time as it was at three.

I COULDN'T DETERMINE if the *Maxim* we came back to was exactly the same as the one we had left or entirely different. The conference room walls were still decorated with advertisements we'd soon be publishing, for Internet gambling parlors located in Latin American nations, ephedra-based dietary supplements, and a revolutionary herbal remedy called Longitude. The bullpen was buzzing over an upcoming feature entitled "*Maxim*'s Guide to North American Girls," in which women were classified into such categories as the "Lipstick Lesbian (*labia experimenteur*)" and "Career Climber (*promotamee legspreadus*)"; readers were taught that such breeds were known for "undressing in front of well-lit windows" and "piercing their taco," advised of one species that "just because these hotties don't eat meat doesn't mean they don't like the Jimmy Dean," and instructed of another that "beer makes *her* horny, too—any line will work."

But on any matter other than the work at hand, the office had gone mute. When computers were turned on, they were less often used to edit copy than to surf soft-core pornography sites, and when telephones were answered, the conversations were conducted in hushed, rushed tones with heads hung down and receivers cradled intimately against bosoms. No one shared information about themselves with their colleagues anymore, for fear of the jealous reactions such news might provoke; every portion of data about your life was fair game to be commodified, collected, and cashed in at a later date, to be turned against you when the time was right. The reduction in chatter also coincided with cuts to the magazine's budget, the loss of several freelance copy editors and fact-checkers, and the discontinuation of the market research reports we once gathered in the middle of the room to read together, which told us precisely how many readers were Very Interested, Slightly Interested, or Not at All Interested in each article, headline, photograph, and caption in the magazine, how old these readers were, and how much money they earned. Things were quiet, and they were about to get quieter.

Two weeks after returning from Los Angeles, I quit. Where I left for was not important—had I truly cared about rehabilitating my dignity, I would have found work teaching the deaf to sign obscenities, reuniting stolen Nazi treasures with their rightful owners, or wiping down the video booths at an adult bookstore; but I just took another magazine job. To accomplish even this much, it had taken weeks' worth of ostentatiously updating my résumé and compiling packages of my published clips, of noisily pressing my industry contacts for freelance assignments and employment leads, of obnoxiously engaging in interviews from my desk, of making it unequivocally known to my office neighbors that I had both the inclination and the means to get the fuck out of here, of doing everything I could to throw it back in their mournful, helpless, frozen faces—to alienate every last ally in this place who might have had any lingering affection for me, for the sake of furthering my own interests. But hey, mission accomplished.

And on the day I gave my notice, it brought me no shortage of unrefined granulated joy to inform Keith that I was leaving—to be the one who called him into Felix's office, the room where the truly important decisions were made, where I could, for once, be in complete control of the tempo and tenor of our conversation—to at last wipe that goddamned smirk off his boyish face.

But he knew why I had asked for the meeting before I could tell him. "So, what?" he asked as we collapsed in slow motion into the designer chairs that adorned the room. "Someone offer you a job or something?"

"Yes," I said, "as a matter of fact, someone did. And I've decided to accept it."

"I see," he said. "And supposing that there was anything we could offer you to stay—and I'm not saying that there is—would you even consider it? Is there anything you'd want?"

What did I want? The same thing every man wants: I wanted what I wanted, when I wanted it. I wanted more responsibility, more recognition, more money, and this might have been the only circumstance in which I could compel my superiors to give them to me. I could feel my tenuous confidence already slipping away as temptation began to pull me back into the magazine's orbit. "Two weeks," I repeated, more for my own benefit than Keith's. "I'll finish out my two weeks, but then I've got to get started at the new place."

"I guess there's no talking you out of this," he said abruptly, opening the office door to allow me out. "Good luck to you." I was relieved that the conversation was over, but I felt no accompanying sense of finality. These would surely not be our last words on the subject.

The challenge to me now was to exhibit an amount of self-restraint I was not sure I possessed. Like any other scrap of fresh gossip to blow into our arid, information-starved workplace, word of my resignation was an empowering piece of property that at the moment only I and Keith could claim knowledge of. And because he did not communicate with anyone, it was mine entirely to reveal, to whom I wanted, when I wanted. If I did this wrong, I risked being cut off from all social interaction between now and the time I departed for good. But if I did this just right, I could savor the distinct reactions of shock and disbelief from the people I was abandoning, over and over again.

Yet, at first, there was no disappointment to savor. Harold and Ethan were so genuinely excited to hear about my transition that they took me out to a celebratory lunch.

"The more magazines the Jews are working at, the better," said Ethan.

"That's how we're going to take over the media," said Harold.

Then I pulled Alicia aside into the employee break room and told her I was leaving. "No," was all she could say. "No." Her voice was trembling, and she could barely look at me. This was exactly the reception I wanted. It felt good.

I thought my final obligation was to Parker; he had brought me into this world, and I could not wait to tell him that I'd be departing it before he did. And Parker was proud for me, hardly the response he would have gotten from me were our roles reversed; although not especially surprised, he was a bit confused by my actions. "I don't understand why you have to quit," he said. "This magazine has been so good to you. I'm sure they could work out a way to keep you happy." Instead, I was the one who was astonished. In his tenure at *Maxim*, Parker had learned loyalty not only to people, but to institutions, to things that were larger than people, regardless of the people who embodied them. If you gave me from now until infinity, I don't think I could learn that for myself.

I had shared my secret with as many people as needed to know about it, justified it to them as best I could, but Keith remained unsatisfied with our morning's sparring session, so that afternoon he summoned me back to Felix's office for another round. For both of us, it was a chance to undo the awkwardness of the previous discourse, and for me in particular, it was an opportunity to leave a job with sentiments of less than total hostility—without feeling the need to destroy everything in my path, without my soon-to-be-ex-employer believing that, if I could, I'd murder him in his sleep. But if that weren't already the case, then why would I be leaving?

"What I don't understand," Keith began, "is why you'd want to leave *Maxim* for a lesser publication, one with a smaller circulation—with less buzz?" This, I assumed, was his last-ditch attempt to convince me to stay, and from the indifferent, nearly accusatory tone of it, it was almost certainly initiated at someone else's behest.

This was a case for which I had spent the previous two and a half years accumulating evidence—the second time in a single day I was being permitted to argue it, having failed so egregiously to make my point the first time—and still the cogent arguments and counterarguments I had neatly organized in my mind spilled out in one big blurt. "Are you not reading your own magazine?" I asked him. "We're running pictures of women lying on their backs, sucking on Popsicles. We're using phrases like 'whiskey dick' and 'stink-finger' and 'Dirty Sanchez.' We would never even have contemplated this a year or two ago. Mike Soutar wouldn't have published this stuff. And you *know* Mark Golin would never have allowed it."

Only the mention of his forefathers, the men who built up the reputation and circulation of the magazine that he inherited, had any effect on Keith. "Everyone who's run *Maxim* has had a different take on it," he said. "This is what I think is in our best interest."

"Does that include the 'Guide to North American Girls' story? Don't you realize that everyone is complaining about this—that people are actually embarrassed by it?"

"I've heard what people have been saying. But I read that story, and I feel it's consistent with the tone of what we've been doing." Keith, in turn, had a few choice words he was ready to lob at me. "You realize that with your current exit date, you'd be leaving before the end of the Close," he told me. "You know," he added, "the whole 'two weeks' notice' thing is really just a gentleman's agreement."

But where were the gentlemen in this room? Our privacy in this part of the office was completely assured, as was the outcome of this meeting; yet for people who prided themselves on their powers of communication, neither of us was saying anything constructive, that did not emanate from our disdain for each other and our disgust at what we had done to ourselves in the service of this publication. In my familiar blustering rage, I think I am forcing Keith to confront his rampant egotism, for terrorizing an innocent staff in pursuit of his own agenda. And in his own nonconfrontational style, Keith thinks he is doing the same for me. But we are both cowards, for whom it is easier to imagine ourselves in love with the thrill of the bluff than to acknowledge we are addicted to the fear of being called out.

"I will make sure that all my work gets done before I leave," I said. "But that's it."

"I'm sorry it came to this," Keith said as he dismissed me a second time. "I just wish we could have talked about this sooner, before you started feeling this way." I wondered if there were some things better said never than late.

While this transpired, Jim was on vacation—the first authentic vacation I could remember him taking in all the time I'd been at the magazine. When he returned, it was my unfortunate duty to inform him that we had four days left in which we'd be working together.

"I already heard," he said. "You could have called me at home to tell me, you know."

"But you were on vacation."

"You could have called my cell phone."

"I don't have your cell number."

"You could have gotten it from somebody."

And then my final day rolled around, with no pomp or circumstance; there were no security guards to escort me from the building, but there was no farewell party for me, either. I was not even treated to the privilege of seeing all my flaws and failings formalized into a parodic *Maxim* cover bearing the worst-possible picture of me that my coworkers could find. I was able to gather a few stray acquaintances for a last round of drinks at Blaggard's, but the group did not include Harold (he and his girlfriend already had plans to leave early for the weekend); or Ethan (couldn't make it); or Parker (couldn't make it); or Gomez (couldn't make it). Alicia was there, but only because some of the Brits were there, and they were there only because alcohol was being served.

In lieu of a parting gift, Jim supplied me with a bit of hearsay he thought I would appreciate, a sliver of a conversation he'd recently had with Keith. "Do you know what he said about you?" Jim related furiously. "He said, 'Let's be glad we're losing *that one.*' "

I did not know why this particular piece of information was being shared with me at this particular time. What I did know is that if it is ever seven o'clock and you are the last person at your own farewell party, then you were probably not well liked within the organization you are leaving. And if you ever find yourself thinking that everyone within a certain group is an asshole except you, then probably the reverse is true.

They come. They go.

Who called?

15.

IS AN ARROW
INTO THE FUTURE

I**N THE SAME WAY THAT I KNEW NEVER TO ASK MY GRAND-** mother about her life in the old country, or my grandfather about his one eye that I suspected was made of glass, my colleagues at my new job innately understood that they were not to raise the subject of my previous employer unless I brought it up first. Still, even among the unassertive, the past has a way of asserting itself.

It had been two months since I left *Maxim,* and on a Friday afternoon in early August I was about to head home from work at the unheard-of hour of five o'clock, in preparation for a weekend in which I had planned no activity more taxing than taking a walk in the park, buying a pair of shoes, and absently running my fingers through the sideburns I had sympathetically grown to match those of my new coworkers. But I was distracted by an e-mail from a former associate, a hastily composed message consisting of the following three sentences:

> are you aware that jim kaminsky left the magazine yesterday?
> a month before his kid arrives? ain't that somehitng [*sic*].

I was surprised only by the news that Jim was expecting a second child and shocked only by the fact that it had taken this long for him to depart. His archaic notions of ambition—his belief that everything, no matter how inherently frivolous or downright awful, could always be improved upon—had no place within the organization anymore. All he had ever done for the magazine was bear it through its most difficult moments on his own fragile back, and all he had given it was everything he had in him. I wanted to believe that he got more in return than just the standard mock *Maxim* cover and a few minutes at the end of the day to pack up his belongings. I hoped he had some well-wishers to see him off, other than the precarious piles of old magazines that surrounded his desk, teeming with the ideas he'd never been able to implement, and the cardboard moving boxes he'd always indignantly refused to discard, a couple of which might now come in handy.

Somewhere between here and suburban New Jersey, I imagined, Keith Blanchard was smiling. While Jim was left to stare into the murky counterclockwise eddy of his future, Keith would have been halfway home and wondering what was for dinner—assuming he'd come into the office at all that day. He had prevailed over his closest rival without ever imperiling a single golden hair on his own head. He was a classic schemer, this Keith, whose drive for self-preservation was matched only by his abhorrence of confrontation. We had more in common than I realized.

For days, I waited to hear how the consequences of Jim's exit would play out, to see the reports in the gossip columns about the internal strife beneath the playful facade of America's most popular men's magazine and the multitude of sympathetic resignations that followed. Then I waited some more. Was it possible that no one else in that drama-deprived bullpen was aware of the Jacobean intrigue unfolding in front of their desks? Or were they turned on to a higher truth than even I realized: that it was too late, and their protests couldn't yield any goddamned results now, and you just didn't do things like that to demonstrate your loyalty to a man—not in this economy, anyway. It was subsequently announced that another *Maxim* editor had been promoted to take Jim's position. Then I went back to doing my job.

A few Fridays later, I was on my way to Westchester for Harold's wedding. Ethan had volunteered to chauffeur me there and back, in our summer T-shirts and shorts, while our suits lay dormant in garment bags in the backseat of his car, not to be revived until we could find a bathroom at the wedding hall in which to change into them. This would be the second *Maxim*-related marriage in several months; Gomez had recently taken a return trip down the aisle, but no one from the staff had been invited to the ceremony—no one except Hiroki, the Japanese art assistant who knew of no English word to describe the event other than "pretty." In the days leading up to his own marriage, Harold had been equally secretive about the occasion, repeatedly asking me not to mention the location or even the date to anyone at the magazine, never once suspecting that I was no longer speaking with most of them.

With fifteen miles of the Bruckner Expressway still between us and the ceremony, and all our remaining avenues of conversation fully explored, Ethan prodded me gently about my current job. "You like the people you're working with now?" he asked.

"Yeah," I said. "The other guys and I go out to lunch together almost every day."

"Good," he said. "It's good when you get along with people. It helps."

"Hey," I said, "you—ah, you talk to Jim lately?"

Ethan made a sputtering sound, like air being released from a tire. "Yeah," he said eventually.

"How did he sound?" I asked.

"How do you think he sounded? He sounded crappy. Have you spoken to him?"

"I tried calling him once. I got his wife, though. She sounded like she was in a hurry to get me off the phone."

"That's probably the hormones talking."

"I asked her to tell Jim I called, but I don't think she gave him the message."

"Yeah, well, I don't think he's returning a lot of calls these days. You should probably try him again."

"I will," I said.

But I wouldn't. What was I going to say to reassure him? "Yeah, I know I'm fifteen years younger than you and I haven't lived long enough to make my first down payment or pass my first kidney stone, but trust me—I know you did the right thing and I got this feeling everything's going to be fine"? Because I didn't—I couldn't say for certain that I was going to make it through another working week, or this wedding, or this car ride, without being overwhelmed by the urge to weep into my shirtsleeve. I had no right to guarantee anyone else's peace of mind.

Harold's wedding was a charmingly rustic, ad hoc affair, in which the DJ was a friend of a friend who was donating his services, as were the string quartet, the caterers, the bartenders, the judge officiating the ceremony, and the parking attendants. There could not have been more than one hundred people present, and from the opening procession to the last champagne toast, the entire function was wrapped up in less time than the average round of golf. In my life, I had been to a grand total of three weddings: The first was for two college friends; it had featured a traditional Hindu liturgy in the morning, a Reform Jewish (which is to say nondenominational) ceremony in the afternoon, and a Grateful Dead cover band at night. The second was Parker's wedding, and we all know how that turned out. The third was Harold's, and I can say without hesitation that it was the best one I have ever attended. Intimacy and expediency were the watchwords of the day—everything had been arranged such that this man and this woman could be joined in holy matrimony in the company of their dearest friends and family members, as inexpensively and as rapidly as possible, with the minimum amount of time wasted on the ritual itself and only slightly more expended on the celebration of their vows. Only if the happy couple had performed their first dance to the strains of "We Are the Champions" would it have been a more perfect realization of the wedding every man would wish for himself; that Harold had seen this dream fulfilled was an indication he was marrying a very special woman indeed.

Most of the guests appeared to be on the groom's side and were all around the same age as Harold, though none of them referred to him by that name. They knew of Hal, the diligent, long-haired English master's student, who had once contributed his research skills to a bestselling book about the history of New York City's newspapers; they spoke of H.T., the picaresque nature lover who spent his summers boating, skin diving, and smoking joints on the waters of New England; and they talked about Harry, the dedicated family man who spent alternating weekends between his divorced parents and somehow found time to have lunch once a week with an elderly grandfather. No one here seemed to have heard of Harold, the magazine editor who picked his nose and sometimes mumbled to himself and who, in private moments, spoke of a day, not all that long ago, when he was so depressed that he wandered into a movie theater to cheer himself up with a double feature of *Philadelphia* and *Schindler's List*. These were personas he shed effortlessly, as if each were a rumpled, armpit-stained chrysalis, and today, the least desirable of these incarnations was going to be abandoned for good.

Then there was Harold himself, a husband for all of twenty minutes, faithfully making the rounds at his reception, dressed not in some intricate, uncomfortable tuxedo—because what man, given the choice, would willingly visit such torture upon himself?—but in a sensible gabardine suit, looking like some local councilman at his election night victory party.

"You did it," I said as I shook his hand in congratulations. "You actually took the plunge."

"*Plunge,*" he said with a smile, letting the word swish around in his mouth like single-malt Scotch. "That's a good description of it. Like being shoved off the roof of a building, only you don't know how far it is to the bottom."

"How long do you figure you can make this last?" I asked him.

"As long as she doesn't find out I'm Jewish, I think I should be safe."

"So you're pretty much finished as of tonight. But then, there's probably a lot of things she shouldn't find out about you. You know," I added quickly, "I'm sorry I don't have a gift for you."

"That's all right, man. There was no expectation of that. At this age, at this point in your life, all you're supposed to do is show up. That's all anyone can ask for."

"I promise I won't leave you empty-handed. I'll send you kids a Salad Shooter or something."

"Davey-Dave," he asked, "how's the new gig going?"

"It's going fine," I said. "If you're interested, maybe when I've been there a little longer, I could ask about having you come over, too."

"Actually," he said in a softer voice, "I think I'm already spoken for."

"What do you mean?"

Harold mentioned the name of a respected and prestigious magazine based in Boston. "I had a two-hour breakfast with their owner the other day," he said excitedly. "I literally charmed this guy's pants off."

"Literally?"

"He took his pants off in the restaurant of the Regency Hotel. I'm expecting a job offer from them like any second. Keith saw me come into the office in this suit—now the guy won't even *look* at me. I love it."

"You'd give up your whole life in New York just for this job?"

"Yeah, me and the new wife have already been talking about it. She'd have to quit her job, too—find work up there. But we'll figure it out."

I was about to make some wisecrack about how any job that required Harold to move two hundred miles away could only be a good thing for all of us, but he had been shuttled away to greet more relatives. With him went any lingering belief in my own superiority; there had been nothing heroic about my desire to leave *Maxim* and nothing special about my possessing the ability to do it. As it happened, Harold had an escape plan of his own, the best one I'd seen so far, one that just might make all the loneliness and self-loathing and late night tears shed silently into pillows that had preceded it worthwhile.

I DON'T KNOW WHY these kinds of stories always end in psychiatrists' offices. Maybe it's because their narrators are so desperate to be accepted that they'll happily settle for the impartial approbation of anyone with more diplomas on their walls than they themselves possess. Or maybe they believe that by relating a series of seemingly unrelated events in the presence of such a person, a logical thread that ties the narrative together must necessarily emerge. Maybe they just like to hear the sound of their own voices, and it's as good a construct as any in which to let it loose. In any case, how can one man stand up against decades of established convention? Who am I to fuck with tradition?

My father and I had been fighting, worse than we'd ever fought before, and of course it had to do with drugs. The way that we fought was to stop speaking to each other entirely, but eventually we decided to start seeing a therapist together. And if you asked us whose idea this was, I'd probably say it was mine, and my father would probably say it was his, but really, it was my mother who came up with the plan and got us both to agree to it.

The first of these consultations did not go well. The therapist charged a lot of money for his services, and my father and I both entered into the session in a mood more combative than conciliatory, and I accused him of being high, right then and there, and he vigorously denied it and volunteered to take a drug test to prove this, and in his agitation he totaled his car on the drive home. We decided that we would seek a different therapist.

When I thought about this later, in between arguments with my sister that this family would never see or hear from me again if that's what it took, I realized what a tremendous burden I had placed on my father and how unreasonable it was to demand that he be able to express calmly, on his very first try, in front of an unfamiliar audience, the difference between who he was and who he might yet want to be. I had an unfair advantage over him: I already knew a word to describe precisely the feeling that came from having a blank canvas on which I could reveal myself to the world, an occasion to present myself in any way I wished to be perceived, to define my identity through my every utterance or action, and that word was *dread*. It was a dread that accompanied the understanding that everything gets noticed, everything gets evaluated, and everything counts—every decision is a decision I can make wrong. And no matter how many choices I make correctly, there is no spare moment in which to savor my accomplishments, because every month that slate gets wiped clean. That collection of pages must be filled again from scratch; the identity must be reconstructed grain by grain, molecule by molecule. So what if I'd blown every opportunity every time it was presented to me? My father never even had the chance to screw it up.

Once I acknowledged this disparity, our next meeting with the new therapist was a snap. All I had to do was make my father understand that in those moments he was most certain that no one could hear him, through the cocaine-induced tirades and the anxiety attacks and the disappointment he could articulate like no other man, there had been someone else who was listening—at the age of twenty-eight, at the age of eighteen, at the age of *eight*—and who was trying to diagnose what these symptoms might add up to, as best he could, to the best of his own experience. And when my father realized this for himself, he took off his glasses so I could see that he was both crying and smiling, and he left that office, with its potted plants, its crooked halogen lamps, and its one-way mirror, feeling hopeful and eager to return to it. And this was only our first session!

He and I were standing outside the door to that room, waiting for an elevator that was just big enough to fit any binary combination of him and myself and our emotional baggage, but not all three at the same time. And here, my father turned to me and stretched out those expressive arms of his, ensnaring me around my shoulders with enough force to lift my feet off the ground, kissed me on the cheek, and said to me with pride, "You're a brave little boy." I realized that's exactly what I was.

New knowledge had been imparted to both of us at the same time, and that had never happened to us before. Not all shortcomings are liabilities. Not all liabilities are failures. Not all failures are absolvable, or even solvable, but most are instructive, and some are even beneficial. There's a certain joy in being small enough that your father can still take you in his arms and hoist you into the air. Sometimes it's a comfort to know that there's someone out there who will always think of you fondly as his little boy.

This, I thought, was the best of all possible resolutions, and far better than I felt I deserved. Certainly, by now, I would have settled for considerably less. I would have been perfectly satisfied, for example, if my Uncle Mustache were here to tell me that he approved of me. I would have been grateful if any one of my many former bosses had said that they were pleased with the work I had done today. And I think it would have just delighted me if Felix Dennis had sat me on his knee, paused to adjust his spectacles, patted me on the head, and declared, "Well done, lad. Well done."

Acknowledgments

The author is extremely grateful for the assistance and
guidance of the following people:

Nina Collins, for making all things possible, and becoming
a great friend in the process, you will always be entitled to
fifteen percent of my heart.

Bruce Tracy, who I suspect knew what this book was about before
I did, and who repeatedly saved me from myself, what more can
I say to express my affection for you than: *dude*.

Laura Goldin, for keeping the wolves at bay with grace and wit.

Mitch, for taking the only picture of me that I can stand to look at.

Robin Reardon, Russian scholar of American descent,
for your invaluable moral support.

AJB, for your honesty, and for keeping me honest.

A special thank-you to John Strausbaugh and the *New York Press*,
for the opportunity.

About the Author

DAVE ITZKOFF is an editor at *Spin* magazine.
His writing has also appeared in *The New York Times*
Sunday Styles section, *Details*, *Playboy*, and the
New York Press. He lives in New York City.
This is his first book.